SUCCESS PRINCIPLES

PROVEN SECRETS FOR ACHIEVING
YOUR DREAMS AND VISION

Dr. Samuel Odeke, DSL

CONTENTS

Contents

DEDICATION

This book is dedicated to God, the Alpha and Omega, the Creator, Manufacturer of all things; the Omniscient, Omnipotent God of all creation and the entire universe – of all which is visible and invisible, in Heaven and on earth. Thank you, God, for your great grace and love. God has been and will always be my sure hope and firm foundation. He is the One upon whom my faith is built – on His solid rock where I stand – and I trust Him for His purpose and plans for my entire life.

This book is also dedicated to my late parents and grandparents who left us suddenly when I was a teenager. God alone deserves the glory for guiding us through the ups and downs of life; through droughts and rains during the short journey on this planet. To my dear Papa: Papa, you left so suddenly and there remains a huge gap and hole in our hearts about you. We have managed to overcome mountains, climbed out of pits and walked through dark valleys – all with the help of God and relatives. Papa and Mum, you introduced God to us as kids, and He has been our Strong Tower and Hope. You taught us to have faith in God and to trust God. You never had a lot of money but you gave us God. You taught us values and principles, which are the foundations of human success.

God surely has plans for us: "For I know the plans I have for you," declares the Lord, "plans to prosper you and not to harm you, plans to give you hope and a future" (Jeremiah 29:11). Nobody knows what God's plans are. We cannot believe everything others have to say but instead we shall believe what God speaks to us through His Holy Word. Our relatives, particularly Uncle Okiria Romano and his sisters, gave us the best they could. Uncle Tegu Joseph (TJ) and Uncle James Peter Aide, I will never forget you in my life time. I want to publicly thank you.

Nobody will separate us except death. No! Not the temporary things in this world; not even things such as money, wealth, property and power. We have grown to know that things change and disappear, but as people we remain with memories. Even now, we still have profound memories of our parents and grandparents. These people had very little resources had no power, but they taught us values and principles and introduced us to the Word of God. The Word of God is a principle and does not change. To every one of you in the world (all 7.5 billion people), this book is for you. My desire is that you live more effective lives by applying the principles contained in here.

You might have encountered challenges, frustrations, obstacles, and disappointments that come with life on Earth as you attempt to reach your dreams. The principles contained in this book will provide a road map that will to succeed in any area of life. Jesus said, "I will give you the keys of the kingdom of heaven; whatever you bind on earth will be bound in heaven, and whatever you loose on earth will be loosed in heaven." (Matthew 16:19). Keys give access, power, authority, control and responsibility. I also use the word, fundamentals in the book, which imply rules and principles upon which all lasting and sustainable success and accomplishments are built.

Putting it another way: "I will give you secrets and principles; when applied correctly you will become successful and effective. I have studied these principles and they have worked in my life. These same principles worked for Biblical leaders such as Moses, David, Hannah, Ruth, Mary, Daniel, Paul and Peter. They were regarded as successful because they did what God created them to do. If you study these great people that God worked with, you will notice what made them successful and effective. Each individual lived effectively and was able to accomplish the most difficult things in their lives. Make a decision today to live your life according to God's secrets and principles that were designed to help you fulfill your dreams and visions. Everyone who obeys and submits to principles will achieve their dreams.

ACKNOWLEDGEMENT

The work on this book has taken over ten years of my life to complete. I wanted to share what I have learned and observed of what makes people and corporate entities succeed. This work has involved my family, friends and colleagues because I wanted to prove that these principles actually work and are true as well as illustrate why I believe and am convinced that they are true. What I learnt has always been an inspiration to me through the years. I want you to know how grateful and appreciative I am for trusting me to share these secrets and principles for living a successful life.

First and foremost, my special thanks to my family. You have stood by me and continue to encourage me to put my ideas and thoughts on paper for the world to know what the most important fundamental principles for effective living, performance and success. Even when I am discouraged, you keep reminding me about the principles. I love you!

My family is my greatest asset and gift. I believe that you will fulfill your purpose with passion and without any fear or guilt in life. You are the reasons I work so hard and I want that spirit and attitude cultivated in you, too. One day, you will understand why this work was given to me by God. I urge you to study and master these principles because they have worked for me and will work even more for you.

Lastly, I would like to thank the team of excellent editors who were led by Mr. Samuel O. Adeyemi of *Media DNA* in Lagos, Nigeria. You did a wonderful job. My special appreciation also goes to Dr. Jason Newcomb, DSL, my classmate at Regent University. You have a special gift in editorial insight. Thank you for the final eyesight and editorial work on this book.

FOREWORD

You will agree with me that we live in a dynamic, complex, multi-cultural and unscrupulous world, which calls for the right mental, socio-economic, psychological and emotional balance. The world is evolving so fast in all facets, driven by the information communication and technological (ICT) revolution. However, though the ICT paradigm shift has come with a lot of positivity in the global village; to a large extent, it has caused adversity in terms of aligning the purpose of life in the world today. People are failing to define success or do not know how to achieve their life's purpose. Many are not aware of or have failed to master the secrets, keys and principles of life that define success or make for a purpose-driven life. It is crystal clear that people are either not following or are wrongly applying the principles of life to achieve their dreams and destinies. No wonder the world is rife with a lot of confusion, conflict, intrigue, destruction, death and failed projects. Against that exposition, there is need to know and understand the cardinal secrets, keys and principles that determine success in this ever-changing world.

The primary purpose of writing this book is to pen down tested and proven secrets, keys and principles that determine one's success and destiny in life. Many a time, people have failed to appreciate the power of principles and values in shaping one's trajectory to succeed and/or achieve one's life's destiny. The bare fact is that life is a game of abiding to the pre-established rules and laws in order to live sustainably and decently in the world. The book is targeted at helping individuals in personal and professional development as well as supporting business entities to grow steadily based on established principles and values for successful business models.

The focus of this book is on defining and unpacking the principles and values that determine the fulfillment of one's destiny based on real life experiences and biblical applications, ranging from: explaining the key concepts — what secrets, keys and principles are — to deciphering the significance of preparation and association in leading to one's success or achievement of life's dreams. In the different chapters, the pivotal secrets and principles of purpose, passion, planning, prayer, perseverance, potential, the power of faith and time management are explicitly explained, underscoring their importance in determining one's success or the achievement of life dreams.

The book follows a narrative, conversational and interactive format, which is very exciting to follow and provokes a lot of imaginative, visualistic and comparative analyses of real life situations on the part of any reader. The content is anchored on the personal life experiences of the writer in his odyssey of work and daily living with his understanding and application of the Holy Scriptures, representing God's law and Word to mankind.

In addition, references are made to literature and quotes of great personas on the Earth. Notably, strong biblical references hinged on God's principles and values form the bedrock of the story as well as divulging the established laws of nature relevant to meaningful living. Real life experiences or case studies are also cited to vindicate the right or wrong application of the laws and principles of life to explain success or failure.

Therefore, I strongly recommend this book as a must-read for everyone who wishes to understand and know the application of the key principles and values of life, which are paramount to achieving one's dreams. I reiterate that the conversations in the book are simply respectfully and logically presented with a focus on the real events and experiences in life, a pointer to the powerful quotes from the Bible and by great personalities in the world and detailed explanation of the fundamental principles of purposeful living.

Finally, I want to thank in a special way all the contributors to the valuable completion of this self-help resource book. May the Almighty God reward each of you abundantly!

Hope you enjoy your reading!

Mr. Michael Omeke
Lecturer, Kyambogo University, Uganda.
November 30, 2017

PROLOGUE

The Power of Laws or Principles

Every country that I have been to in the world have laws. Every citizen of that country is expected to obey and follow the laws. Visitors or non-citizens are also expected to obey law. Why? Without law there is no order, peace and development. Law is the foundation of life and all creation. God is first to set laws which I refer as first laws. Law is what God gave to Adam before the fall and repeated it to Moses. God never gave man power, fame, wealth, property or the things we are fighting for in the world today.

In my research, successful individuals obeyed law and were guided by principles or the first laws. This is the reason, David many times prayed to God saying teach me thy precepts, ways, laws and commandments. In other words, David was saying teach me thy laws. Why did God give Moses laws in Mount Sinai? God was building a nation. God wanted order so that people could live effectively at peace and develop themselves. Why did God give people who had been oppressed for 430 years in Egypt laws that we call commandments in the wilderness? The Israelites had been in bondage and oppression for many years but God calls Moses and gives him laws for the people who were now "free" in the wilderness without Pharaohs. Why? Does it mean that God wanted to restrict them? Does it mean God did not want them to enjoy the freedom after coming out of slavery or oppression?

To me God gave laws to protect His people. Why;
- Everything exists by law.
- Everything exists on law.
- Everything exists for law.
- Freedom is a good thing and you are free to do whatever you like but must be with limitations. A fish is free to swim but must obey the water laws and so is with human as well.
- Enjoy the freedom within given boundaries set by laws.

PREFACE

We, as humans, are alive at a very critical time in history. People are faced with many challenges such as terrorism, globalization, ideological confusion, culture clash, unemployment, poverty, high rates of population explosion, conflicts and wars in every continent. There are opposition groups and terrorists that are beyond human control. We are also experiencing global warming, climate change, religious and ethnic conflicts everywhere, leaving leaders confused. Nations are passing laws that grant one-man permission to marry another man, women are marrying each other and value systems have been abused.

Humans are witnessing global, regional and national meetings or conferences where leaders are not able to reach conclusive agreements and find solutions to all issues. If the world continues this way, what will happen to the next generation of people and how will they live effective and productive lives? I believe, with all my heart, in the Word of God and believe that people need to go back and study the power of principles. The cause of most of the world's problems is the application of wrong principles and values among people. This includes those who are terrorists and no longer value human life.

People who steal billions of dollars for personal gain, which should be used for service delivery and provision of social services, have lost the value for human life. The people who are fighting and supporting terrorists or wars no longer value peace and freedom, human rights, or dignity, as God the Creator intended humans to live. Our leaders are also people who have lost direction, with some of them more concerned with power, benefits and their privileges. Our leaders are not interested in people but power and privileges. They want to use people for their own selfish interests and to stay in power.

There is need to make adjustments in our thinking so that the focus is on people and not power. In order to change what has gone wrong and correct problems, we need to go back to study the concept of principles (I mean the correct principles and values) and apply them to our lives and also teach these principles to our children. Organizations, too, need to apply these principles, be it a firm, company or personal consultancy.

What do I mean by the word principle? I have often talked to people about principles in many different contexts and situations. As I have worked with people on different projects and programs related to humanitarian and development work in different communities and countries, I often hear statements like "I have my principles" or "I cannot break my principles" or "That man is principled." I have always wondered whether people actually understand what principles are and what role they play in human life, in creation and what the source of these principles is.

God defined and determined principles because of His goodness and mercy. When God created the first human beings He put them in the Garden of Eden, which was an orderly environment where God could walk and speak to His creations. He gave them instructions on the things they were permitted to do and those they were not allowed to do. God set boundaries; God gave restrictions; God gave guidance on what was acceptable and not acceptable for man to do.

For example, God said, "Do not eat of the tree in the middle of the garden." (Genesis 2:16 - 17). Sadly, this text has been misinterpreted by millions of people, and even I was once a victim of the same confusion. As a child in primary school, I remember we were taught stories about the Garden of Eden with a focus on the "tree" in the middle of the garden, which man was not permitted to eat.

Permit me to draw your attention to this natural law. God made trees to be attached to the soil in the ground and if trees are uprooted, the trees will naturally die. God made a law that a tree must always remain attached to the ground if it is to live, remain successful and bear fruits. God gave Adam laws to protect him but when he disobeyed and failed to keep the law in the Garden of Eden, God said "You will surely die." I therefore say with confidence that God gave laws for the good of creation. And this is true also with man. When laws are broken in any country, there are consequences. In your country, the police are mandated to ensure law and order, which is good for the citizens. Without law and order, there is chaos, disorganization and confusion. Do you agree? Laws are given to protect people and organizations. Laws bring order and effectiveness to people and corporations. When a child is restricted from touching a live electrical wire, the aim is to protect the child. When a corporation sets laws, it is for the good of both employees and the organization.

This book is written for you to think about these principles in your life and organization. How many principles have you violated? What happens when you violate the laws of your country? The police will prosecute you for breaking the laws. The same is true about these principles and secrets; when you violate principles, you automatically subject yourself to the consequences of your actions. However, if you obey them, you will enjoy the benefits. Similarly, there exist secrets and keys which are as important as principles in achieving success. In the Introduction (next section), I will explain in detail what keys are and the importance of keys to humanity and organizations. You will agree with me that without keys, you have no access, authority, authorization, ownership, control, power and influence over a thing.

INTRODUCTION

"Try not to become a man of success,
but rather try to become a man of value"
~ Albert Einstein

This book is written to be a guide both for the over 7.5 billion people in the world today and for future generations. There are millions of people, young and old, who are wasting their lives away. Drugs, confusion, sex, HIV/Aids alcohol, etc. have robbed them of the joy of achieving their dreams. They are failing in life because they have no knowledge of principles that God designed in creation for everything to become what it was supposed to become. Millions of people need this book and I encourage that you give this book as a gift to those people you interact with so that they can live effectively and succeed in their lifetimes. This book is recommended for all parents irrespective of religion, race, tribe, colour, country, and political affiliation. Principles are universal and apply regardless of which country you live in. Principles are the same everywhere. It means every human being needs a knowledge of principles. Gravity, for example, is a universal principle. If a stone or object is thrown into the air, it will come down no matter in what part of the world this exercise takes place. Integrity is a principle. To me, there is nothing more permanent than principles. Everything will change on Earth, but principles will never be changed by how humans choose to interact with them.

The ideas that are shared within this book are highly recommended for your family, friends, students, and corporate entities including nations. Please take note of all the principles and practice them in your lives, families, societies, organizations and corporations. Success is possible when you apply principles, laws and have values. Values can be personal or corporate. Each person has values and every corporate entity has its values. The book is based on my own experiences and lessons learned from others whom I have observed, interacted and also read about. These people have been an inspiration to me and changed my outlook on life. .

I have applied these keys in my own struggle for success in life. They have helped meet the demands of life in an attempt to fulfill my calling, reason and purpose. Whoever applies these laws and keys will surely achieve greatness and fulfill their destiny. When you obey laws, you never worry about going to jail. People who break the law are taken to court and made to face the consequences of the violation of these laws. They are punished because they disobeyed the laws and not because of their race, culture or ethnic background. There are even cases in which punishment is meted out despite that there is the prevalence of bad governance, dictatorship and lack of rule of law in that country.

When people break national laws or even traffic laws, they get punished for breaking the law. The punishment could be a fine or imprisonment or both. Within an organization too, you will always be secure, safe and protected when you obey the laws. Laws are not bad; they are meant to guide you into effective living, success and performance. Laws have benefits and once you live according to the law, you never worry about the results and outcomes of living on Earth.

Throughout my journey through this world, I have observed how human beings function and operate. All have the same basic needs with an inherent desire to become successful. Everyone wants to be successful. Everybody wants to succeed but often do not know how. The same applies to corporate entities; all need success and desire to achieve results. If you obey principles, success will never elude you. It might delay, but you will experience it. If you obey the laws of your nation or any corporate entity, you will never suffer the consequences. The consequences of disobeying organizational laws could include job loss, demotion or loss of public trust.

Anyone who follows these basic laws, and keys will make it in life, achieve dreams, and experience success like never before. This book is not written because I have already succeeded. Rather, I share my life experiences because I want to see people discover their true purpose without any delays or setbacks for lack of knowledge. This will enable you to live a purposeful life. My desire is to help you avoid the pitfalls of living an unfulfilled life.

No one has ever climbed the success ladder without help from others. Joshua worked with Moses. Peter worked with Jesus. Elisha succeeded because he followed Elijah. There are millions of people who are stuck in a pit and need help. Through biblical principles and my life experiences, I will show you what principles and laws unlocked success for me. Be determined not to allow your ideas and plans fall into an early grave. Apply these principles and you will start to experience increase in every area of your life such as in your finances, businesses, homes, schools, and much more.

The Power of Keys

What are keys? A key is "a thing that provides a means to access or entry. It is a small piece of shaped metal with incisions cut to fit the wards of a particular lock, which is inserted into a lock and turned to open or close it." A key gives you instant access to everything that the key opens. The secret is to know which key to use and avoid trial and error or experiments. A key also gives authority and authorization. It means that if you have the key to a safe in the bank or house, you have been authorized to access the valuables in there. Furthermore, having a key means you have control. If you are the one holding the key to something, it means you are the one in control. You can control when or whether to open or close it.

Another benefit of having the key is that it shows you have ownership. If you hold the key to the house or a safe, it simply means you are the de facto owner of whatever the key can open. Therefore, if you have the key, it means you will have ownership. Jesus said in Matthew 16:19: "I will give you the keys of the Kingdom of Heaven; whatever you bind on earth will be bound in Heaven, and whatever you loose on earth will be loosed in Heaven."

Let me give an example. Suppose you were once employed and you lost your employment. You do not have to worry. Jesus gave you the keys of the Kingdom of Heaven. Go have a celebration party because you have ownership of part of God's property as a child of God. In addition, having the key means you have the power and freedom to open and close. The key to your house means you have power to enter and open it. If you have the key, it means you can lock and unlock or open and close. The freedom is in your hands.

26

Keys are laws that remain fixed, stable and never change. And when you use them in a correct manner, they will always work for you. Keys are principles.

Jesus spoke of the keys of the Kingdom of Heaven and not about physical keys that open the locks physically. Keys are the ways and systems by which we operate and are fixed. If you know and understand the keys, then everything in Heaven is accessible. The key to your car can activate the car to function so you can move from one location to another, if every other thing is okay. A key causes the car to function as designed. Our goal in life should always be to seek insight for better understanding of the importance of secrets, keys and principles.

From the foregoing, we see that God instituted a law for the first man to operate and live in the Garden of Eden. God gave this law to man and charged him with a responsibility and management mandate. God set boundaries by which man was to live and the failure to do this attracted consequences. The law was meant to keep man safe, alive, peaceful, and secure. It was to protect man from death. God was essentially saying, "If you obey My law, you will live." Living means to attain full potential. It means to mature. Living means to multiply and fill the earth and subdue it, which is the big responsibility given by the Creator to man. When you obey this law, it means you are responsible. A responsible person is trustworthy, stable, and dependable. I invite you, therefore, to learn and do all that makes you a responsible person.

God designed principles by which humans are to live. When kept, they will protect safeguard and enable you to perform effectively. Let me give you an example of a law, which I will refer to as a natural law. God designed fish to live in water. The fish did not decide on its own to live in the water, but it was decided by God, Who created the fish. If the fish decides to say, "This water is restricting me. I want to get out of the water;" there is nothing else you can do but wait to bury. The fish will die and nobody will take responsibility for this, as nobody can be blamed.

Concluding Thoughts

I have deliberately put this at the end so you will know the benefits of obeying and submitting principles. If you learn these principles and apply them you, success will be guaranteed. There must be constant effort to rethink, renew, recognize and reorganize for the future.

CHAPTER ONE

THE FUNDAMENTAL PRINCIPLE OF PURPOSE

"The purpose of life is to contribute in some way to making things better." ~ *Robert F. Kennedy*

The Gatekeeper's Story in Nairobi, Kenya

I want to begin this chapter with a true story out of Kenya. These stories will serve as a reminder of the facts that will guide us in understanding our lives. This story will serve as a reminder of the fact that very few people truly know themselves. People do not know who they are, why they are on Earth or where they came from to this planet. I have met people who think they are useless and unimportant in this world. And, I want to use this story to correct that misunderstanding.

One day, I was in the Kenyan capital in Nairobi and preparing to travel back to Kampala, Uganda on a Kenya Airways midnight flight. A young man who worked as a gate keeper came to me as I was making a cup of tea. He indicated he wanted to talk to me and we ended up discussing for about three hours before I headed to the Jomo Kenyatta International Airport. Unfortunately, the flight was postponed until the next evening, but this only gave us more time to discuss. The young man in this true story had worked in this hotel for three years and I had known him for as long as that, too. He said, "I don't think my life is important. I am useless and I do not know why God created me. I feel God does not love me. I feel life has no purpose and meaning. I make money, but it does not satisfy. I don't feel excited." He had been a watchman for many years. Before coming to Nairobi, he was in Kisumu doing the same type of work. He was a guard. He had a lot of regrets about the way things had gone. He said that he had reached a point in life where he wanted to go hang himself and die. As I listened to this young man, my heart begun to beat heavily. I told him that I was going to become his mentor and coach.

He said for three years, he had observed me and admired me and wanted to be like me. "Why is that?" I asked him. He said he thought I had everything and was successful. His declaration reminded me of the irony in the world we live – where young people, who ordinarily should be more optimistic about the future, are confused and perplexed about success. I asked him about his religion and he told me he is a Christian. I then asked him whether he believed in God and in His Word. It turned out this young man believed in God but not in His Word. He believed God is selective and wondered why God makes some people rich and others poor.

I told him God's Word is like a memo or an e-mail from God to people living on Earth. God does not speak many words. He does not always explain things verbally but can choose to put the explanation in the Bible. I told my young friend that if he will commit to studying the Bible, he will become successful. When he asked why this was my recommendation, I showed him Hosea 4:6:

> *My people are destroyed for lack of knowledge. Because you have rejected knowledge, I also will reject you from being priest for me. Because you have forgotten the law of your God, I also will forget your children.*

So I asked him, "What destroys people?" He said, "It is lack of knowledge." And, that is correct! People die because they deliberately reject knowledge.

Note that lack of knowledge does not imply that knowledge is not available. In fact, it is more available today than it was several decades ago. We live in the Information Age and so much knowledge is available everywhere. But, real knowledge is only for those who are willing to seek it. Information is not necessarily knowledge. However, when you get information, you are closer to getting the knowledge and wisdom which will help you to live and make right decisions. Even though information is available, it does not mean you possess knowledge. Information becomes knowledge when you understand it and becomes wisdom when it's applied. It becomes personal or yours when you are able to apply it to your life and make informed decisions and choices.

Furthermore, as Rom. 1:18 - 21 reveals:

> *The wrath of God is being revealed from heaven against all the godlessness and wickedness of people, who suppress*

the truth by their wickedness, since what may be known about God is plain to them, because God has made it plain to them. For since the creation of the world God's invisible qualities—his eternal power and divine nature - have been clearly seen, being understood from what has been made, so that people are without excuse. For although they knew God, they neither glorified him as God nor gave thanks to him, but their thinking became futile and their foolish hearts were darkened.

Have you seen this scripture before? It is so loaded and requires that you think about it a little more deeply. It means you have no excuse anymore. As I listened to the story and questions on the mind of this young man, I made some notes in my notebook. Clearly, we would need to have a lengthy talk about these important life issues and I told him as much. Together, we looked at Genesis 1:1: "In the beginning, God created the heavens and the Earth." I helped him to see that God created all things and nothing came to this Earth on its own. Everything is a creation of God. God does not forget what He creates. He created everything and the account of this is given in the first two chapters of Genesis. We discussed Chapter ONE on that day and at the end of the discussion, he said that nobody had ever taught him the Bible.

One of the things he found interesting was the principles that God has put into creation. For instance, God created fish to live in water and therefore, it must stay in water to remain alive. Trees have to stay in the soil or else will they die. The same is true for humans. We came from God and must stay connected to the source of life to truly live. Anyone who declares independence and disconnects himself from God has declared death upon himself. I told the young man that the first thing he needs to do is remain connected to the source of everything and that is God.

Let me share with you another principle in connection with the above. John 15:4-8 says:

> *Remain in me, and I will remain in you. No branch can bear fruit by itself; it must remain in the vine. Neither can you bear fruit unless you remain in me. "I am the vine; you are the branches. If a man remains in me and I in him, he will bear much fruit; apart from me you can do nothing. If anyone does not remain in me, he is like a branch that is thrown away and withers; such branches are picked up, thrown into the fire and burned. If you remain in me and my words remain in you, ask whatever you wish, and it will be given you. This is to my Father's glory, that you bear much fruit, showing yourselves to be my disciples.*

The next day, I sat again with this young man and we talked about success and how a person becomes successful. I showed him a newspaper article in which I had read that an ambassador of Libya to Tanzania was found dead, hanging in his office in Dar-es-Salaam. I gave him the article to read and asked him, "What do you think happened? Why did he kill himself? Was it about not having money? Who did he leave behind? He possibly left behind his wife, children, parents, friends, brothers, sisters or workmates. How would they feel about his act of suicide?"

Our discussion could not address all the universal questions exhaustively. But I showed him that life is not about material success itself, but about what you donate to the world. Life is not measured by duration, but donation. It is about doing what God wants you to do. You can have everything including wealth and still be a failure in life. Jesus Christ did not live long. He lived for 33.5 years and died. However, His impact on the world can never be erased from history. Compare Him to Methuselah who lived 969 years and yet, there is not much that is written about him in the Bible. Examine your life. How old are you now? What will people remember you for? It is not how long that you live on Earth that matters but what you do. Genesis Chapter 5 is where you find the story of Methuselah (referred to earlier) who lived 969 years, yet his name is mentioned only once. I believe he did not do much with his life. In contrast, Jesus Christ had accomplished the purpose for His life by 33.5 years of age.

Every human being has dreams and visions that come from his/her mind and heart. We are destined by God to accomplish a specific purpose in life. There is no human being who is useless on Earth. Look around you and you will see that everything has a purpose. Man-made things such as a phone, computer, car, house or radio — everything has a purpose. God gives every person the potential and the power to accomplish their dreams and visions, but only a few are able to do so. Most die day-dreaming and thinking that dreams will be achieved without hard work, drive, passion, sacrifice, determination, and commitment. In order for you to become successful and to make it through in life, you need to understand your purpose.

Before I proceed, I need us to understand the meaning of "purpose" and why purpose is important for all human beings. Why are we living on this earth? Why were we born? Why are you alive? Why are you living on earth? What difference can you make so that the next generation will benefit from your life? What difference can you make in the world? What will be your contribution? What will the next generation get when you are no longer alive? What will they remember? Do you even want to be remembered?

Genesis 1:29 - 30 says:

> *I give you every seed-bearing plant on the face of the whole earth and every tree that has fruit with seed in it. They will be yours for food. And to all the beasts of the earth and all the birds of the air and all the creatures that move on the ground —everything that has the breath of life in it – I give every green plant for food.*

God is a great God. Every fruit has a seed in it just like every seed has trees and fruits. He puts the future of every fruit inside it. A mango fruit has a seed inside of it and this is its future to produce. To be effective in life, you need to change your mindset and realize that your future is inside you as a seed. Your future is not a head of you, but it is hidden inside you. It's trapped like the seed concept.

Your future is not ahead of you,
but it is hidden inside you.
You are like a seed.

What is Purpose?

Purpose is the reason for the existence of something. Purpose is the reason something is created or the main reason for its existence. Purpose is the original intention that motivated God to create us. Purpose is always related to the one who made a product or a thing. Purpose is a goal or your destination that leads you to your vision. Purpose is the reason why something is done, created or exist. As for human being, purpose is the knowing and understanding what you were born to accomplish on Earth. Vision is when you see your purpose in pictures or imaginations. The discovery of purpose is related to your vision or understanding of the world. The first task for every human is to find out why God made them, what His original intention was? Why did the creator send you to the world?

The Power Of Organizational Purpose

After I left the university, I was blessed by God to work with several organizations. Among these were World Vision International, United Nations World Food Program and United Nations Children's Fund, among others. One thing that is common to all these organizations is that they all work to support people who are vulnerable: children, women or people living in poverty or affected by crisis. Despite this common purpose, I noticed something about them to which I want to draw your attention: Each organization had a unique corporate purpose.

Every organization has a unique and distinct purpose and mission even though they might be helping children, women or elderly. When you open the Compassion International Website, you will see a statement "releasing children from poverty in Jesus Name." This statement is about the mission of Compassion, why the organization exists. In the same way, World Vision International's mission is "a global Christian relief, development and advocacy organization dedicated to working with children, families and communities to overcome poverty and injustice."

Have you wondered why every organization has a corporate purpose? Have you wondered why each has a specific mission statement? It is because purpose serves as a guide to the desired destination. Each organization will always have a unique and distinct vision, values, purpose or mission. To guarantee success, they pursue their purpose or mission, keeping their values intact.

No individual or corporate entity will succeed that tries to do everything. You were not born to do everything but one thing or a few things. This is an important truth to bear in mind. You need to think of your mission or purpose hard enough. As a spring-off of the purpose, you come up with your goals, activities and strategies. Then identify what you need to accomplish these goals. When you do this, your dreams will manifest and your potential will be maximized.

You were not born to do everything but one thing or a few things.

Understanding the Concept of Principle

Perhaps, we have heard people talk about having principles. "You have got your principles." Or, "Where are your principles?" Many people don't seem to understand the principles behind natural laws at all. A principle is the foundation upon which everything operates or functions. A principle is like the roots of a tree. The root system of a tree is a complicated web of shoots going down into the soil to bring up the needed moisture.

Principles are no respecter of persons, in the sense that they are established in their own right and are not swayed by who people are. Violation of principles can result into chaos, disaster, disorder, confusion, crisis or even death. The world today is in chaos because people have wrong principles and values. Corruption is due to a loss of moral principles and laws.

Purpose gives you guidance as to the way to live on Earth and what to do. Each person living on Earth must have a personal purpose, mission, and a reason for living. I have observed that all successful people have a personal vision. I call this a glimpse of destiny or the end of a person's life. Knowing your purpose enables you to transcend the problems of everyday life. I believe God created everyone for a purpose. It is a life-time assignment and responsibility to find that purpose. The lack of responsibility and consistency leads to failure in fulfilling the purpose and therefore, an inability to make a difference. Millions of people are so irresponsible and inconsistent. That is why God says that to everything there is a time and a purpose under the Heaven (Ecclesiastes 3:1).

God created all things and man was fashioned in His image to rule over the universe. I believe God created you and everyone living on Earth to have an impact and make a difference in this phase of history. Whatever God created you to accomplish your purpose. Your vision is a glimpse of destiny. Vision makes the invisible to become visible.

The lack of responsibility
and consistency leads to failure
in fulfilling the purpose
and therefore an inability
to make a difference.

How Do You Discover Your Purpose?

God is the Creator of purpose and does things as per His purpose. This means God is always driven, guided, and motivated by His own purpose. God does not create or make things happen without a purpose. God does things for a reason. There is a purpose for everything and for all things. God is a purposeful God. He allows both the good and bad things to happen for a reason. For instance, the loss of a job might mean God is preparing you for a better job. If you lose a relative, spouse or family member, God will only allow it to happen to reveal His purpose for your life. I would like to link the above with what manufacturers do. Manufacturers do not make a thing for the sake of itself. They do it because they have reasons to. When Japanese manufacturers make cars, they do it for a reason. When Apple Corporation makes Apple products, they have solid reasons for doing so and they release the products to customers to accomplish a certain purpose. When the product has any defect, Apple Corporation will recall the product back to the factory and fix it first before it is released to the market again for the benefit of customers. When Japanese cars are observed as defective, the corporation recalls all the defective products to the factory.

The same is true with God and you. God created you for a purpose. God, not your friends or associates, knows the purpose for your creation, even though your family or friends "assume to know you.". God knows how you are to perform and the capacity He gave you. He might give you an assignment because He is preparing you for a greater purpose. You will never know that purpose until you are obedient to God and His principles. For instance, David was supposed to look after the sheep and goats before becoming a King. God will speak to you and create a desire in your heart about something you want to achieve. This will never go away from your thoughts. It will occupy your mind for a long time. It can take days, weeks, months, years or even decades. When you find purpose, you become different and confidence increases. You become invisible and unstoppable. When purpose is discovered, you become complete, confident, careful and disciplined.

A corporate organization that knows its purpose is careful in all it does and follows a set of laws to achieve its goals.

The Story of Joseph: Slave, Prisoner, and Ruler

One example that has inspired me is the life of a younger son of Jacob called Joseph. As a young man, Joseph got a revelation that he was feeding his family. He saw his family eating from him. As a young boy he ran to his father and told his father about what he had seen in the dream. When he told his parents about this, they were surprised. In fact, the Scripture says in Gen. 37:5–7:

> *Joseph had a dream, and when he told it to his brothers, they hated him all the more. He said to them, "Listen to this dream I had: We were binding sheaves of grain out in the field when suddenly my sheaf rose and stood upright, while your sheaves gathered around mine and bowed down to it.*

Joseph revealed yet another vision or dream that he had seen to his family and this caused conflict, hatred and dissent within the family. This time, it was a dream about the sun, moon, and stars bowing down to him. This was a terrible mistake that cost him hugely and led him to be subjected to physical and social isolations, emotional abuse and cultural abuse. Joseph was sold by his own siblings to slave masters from Egypt. The brothers who were involved went back home and lied to Jacob about what had happened to Joseph. This is true even today. Some people keep telling lies about you and their friends. Watch out for this.

Sometimes, when people are against you, they will say all sorts of things that can discourage and hurt you. They could even be people who are close to you. The greatest lesson I have learned from these stories is that most of the people that you live with, whether they are close family or friends, think that they already know how far you are going to get in life. But, the truth is, nobody knows you except the God Who created you. If you share your visions and dreams with this inner circle of your life and they accept it, that is great. But, they may reject it and this may be a challenge for you. You may face disgrace. Joseph went through this rejection and it seemed a hopeless situation. But with faith in God, he reached his destiny. We will visit Joseph again later in our study.

You may be humiliated, attacked, abused or isolated when you decide to pursue the dreams that you have in your life and fulfill your purpose. Those closest to you could do that for any the following reasons: jealousy, fear and greed. I have learned that God may show you a glimpse of your destiny or the vision for your life. But He does not always show you the tough journey ahead – the mountains or the valleys in which you will tread. There will be valleys that you are going to walk through by yourself and not with your parents, friends or family; mountains or hills you will have to climb; the cold you will have to endure; the wind or the hot sun you will have to face in order to reach the end of your purpose. As you live on this planet, you are going to be confronted by many forces, choices, obstacles and challenges that will attempt to make you give up on your dreams and vision.

God may show you a glimpse of your destiny or the vision for your life. But He does not always show you the tough journey ahead – the mountains or the valleys in which you will tread.

Your greatest challenges could be those closest to you or they could be your own fears. Do not be intimidated by this and never give up. Deal with these things as they are merely the price you pay to reach the end of your purpose and to fulfill the vision God gave you. You are going to receive negative and positive comments – but mostly negative ones. They may say, "Who do you think you are?" Or, "You are proud and crazy!"

Sometimes, when you face resistance, it is an indication that you are right and you should never give up. You need to know that purpose sometimes separates you from your family and friends. When you start to do things that God created you for, your close friends or family will disapprove of it and may even distance themselves from you or cut off all relationships. However, do not let that discourage you. Keep doing the right things you believe is your purpose.

My challenge to you is that you and those who read this book should discover and get to know the purpose of your life and have a personal sense of significance. You have to find your purpose for life, pursue it and dedicate your time to achieving that purpose. No matter what happens in life, you should run after your purpose and not get distracted by problems, challenges and life's experiences. Challenges are good for people with a purpose. Problems are good for leaders because they help them get stronger. You will never be successful unless you have overcome challenges in life and have paid a price. If you study people in history, those who faced lions, the furnace, were thrown in prison or valleys are considered to be great. Do you want to be great?

Problems are good for leaders because they help them get stronger. You will never be successful unless you have overcome challenges in life and have paid a price.

Vision Has An Appointed Time

The book of Habakkuk 2:2 - 3 says:

Then the Lord answered me and said: "Write the vision and make it plain on tablets, that he may run who reads it. For the vision is yet for an appointed time; But at the end it will speak, and it will not lie. Though it tarries, wait for it; because it will surely come. It will not tarry.

This Scripture quoted above teaches us to write a vision of the things we desire. When you write something down, it is easier to remember. It becomes harder to forget. When you write your vision down, you will start to work towards it and this will be your purpose. Without purpose, which leads you to your vision, you will perish and become disorganized. That is why it has been said that without vision people perish. In fact, the Bible says, "Where there is no revelation, the people cast off restraint; but blessed is he who keeps the law" (Proverbs 29:18).

Notice that it does not say without a leader, people perish. This statement is powerful. It means that vision is more important than leadership. Purpose is even more important than anything else. It also means that without knowing your final destiny, you will take the wrong paths and get lost or perish.

Another example of this scenario is the way pilots leave the airport for a new destination. Pilots all over the world will never depart an airport without a clear purpose. They know where they are going and are on a definite route to get there. The New International Version of the Holy Bible puts it this way in Habakkuk 4: 2-4:

> *Write down the revelation and make it plain on tablets So that a herald may run with it. For the revelation awaits an appointed time; it speaks of the end and will not prove false. Though it linger, wait for it; it will certainly come and will not delay. See, he is puffed up; his desires are not upright — but the righteous will live by his faith.*

The word revelation means something that is covered and unseen but when it is opened, it gets seen. It is the same as vision that comes from inspiration by God. Revelation is an act of revealing something. God has the divine power to reveal things to humans.

Principles

- God is a God of purpose.
- God creates everything for a purpose.
- God creates everything to fulfill its purpose.
- God is motivated by His own purpose.
- God is obligated and responsible to His purpose.
- God is more concerned about His purpose than man's plans and ideas.
- God's purpose is permanent and does not change.
- Everything has a purpose but that purpose must be discovered.

The Story of Helen Keller

Keller Helen (1880-1968) is an outstanding example of a person who conquered physical disabilities. A serious illness, which her doctor called "acute congestion of the stomach and brain," destroyed her sight and hearing at the age of about 1 1/2. Because of this, she could not speak and was entirely shut off from the world. But she rose above her disabilities to gain international fame and to help disabled people live fuller lives (World Book Encyclopedia).

Keller was afflicted at the age of 19 months with an illness (possibly scarlet fever) that left her blind and deaf. She later learned to read and speak slowly and using her fingers to interpret things around her world. She was assisted to go to school and she completed her studies. During those years, she had developed skills. Keller began to write of blindness, a subject that then was a taboo in women's magazines because of the relationship of many cases to venereal diseases. She is credited for producing some of the best books and received awards.

The Lessons from Helen Keller's Life

The story of this lady is an amazing one. Keller was born a normal child, but got an early childhood illness, which made her mute and unable to speak normally. But she did an amazing thing during her lifetime. She wrote poetry and received many awards. Keller found her purpose. She was able to know and do something in her life time. How many of us can succeed just as Helen Keller did? But she rose above her disabilities to gain international fame and to help disabled people live fuller lives (World Book Encyclopedia). In one of her writings, she says "When one door of happiness closes, another opens; but often we look so long at the closed door that we do not see the one which has opened for us." Remember, Helen Keller was born with a handicap. She could not hear. She could not talk. Can you imagine that Helen Keller wrote poetry despite being handicapped? She was able to overcome the fear and stigma of her situation, wrote poetry and received prizes.

Many people sought her counsel and she provided it in spite of the handicap or disability. As a matter of fact, Keller received many awards of great distinction. They included the Chevalier's ribbon of the French Legion of Honor, the Alumni Achievement Award of Radcliffe College, and decorations from many governments (World Book Encyclopedia). The play based on her life, The Miracle Worker, won the Pulitzer Prize in 1960 and was made into a movie. How many eyes do you have? Do not answer this question because it is a rhetorical question.

Yet, how many people have two eyes and have done nothing? How many people have ears and have done nothing? How many people have the mouth but only talk nonsense? Many people do. I would like to say, each and every human being needs to get out of their closet and get to work. Do something important and let us remember you for something you did before you die, before we put you in a cemetery to be forgotten. What you want to be remembered for is what you have done, what you have left behind and your character. Hopefully, when you die, you will be known for something. That something is what I call purpose or doing what we were created to do.

The Value And Significance Of Purpose

When you discover your purpose for living and the reason God created you, the following are the benefits:

1. Purpose will defend you against many challenges and problems.
2. Purpose will keep you going and committed.

3. Purpose will guard you.
4. Purpose will shield you from danger and crisis.
5. Purpose will shelter you.
6. Purpose will be like the armor and cover you.
7. Purpose will protect and defend you.
8. Purpose is your shield, security, and safety.
9. Purpose will give you fulfillment, satisfaction, happiness, joy, and freedom.
10. Purpose helps you to identify with the right people and not merely good people.
11. Purpose enables you to discipline yourself for victory and success.
12. Purpose enables self-control, self-restraint, and an awareness of your decisions and actions.
13. Purpose will keep you on track and enable you to follow the right path. This also means that purpose enables you to stay on the right path without deviation.
14. Purpose enables you to hang in a situation even when the going gets rough and tough. It enables you to rise to endure the challenges of life. It gives you reason for living and surviving.
15. Purpose is a source of inspiration when you are discouraged and downcast. Purpose will give you the stimulus to continue to be motivated towards your mission and vision.
16. Purpose will give you self-discipline and corporate discipline.
17. Purpose gives you focus and direction.
18. Purpose determines your friends and associations.
19. Purpose will drive you to persevere even when life seems useless and meaningless.
20. Purpose makes you wise and have wisdom; you will know who to associate with and who to avoid.

My challenge is that you write down your purpose, visions and goals. Take this opportunity as a significant moment of your life. Go ahead and make the most of this. You can also write down the goals that you want to achieve in your lifetime. Ask yourself:

- What kind of future do I envisage?
- What do I want to do with my life?
- What am I going to do to reach that desired or preferred future?
- What is the main problem that needs to be solved?
- How can I solve that problem?

Most people are concerned about connection, relationships, or favours. I recall when we graduated from the university, we expected our leaders to help us secure jobs. One of my relatives was actually led to believe that someone else would assist him to get fees to complete his degree at Makerere University. But it did not happen; the funder abandoned and ceased supporting him.

Another Person Had a Similar Fate

One of the things I learned from this experience is that the future of everybody is not ahead of you, but it is within you. It is trapped within you and based on your day-to-day decisions, your actions or interests, your goals and desires. When you start making the right decisions, you will realize that your life starts changing and you will experience the good life. Bad decisions will always produce bad quality of life and good decisions will also produce good life. When you change your actions to do the right actions, you begin to advance towards your desire and purpose. When you set the right goals and work towards the achievements of the goals, your life begins to change for the better and over time you will see dramatic changes.

Bad decisions will always produce
bad quality of life and good decisions
will also produce good life.

When you change your desires, you will improve and your life changes. It is important for you to sit and examine your decisions and review whether you have been making the right decisions. When you review your decisions, you may realize that bad ones outweigh good one. This realization is your life's outcomes. Good decisions will lead you to good life and bad decisions will lead you to bad life. Wrong decisions lead to wrong destinations where you do not want to reach. Most people have made bad decisions that have wrecked their lives and they are miserable.

Thefuturedoesnotdependonexternalconditionsorenvironment, but it is determined by attitude, belief, faith and decisions. In life you will find that there will always be some people who will not like you for whatever reason: your skin colour, ideas, education, skills, knowledge, background, race, or tribe. You may not be the same as they are! That is okay. We are all created differently. And you do not have to be liked by everyone! Accept your uniqueness. You will never be loved by everyone. That is life but the most important thing is for you to love yourself and do not hate yourself because somebody rejected you.

Only God can love you despite your shortcomings and sins. You might have made mistakes in life; it is okay; change your life; avoid making the same mistakes and God will forgive you. Pray to God for forgiveness of your sins and God will restore you. You should have self-esteem and love for yourself first before you can love others.

But what is most important is that God created you as you are and He has got a purpose for you in this world. Once you realize this, then it is all about how effective you will live your life and how goal-oriented you are towards your ultimate end. What do you do when you start to understand your purpose in life? Everything you do and especially the people you associate with should align with your purpose in life. You may need to disassociate yourself from bad influences. There are people who will not help you advance your goals in life and will always try to pull you down.

You may need to make new friends – the people that you can learn from and to help you get to where you want to go with your life. Another thing is to read or do things that will enable you reach your life goals or destiny. Read books that are connected with your interests, aspirations, vision and dreams. Stop buying books that are useless to you and not connected with where you want to go in life. Listen to MPs and videos and get closer to mentors in your area of interest. It is important you make the right choices and take the right opportunities and make the right decisions.

Every Purpose Has Its Own Timeframe

Ecclesiastes 3:1 says, "There is a time for everything, and a season for every activity under heaven" (NIV). Every action you want to take has a timeframe. If you want to study to bag a degree, there is a time allocated for it and not forever. If you want to build a house, you do not have forever to do it. Everything has a time attached to it because it is under the heavens. In heaven there is no time, it is called eternity. It is timeless and time you cannot be measured. The New King James Version (NKJV), it says "To everything there is a season, a time for every purpose under heaven." I love what the King James Version says in the above Scripture that everything has a season. Everything has a time. All things have seasons. I love this Scripture because in it, there is life and success. Why? Everything has its own season.

There is nothing that lasts forever except God and His promises. If you have no money right now, it is just a season. If you are rich right now, it is just a season. If things are rosy right now, it is a season. If you are a professor now, it is just a season. If you are a teacher, it is just a season. If your spouse has divorced you, it is just a season. If someone has died, it is just a season. I love this statement because life is seasonal. A secret to life is that it is seasonal; situations are seasonal. Problems are seasonal and they come in seasons. People come in seasons. Poverty is seasonal. Riches and wealth are seasonal and never last forever. Power is seasonal and has a timeline. Power will not be in the hands of dictators forever. Authority is seasonal and does not last forever. Things like human problems, happiness, marriage, riches, or poverty are seasonal. All things are seasonal. Relationships go through seasons. Even marriages have seasons when couples do not speak to each other. Things are seasonal.

These are all seasonal because to everything there is a season. Let me say something. There are leaders whom we know and who thought they own the world or their countries for example (Muammar Gadhafi, Hosni Mubarak and Saddam Hussein among others). These people are no longer presidents; two of them are dead; and Mubarak is out of power. They had power, but they forgot the principle that everything is seasonal. If things are going well right now, you must remember it is seasonal and it is not forever. If you have got sickness, remember it is not permanent. If you have no job at the moment, it is a temporary experience; there could be a job coming your way next year. Do not do stupid things that you will regret because of temporary challenges or bad experiences in life. The second part says, "There is a time for every purpose under heaven." God sets time for everything. Every purpose has its own time frame allocated by God. There is a time to be born and a time to die. A time to work and a time to rest. A time to lead and a time to give up power. A time to mentor and a time not to mentor. A time to teach and not to teach. There is a time when you will have problems or challenges, but there is a season when there seems to be no problems.

The life we have on Earth came with an eternal purpose. Every purpose has its allotted time and it is not going to happen forever. God created us for a time to fulfil a purpose. When you know your purpose, it will keep you going amidst problems. You will be motivated and challenged to work hard. Can you think a bit about the meaning of the part of the sentence "under heaven?" This to me means time is only applicable on Earth and that under heaven and above heaven there is no time. It also means in heaven time is cancelled. That is why the Bible says God lives in eternity or in heaven. Humans need to understand the essence of time in that God who lives in heaven and has allocated everything a specific time here on Earth (under heaven). We must remember this all the time. When you know your purpose, time becomes a constant discussion and concern because you do not have forever to do it. Nothing lasts forever. The person reading this book should know that everything has a time and that purpose is only fulfilled within the time limit set by God.

No additional time will be given to you. Therefore, stop wasting time and stop thinking that you have plenty of time. The time you have now is the only time that you have and must use effectively.

Maximize the time in your hands. If you waste the time you have now, you may not get another chance. You cannot recover it. Many people waste the time by doing things that are not beneficial in enabling the accomplishment of purpose. Do you waste your time? Ecclesiastes 3:11 says, "He has made everything beautiful in its time. Also he has put eternity in their hearts, except that no one can find out the work that God does from the beginning to the end." When you complete your purpose, God says He will make everything beautiful. Beautiful means mature and perfect. God will make things perfect at His appointed time. God decides when the time will be good, better, and excellent. God will decide when you will achieve your dreams. Purpose and vision are connected; purpose leads you to the vision that God places in your heart. Without purpose and vision, you will have time without knowing how to use the time God has given you. A vision given by God requires it to be written so that it is not forgotten. Purpose that is written leads to the vision.

Time For Purpose Completion

Most people hurry with their purpose and want to start doing things even before it is the right time. If you try to rush or hurry it up, you could end up failing or not succeeding. Jesus told people who were attending a wedding function that His time had not come. Jesus' mother, Mary, said to Jesus, "They have no wine." Jesus said to her, "Woman, what does your concern have to do with me? My hour has not yet come." The principle here is always being careful not do things before the appointed hour and if the hour comes, you will do and it will succeed (John 2:1-4). However, Jesus came to a realization of himself in the process of the wedding, that this was in fact the beginning of His miracle ministry.

Jesus Repeated The Same Message

In John 7:6, Jesus said to them, "My time has not yet come, but your time is always ready." The point to note here is that until the time has been set and permitted by God, it means you are not ready. Even Jesus, the Son of God accepted this fact that the time had not yet come. This also implies that some of the things you want, you might not get them because you are not ready. For instance, you might want a Mercedes Benz because you see people who own them; the car looks good and people enjoy the Benz. God will not give you the Benz because you might not have the capacity to maintain the car through paying for expensive spare parts, service fees, and high insurance and manage all the expenses related to the Benz. When the time is right, God will give you the grace to manage challenges. God's time is different from our time.

Also John 12:27 says, "...Father, save me from this hour? But for this purpose I came to this hour." When the hour to fulfil your purpose comes, you will know it and it means your true self will be manifested. Jesus said that the Son of Man should be glorified. Glory means to reveal or show the true nature and essence of God. The person who finds purpose brings glory to God. On the other hand, those who are yet to discover their purpose do not bring glory to Him. In addition, when you know your purpose, you will know it and you will have confidence. Time is given to you to fulfil purpose at the appointed time. John 17:1 states, "Father, the hour has come. Glorify your Son that your Son also may glorify you." To fulfil your purpose, you need to have time to pray and work with faith fixed on God. You cannot fulfil the purpose of God without God. God has to be consulted. Everyone in the world, Christians and non-Christians, all have 24 hours every day. Rich or poor, people have the same hours every day.

You cannot fulfil the purposes
of God without God.

Practical Advice To Apply

The practical advice is for you to learn to count your days. Psalms 90:12, "So teach us to number our days that we may gain a heart of wisdom." When you do not know how to use time, the Bible in this text says you cannot gain a heart of wisdom and you are you are unwise. Learn to count the days or put it this way. Learn to plan how your day will be used through what is call time management. The biggest reason people have problems is because they lack management skills, which I call mismanagement.

From today on, you will need to go back and look at the reasons why you are that stuck in the same position without progress in life. You will find that your biggest problem is mismanagement of time, resources, and opportunities. What I came to learn in life is that what you mismanage you will lose. When you mismanage your life, you will lose it. When you mismanage your money, it will be lost. When you mismanage your marriage, it will be lost. When you mismanage your health, you will lose it. Mismanagement is a problem that causes people or organizations to incur s or fails. You must address it and fix the way you manage your time and resources. Management is the solution to mismanagement.

What I came to learn in life
is that what you mismanage you will lose.
When you mismanage your life,
you will lose it. When you mismanage
your money, it will be lost.

Everything Created Has Its Intended Purpose Or Purposes

Proverbs 20:5 says, "The purposes of a person's heart are deep waters, but one who has insight draws them out." Look at this statement more carefully. The Scripture is telling us that a person's heart is deep water. To get the purpose from the heart requires insight. Insight means wisdom and understanding. This means that purpose cannot be achieved without knowledge, understanding, and wisdom. There is nothing that can be accomplished without getting knowledge, understanding, and applying wisdom. As you begin to think about your purpose, you need to check yourself if you have knowledge. Once you understand that, then you need to be wise enough to apply it. Without knowledge in your purpose, you will not be able to fulfil it and you will gamble your way.

It will be like a doctor who gives wrong prescription to treat a patient. You might be having great ideas that you need to achieve, but if you do not have knowledge, wisdom, and understanding you will not be able to get your purpose achieved. You need knowledge, wisdom, and understanding to accomplish your plans. If you do not have knowledge, you need to go back to get knowledge, understanding, and wisdom to achieve your purpose. There are millions of people with empty minds, without knowledge and wisdom who pray to God to help them. However, God says He cannot work with you until you get wisdom and knowledge. God works with people who have found wisdom and knowledge.

There are millions of people with empty minds, without knowledge and wisdom who pray to God to help them. However, God says He cannot work with you until you get wisdom and knowledge. God works with people who have found wisdom and knowledge.

Every Individual Is Created For And With Purpose

Ecclesiastes 3:1 says, "To everything there is a season, a time for every purpose under heaven." Previously, I emphasized the season aspect in this verse. Now look at the purpose aspect. There is nothing on Earth that has no purpose. Everything that you see has an intended purpose. Even the smallest insect has a purpose. Everything has a purpose. Anything that has no purpose is thrown away. If you had no contribution to make, God would not allow you to be born on Earth without a purpose. God does not create humans for beauty alone but with a purpose and for a purpose. The danger is most humans do not establish this purpose.

Dream Big Dreams

Genesis 37 reveals a powerful message of great dreams of purpose. Joseph dreamt of greatness and spoke about his dreams to his family, parents, and went to his brothers who were looking at their flock in the field. Joseph saw himself as a ruler. Most people do not know why they are created and that is still the reason they have not found their purpose and have not even dreamt about it. Take a moment to dream and think about the purpose that you want to achieve. Take note and write it down. What is something that is so great to be achieved for God? What is your desire? Are there some things you keep thinking about? Write those ideas down.

Most People Are Afraid To Pursue Their Purpose

God is so good because He says the beginning of a thing is not important as the end of it. It does not matter where your life started, but what matters is where it ends. Take a look at Job 8:7, which says, "Your beginnings will seem humble, so prosperous will your future be." The reason I am presenting this Scripture is to remind you that no matter where you start to pursue your purpose, whether big or small, if you have a vision, you should not be afraid of how you will achieve it. Follow through with it and you will overcome your fears.

People fear to pursue their purpose and vision because they lack knowledge, information, resources and generally are afraid of people's opinions among many others. You might be a junior officer in your office or organization. You might be a cleaner or driver. You might be at the low end of things, but believe me, your situation can change. You might start out small, but in the end you can be much greater. Don't worry; you will not die doing what you are doing today! Things can change. Your bank account will grow. Your wisdom will increase. Your opportunities will increase irrespective of the fact that you were not born with a silver spoon. Your humble beginning should be an advantage.

My experiences during my childhood propelled me to start fulfilling my purpose. I remember when there was a war in my home district of Bukedea in Uganda. This war shaped my mind and I resolved that when I grow up, I would work with an organization that help people affected by war. To the glory of God, I have been able to fulfill this purpose in my lifetime. I believe am still going to do greater works than I can imagine.

You too have the ability to start whatever you have been dreaming. Do not fear but suspend any disbelief you have and start now. I had no idea of working with this organization when I was growing up in the slums of Mbale and in the rural areas of Teso in Eastern Uganda.

Challenges Are Just For A Season

The message of Job 8:7 has transformed my life. I remember the days when I was a high school student, and there was war in my home region of Teso in Uganda. Hundreds of people were displaced and many others died. These people died without fulfilling their purposes. As a teenager, I read that part of the Scripture and it made no sense to me at that time. After years in high school, I was admitted to Makerere University and completed my degree studies. I kept on reading this wonderful book called the Bible and I can't recall the number of times I read this Scripture. It began to make sense to me and the Lord applied its true meaning in my life. I saw an immediate improvement in my life. My beginnings were changing and so was my life. When I left the Makerere University, I got a job in Eastern Uganda, and we were implementing a project in the remotest and poorest villages of Uganda. I used to go to work on a bicycle, sometimes with no food at all, but I kept on working hard. I was faithful, committed, and determined. I went to that local community, taught children and worked with community leaders. Sometimes, I got so discouraged, but what kept me going was that Scripture from the book of Job.

It was very challenging. I used to walk through the swamps of dirty water, sometimes beaten by rain or hailstorms, but that Scripture reminded me that the future was going to be different and present conditions were not permanent. My future would be great, better and prosperous! At that time, I could not afford even a car, but as I write today there are four cars parked at home in Kampala for my use when I need them. As I write this, I travel both by road and by airplanes most of the time. I have been to places I never expected to be. And stayed in expensive hotels and apartments. I have been to South Africa, Ethiopia, Nigeria, Kenya, Senegal, Spain, Belgium, Netherlands, Rwanda, and other countries around the world. I believe with all my heart; more is yet to come. It takes faith to believe in God's word.

Who can do all these things? To me, it is only God who can do that and make you great. God can make your beginning seem humble and yet He has a great and beautiful future for you. Only God can make a shepherd boy like David a king. Only God can make someone who had been a murderer into leader and deliverer of His people, and his name is Moses. Only God can do things that man cannot do. You might be in a situation where you think you are failing or things are not working. But my advice is this: Do not underestimate the situation where you are right now. Believe me, God can change the situation and make you rise above that situation and achieve your dreams and visions that are in your heart. You need to start a new relationship with God. In the last section of this book, there is a prayer of reconnection with God and if you pray that prayer, God will begin to work with you and make you successful.

Paul and Peter were both apostles, but with different missions, or purposes. These two men are among the apostles of Jesus Christ. However, both have unique histories about their lives. Paul, as we all know, was a chief planner and architect in the killing of the first disciples and followers of Jesus Christ. He planned and witnessed the stoning of Stephen. You will find the full story in Acts 8. On the other hand, Peter was one of the twelve disciples who spent three and a half years with Jesus Christ. He witnessed all the miracles that were done by Jesus. He also witnessed the appearance of Moses and Elijah on the night Jesus Christ was transfigured. He promised never to desert His master. He promised to die with Him when Jesus Christ talked about His death. Peter, however, denied his master when the master was arrested. But the interesting thing about these fellows is that God created them to fulfil their purpose. They were created to take the gospel to the circumcised and uncircumcised, the Jews and the Gentiles. Peter and Paul had different purposes. So it is with you. Galatians 2:7-8, states,

> *On the contrary, they recognized that I had been entrusted with the task of preaching the gospel to the uncircumcised, just as Peter had been to the circumcised. For God, who was at work in Peter as an apostle to the circumcised, was also at work in me as an apostle to the Gentiles.*

From this Scripture, we see that Paul was aware of his purpose and mission. He was assigned by God to preach the gospel to the uncircumcised or those who were also known as the Gentiles. In the same way, Apostle Peter was responsible for passing the good news of the Kingdom of Heaven to the circumcised, the Jewish people.

Purpose Might Be Completed In Phases

The greatest discoveries and revelations I have come to know about purpose is that purpose can be in multiples. When God created the Sun, in Genesis 1:14-18, the purpose was manifold. God created the Sun to divide the day from night, divide seasons and rule the day and night. We also see in Genesis 1:26-28 that man was created to dominate, fruitful and multiply. God created man to dominate and have control. God created man to be fruitful. God created man to multiply. In this alone, you can see man was not created for a single purpose, such as to dominate. God created man to accomplish multiple purposes.

The iphone Has Multiple Purposes

Another practical example is an iPhone which has multiple purposes. A manufacturer makes a product but gives it the ability to perform multiple purposes. An iPhone can be used for communication, sending and receiving messages, get weather forecasts, taking pictures, playing music, as a calculator, and among other things. This is true for even humans. Genesis 2:15 states, "The Lord God took the man and put him in the Garden of Eden to tend and keep it." There were many reasons why God created man and this is true with everything that God created. The difficulty in living is that most people cannot establish the purpose. You were born to do so much. Therefore, do not sit around complaining or lamenting. God has many purposes for you.

A manufacturer makes a product but gives it the ability to perform multiple purposes.

Jesus Christ, The Only Son Of God

Another example is the life of Jesus Christ. Jesus Christ was born for a reason, but before the final purpose was fulfilled on the cross, He accomplished several purposes that led to the ultimate purpose. One of Jesus' purposes was to teach that you and I can overcome temptations. Jesus' purpose was also to raise up men and women who would preach the Gospel of the Kingdom of God (Matthew 4:18-19). Jesus' purpose was also teaching His followers about the Kingdom of heaven (Matthew 5). Jesus' purpose was to teach humans that you can love your enemies (Matthew 5:43-45). Jesus was on Earth to teach and give lessons about prayer (Matthew 6: 8-13). Jesus' purpose was to teach about faith (Matthew 8). He taught about the narrow way that leads to life (Matthew 7: 13-14). There are multiple purposes that Jesus came to Earth fulfil. Therefore, we too have multiple purposes.

Purpose Sometimes Require Teamwork

I have come to realize that nothing can be done without people, but it must be the right people. Nothing happens in isolation. Nothing happens alone. For instance, a tree cannot survive without being attached to the soil for it to be able to live and grow. This is the same for all creation, including you. This is why children are dependent on their parents or guardians before they become independent and interdependent. Let us look at the next Scriptures. In Matthew 10, Jesus called His disciples and gave power over unclean spirits. Jesus sent the disciples out to preach and carry out an outreach ministry. Jesus did not do it alone but chose to do it.

He even left them to continue with purpose. The Great Commission:

> *Go and make disciples of all nations, baptizing them in the name of the Father, the Son and the Holy Spirit, teaching them to obey everything I have commanded you. And surely I am with you always, even unto the end of the age.* (Matthew 28:19-20)

Romans 12:4-5 says, "For as we have many members in one body, but all the members do not have the same function, so we being many, are one body in Christ..." To achieve purpose, members must come together to do the work. No single person can fulfil his purpose alone. Moses had to work with Aaron, Joshua, and Mariam. Jesus Christ had His disciples, Peter, and the apostles. Paul needed to work with Timothy. Paul had to work with Silas. This is a great lesson for those of you with a desire to accomplish something in this generation.

God's Purpose Is More Powerful Than Man's Plans

God will prevail over man's plans. I want to highlight here how people think they are smarter than God. I have met people like this. Some people think they can play games with God. Some men and women think they can come up with their plans and achieve them without God's approval. I would like to advise you before you begin to do anything, you need to establish a relationship with God and dedicate your plans before God and seek the counsel from God the Creator of all things.

God's Purpose Will Prevail Over Man's Plans

Proverbs 19:21 says, "Many are the plans in a man's heart, but it is the Lord's purpose prevails." It is important for a man or woman to consult God through prayer if they want to succeed in their plans. Many people make beautiful plans that are not in line with God's purpose and that is why plans fail to become a reality and achieve the intended results and outcomes. People's plans fail because they are not aligned with God's purpose for their lives and this is why God does not answer some prayers or God says, "Not yet." God does not answer your prayers until it is in line with his will or purpose. God's purpose is more important than your plans. It is God's purpose that you succeed and not the plans of man. The key here is to align your plans with God's purpose. Many times people come up with their plans without consulting with God and God does not support the plans to succeed. The reason or cause of failure could be in this message. As you begin to develop your plans, you need to consult and make contact with God to be assured that your actions are in line with his purpose for your life.

God's Purpose Will Stand As Planned

Furthermore, Isaiah 14:24 states, "The Lord Almighty has sworn, 'Surely as I have planned, so it will be, and as I have purposed, so it will stand." If God has purposed something for you, believe God and not man for His purpose for your life. God's purpose for you will stand and nothing can change it. From Scriptures, we are made to understand that God's plans and purpose are decided by him. The purpose of God stands forever and it means purpose is permanent and does not change. God's plans never change. In addition, God usually develops and designs plans for everything to accomplish His will. No matter how you plan, unless it is in line with God as He has planned from the beginning of time, it will be difficult to achieve that plan. Also, what God decided is what will happen and what God purposes will be the end result.

God Knows The End From The Beginning

Furthermore, Isaiah 46:10 says: "I make known the end from the beginning, from ancient times, what is still to come. I say: My purpose will stand and I will do all that I please." It is only God who knows the end from the beginning. God declares that only His purpose will stand and all other purposes done by man through their own schemes and ways cannot stand. God already knows your future. God knows your destination and the end of your life. God knew your end before He began creating you. God knows your end. God knows your mission. God knows the vision for your life. Your future is God's past or history. God will only do things that please Him in regard to your purpose and potential. God will do what pleases him in regard to your future, vision, and destination. God does things according to what pleases Him and His will. This means that you need to align yourself with God's purpose. If God is pleased with you, then he will do what pleases him to make you reach your destiny and fulfil the purposes that he created you for in this earth.

The Lord's Purpose Stands Forever

Psalms 33:11 says; "The purpose of the Lord stands forever, the plans of His heart to all generations." God's purpose for your life will stand forever, but you will discover that purpose by going back to God. The purpose of God does not change or get affected by changes in time or context or challenges that you have experienced or failures of your life or mistakes that you have made in life. God does not care what you have done provided you are willing to come back to Him with commitment and determination to follow him. God will use anybody who comes back to Him. That is why God used Paul (formerly called Saul) for His purpose. Paul's ignorance and lack of knowledge about God's purpose could not stop him. No one can change the purpose of God for your life. If God has chosen you to do His will, His purpose will be achieved because it will not fail but stand forever. In addition, the plans that God has for you and your descendants stand for all generations. Abraham is an example of a man that God worked His purpose through and the plans are for all generations of Abraham. The secret to success is having faith in God's purpose to stand forever.

The Words Of Jesus Christ
To His Disciples And Friends

I believe that these Scriptures should give you great insights of how it is important for you to remain in Christ. You can see both the benefits or costs or even what happens when we choose to refuse to abide in Jesus Christ. The key is to abide in the "true vine." I will show what this means. When you abide and the words of Jesus Christ remain in you, then you can ask whatever you desire and it shall be done to you. I want us to study each of the verses and see the comments that I have posted below each of the Scriptures.

Remain Attached To God
As A Branch To The Vine

John 15:5 says, "I am the vine; you are the branches. If you remain in me and I in you, you will bear much fruit; apart from me you can do nothing." In this text, there is a condition that anyone who remains in Jesus Christ will bear much fruits and without Him, you can do nothing. Notice the words, "bear much fruit." "Much fruit" means multiple fruits. The next word is nothing. Jesus is not saying something. Jesus is clear: nothing. The word "nothing" means zero. The key lesson here is we cannot be outside of God and expect to succeed. It is impossible.

Besides, John 15:6 says, "If you do not remain in me, you are like a branch that is thrown away and withers; such branches are picked up, thrown into the fire and burned." It is important to note that when you disconnect yourself from Jesus Christ, you will be thrown away, withered and burnt. Most people think they are clever and never believe in having a connection with Christ. The key to success, to avoid being thrown away and burnt is connection with Christ. When a branch of a tree is cut off, the branch dies. But if it stays attached to a tree, it will continue to be a live because it will receive food from the roots and oxygen from the leaves. This gives you a clear understanding that without connection, the branch dies. Without connection with Jesus Christ, humans die and are helpless.

Bearing Fruit Is Only Possible Through Attachment To God

Also, John 15:10 says, "This is to my Father's glory, that you bear much fruit, showing yourselves to be my disciples." This is interesting for me. Jesus is giving the reason. He is answering the questions, "Why? What is the reason for fruit-bearing?" Glory reveals the true nature of God. Glory reveals what God can do. Glory reveals God's power. Glory reveals God's true ability and nature. Glory reveals that God desires that we bear much fruit and be fruitful. We have to remain attached to God through fellowship, prayer and obedience to His word. On the other hand, we disconnect ourselves from God through disobedience. Disobedience means we will never bear fruit. When you detach or disconnect from God, there are no fruits that you will bear.

God Choses And Appoints

John 15:16 says, "You did not choose me, but I chose you and appointed you so that you might go and bear fruit – fruit that will last – and so that whatever you ask in my name the Father will give you." God chose us before the foundations of the Earth were laid. You did not come to the world by your own choice and decision. God has that authority. God has that power. When you understand this in your life, you will begin to enjoy God and have peace on Earth. God also appointed you. He knows what your purpose is here on Earth. God will deploy you to fulfil his appointment. God gave and placed in you a seed that is supposed to bear fruit that will last forever. You cannot have an appointment without a seed in you. In every human being, there is a seed that is supposed to bring forth fruit to last. God therefore, placed the future of everything in itself and in the seed.

Enemies of Purpose and Vision

There are many enemies.

1. The "Thief"

John 10:10 says; "The thief comes only to steal and kill and destroy; I have come that they may have life, and have it to the full." In the KJV, it says "abundantly." Many times, I have read this Scripture and many pastors, preachers and evangelists use it to brand the devil or Satan as a thief. This is true. However, the thief is capable of stealing, killing, and destroying your purpose and potential. The thief could be your bad character, lack of discipline, pride, bad company, associations, friends, bad family, poor relationships, and non-supportive networks. Furthermore, the thief could be fear, past success, challenges, obstacles, and problems.

2. Pride, Arrogance, And Power

One of the greatest problems the human race has failed to deal with is the intoxication of pride and power. The majority of humans are "proud" and love power and want to exercise it in a wrong way.

There is a saying that "absolute power corrupts absolutely." One sad example is Idi Amin, the former Ugandan President who became a dictator and was consumed by pride and power. Furthermore, pride comes before a fall and destruction.

My advice to you is that you need to learn how to deal with pride. How you handle pride will determine how high you fly and how long you will travel in the long journey of life.

The same with power, when not handled properly and managed, it destroys humans. God Himself will use His power against man. Job 24:22 says, "But God draws the mighty away with His power; He rises up, but no man is sure of life." God draws away from those who think they are powerful. They do not even know and are not sure about their lives.

3. Doubt And Disbelief In Yourself

The next enemy is doubt. Doubt and disbelief are two related enemies that will affect you in your pursuit of purpose in fulfilling your greatest potential. Doubt is disbelief. Doubt is an enemy. When you doubt, it will create fear and you lose confidence. Whenever you doubt something, it means you have no belief in it.

4. Lack Of Self-Confidence And Self-Doubt

Lack of self-confidence is another enemy with which you have to deal. Confidence is created by your belief systems and when your belief systems are challenged and tested, you will become weak, wavering, losing your concentration, and commitment. In order to avoid this problem, you need to keep your faith. Do not lose the faith that you have because it is the source of confidence.

5. Wrong Associations

Another enemy is the type of people with whom you spend your time. These people will determine the achievement of your dream and vision or purpose in life. The story of Joseph's family reminds me that His own family turned against him when he spoke about his dreams, vision, and plans. They said things that were an indicator of their unhappiness towards his ideas. "When he told his father as well as his brothers, his father rebuked him and said, 'What is this dream you had? Will your mother and I and your brothers actually come and bow down to the ground before you?" (Genesis 37:10).

The same can happen with you today. Your life may not be improving or changing because of your associations or the people you keep company with. This calls for you to thoroughly review the people with whom you share your time and life with. They could be a reason why you are stuck and you cannot save yourself. The way forward is to dissociate yourself carefully and start to be with people who encourage you when you talk about your dreams, ideas, plans or visions. The people who encourage you are the right friends, but those who discourage or attack your ideas are bad or toxic people. Leave these people immediately if you are passionate about your vision.

Purpose Will Make You Develop Psychological Hardness

Some people never get to know their purpose until they encounter problems. In Jonah 1:9, God told Jonah to go to Nineveh, but he did not agree to go at first. He developed psychological hardness. He became stubborn. He rejected God's instructions. He had chosen to do his own things. This is true for most of us. It is when you get into trouble that you run back to God. Jonah was stubborn. But

God had to take him through the storms of life, under water, inside the fish before he could go to fulfil the purpose of God. Some of you are going through storms, you are under water, and you are inside the belly of the fish. You are facing some challenges personally or in your organization. Do not behave like Jonah. Go back to God. Humble yourself and God will lead you to "Nineveh" (although it may not be what you want to do!). God will guide you to your purpose and you will gain peace and find meaning for living.

Past Behavior Never Stops Purpose

Many people are also trapped by their past lifestyle and never think of doing anything for God. For instance, you could have killed a child through abortion. You could have been in jail. You could have been a thief and now this is holding you back. Today, I tell you to never allow your past lifestyle and conduct stop you from doing or accomplishing your purpose. In Exodus 12:3, God called Moses to lead the Israelites. Before God called him, Moses had murdered an Egyptian (Exodus 2:12). In our societies people would never want to associate with a killer and this man Moses would be called a murderer. That is not how God sees you. In fact, this man Moses is the author of the first five books of the Bible. I wonder how you look at people today who have done evil things around you.

The Life Of A Samaritan Woman

Another example is a Samaritan woman who met Jesus as she had gone to collect water from the well. The Samaritan woman had five husbands (John 4:16-24). In our culture today a woman with five husbands is considered an outcast or a sinner, but Jesus did not see her that way. Jesus had a conversation with her and even asked for water. Jesus revealed a powerful message of true worship to the Samaritan woman. Jesus said in John 4:23-24 "... True worshippers will worship the Father in spirit and in truth; for the Father is seeking such to worship Him. 'God is Spirit, and those who worship Him must worship in spirit and truth."

It does not matter what you have done; God can do anything with you. He can make you a leader of his people. He can make you an author of books for Him. He can give you a message that no one else will get. God can do anything and He does not look at what you have done, but He is concerned about what you can do for Him. The principle is to never allow what you have done in the past to stop you from going on to achieve your dreams and vision that God placed in you. Be willing to obey God when He approaches you and always prepare for the challenges and obstacles.

Saul, Whom We Call Paul, Was A Murderer

Likewise, Acts 9 shows us a story of Saul on the road to Damascus and how he was converted. Saul was a leader of people who were persecuting the early church. He was a mobilizer. Saul was an organizer, a speaker, and talented person. Saul planned to destroy the church by killing the followers. He witnessed the killing and the stoning of Stephen. (Acts 7: 57-60; 8:1)

The story of his conversion is in Acts 9:4: "... Saul, Saul, why are you persecuting me?" and he said, "Who are you, Lord?" Then the Lord said, "I am Jesus, whom you are persecuting." Act 9:6 states that "... Arise and go into the city, and you will be told what you must do." This is an example of what I call purpose. Saul was to be told what to do. Acts 9: 16 says, "For I will show him how many things he must suffer for my name's sake." Everything happens for a reason, which only God knows, and not your friends, family, pastor, or bishop. God does not care about what you have done, but He is concerned with what you are capable of doing and His will. He is concerned about His name.

In other words, God is concerned about His purpose. God used Saul after his conversion in many ways. He became a witness of God's grace, goodness, love, mercy, faith, redemption, and salvation. God used Saul (renamed as Paul) as an author of many books in the New Testament. It does not matter what you have done as an individual, God is God and He can use you even with your mistakes, errors, bad motives, and past actions. He has the capacity to transform you, change your past and use you for the glory of His name. God can use a former murderer as a preacher, teacher, and a writer and to become a witness of His greatness.

Look at what Paul says in 1 Corinthians 15:9-11:

> For I am the least of the apostles and do not even deserve
> to be called an apostle, because I persecuted the church
> of God. But by the grace of God I am what I am, and his
> grace to me was not without effect. No, I worked harder
> than all of them –yet not I, but the grace of God that was
> with me. whether, then, it was I or they, this is what we
> preach, and this is what you believed.

Most people think that all this was happening without God's knowledge. I believe God knew everything and watched all the evil scheming that was going on. When Saul was carrying out his acts and plans, God was watching, but God wanted to show that He can work in spite of what was happening. He can use you to take his message even when there is opposition. God wanted to show that your mistakes and carelessness are not important, but He can use you to fulfil His purpose.

Acts 8:3 says: "But Saul began to destroy the church. Going from house to house, he dragged off men and women and put them in prison." We all know that God is omnipresent and omniscient. God is present everywhere and all knowing. There is nothing that happens, of which God is not aware. Saul's terrible behaviour is described as "havoc" in the King James Version. Havoc means chaos, mayhem, destruction, turmoil, disorder, devastation, confusion and a mess. Paul caused chaos, killed, and destroyed believers. He disorganized followers of Christ and messed up everything. But something I love about God is that no matter what you have done, He will use you to fulfil His purpose just He did with Paul. Like Paul, God knew you before you were born.

God Knows Your Purpose

Jeremiah 1:5 says, "Before I formed you in the womb I knew you, before you were born I sanctified you; I ordained you as a prophet to the nations." Whatever you are born to do, you are set apart. God knows everything that you are to do even before you came to this world and that includes your purpose. Only God knows our purpose and therefore each human being needs to find that purpose. God knows who you will become in life. God knows the end of your life and nobody else knows that. John 9:3 says, "Jesus answered, "Neither this man nor his parents sinned, but that the works of God should be revealed in him."" This is an interesting message. The man was born blind, but the purpose of God was to be fulfilled through him. Jesus said, the works of God were to be revealed. Revealed means to be exposed, made open, or publicized and disclosed. God does certain things in life that will only happen according to His will. God can allow you to be born blind, but there is a reason for that condition.

God Gives You Purpose
Together With The Potential

Meanwhile, Genesis 1:11 states that, "Then God said, 'Let the earth bring forth grass, the herb that yields seed, and the fruit tree that yields fruits according to its kind, whose seed is in itself, on the Earth." God has designed humans with seeds in it and this seed has the potential, ability to multiply and be fruitful. The greatest tragedy is that millions of people die without multiplying and becoming fruitful. How sad is this? Never die before you accomplish the task God brought you to the earth to accomplish. You are here to dominate, multiply, and be fruitful.

Most people think that the future ahead of them is something that is very remote and far away. They are hoping to go there someday. I would like to advise them that every seed has its future inside itself. The potential for the future is built in creation. The future of the mango seed, which is a mango tree, is trapped in the mango seed. The problem is that you might be in the company of wrong people, wrong environment, or wrong associations.

God Mandate Us To Be Fruitful, Multiply
And Have Dominion Over The Earth

Furthermore, Genesis 1:27-28 says,

> So God created Man in his own image; in the image of God
> He created them. Then God blessed them and God said to
> then 'Be fruitful and multiply, fill the earth and subdue it;
> have dominion over the fish of the sea, over the birds of the
> air and every living thing that moves on the earth.

But how can God create two people and just give the assignment to be fruitful, multiply, fill the Earth, and subdue it? Why didn't God just fill the Earth with humans all at once without asking the two to multiply? This means God knew that two people had the potential to be fruitful, multiply, and have dominion on the Earth and not in heaven. God gave man the power to determine what happens on Earth and not to make our way to heaven but religion teaches people the opposite. Most people think we are on Earth and waiting to go to heaven, but actually we have to dominate the Earth and subdue it and that is the mandate. We are here to make a difference before we can return to eternity.

How can God ask two people to fill the whole Earth? All the billions of people on Earth originated from two people who were created first, Adam and Eve. God placed seeds inside two human beings which have produced all the populations of the world. God gives humans the ability to multiply. This ability is called potential.

God Use What Is In Your Hand To Fulfill Purpose

Exodus 4:2-4 says,

> *So the Lord said to him, "What is in your hands?" He said, "A rod." And He said, "Cast it on the ground." So he cast it on the ground, and it became a serpent; and Moses fled from it. Then the Lord said to Moses, "Reach out your hands and take it by the tail." And he reached out his hands and caught it, and it became a rod in his hands.*

When I was working in World Vision (a world relief organization), it was a custom for members of staff to gather for morning devotion every day before we embarked on the day's work. On a fateful day, this Scripture from Exodus was shared and it was the quote of the day. As we completed the devotion and returned to our offices, the still small voice of the Holy Spirit asked me, "What is in your hands?" As I quietly sat in that office, it dawned on me that it was the job that I was doing. God told me that the job I have will be the weapon that will be used to fulfil my dreams and achieve the desires of my hearts.

God told me to keep the job and protect it. Believe me, it was the experience in that job that enabled me to get another job with World Food Program in Northern Uganda and several other jobs in other organizations such as The United Nations Children's Fund (UNICEF).

The job was in my hand and God used it to raise me to a level where I am today. What do you have in your hands? What has God given you? Do not throw it away, but use it to do what God desires. The rod that Moses had in his hands is what God used to make people believed God. Sometimes, Christians do not know what is in their hands and God will use it to accomplish purpose. God can use what you already have to fulfil His purpose even though you do not know it. Moses had a rod in his hands, but did not know that the rod could become a snake. I believe that all humans on Earth do not know what they have. God has given you things in your hands, but you may be unaware of their potential.

You do not know what they can do or what will happen when you use them. The practical advice is to be very careful with what God has placed in our hand and use it carefully. He has entrusted you with your family, children, relatives, friends, jobs, education, money, assets, property, land, buildings, cars, and many others things that you possess or own. God used Moses with his rod to deliver the Israelites to the Promised Land. It was the same rod that Moses used to strike the Red Sea to create a passage for God's people on their way to the Promised Land. God's purpose was to deliver Israelites to the Promised Land.

God Never Healed Moses From Being Unable To Speak Well

Furthermore, Exodus 4:11-12 says, "So the Lord said to him, "Who has made man's mouth? Or who makes the mute, the deaf, the seeing or the blind? Have not I the Lord? Now therefore, go and I will be with your mouth and teach you what you shall say." This is interesting and I love it. God says no matter what excuses or reasons you will give, God will stand with His purpose and He even promised Moses that He was going to be with his mouth and teach him. In other words, God is a teacher. He can teach us what we do not know and make us know so we can say it to fulfil His purpose. God does not allow various reasons to interfere with His purpose. That is why you should not be afraid to obey God when He calls you.

I have seen people who have given up in life because of a disability or some inadequacy in life. Some say I do not know how to speak very well. Some say they are not gifted and talented. They have all these reasons and excuses. You have to know that God does not make a mistake during creation. He creates you with the ability and gives you the potential. God creates you to fulfil your purpose. He will give you the amount of ability that is commensurate with your purpose. Do not blame or stop believing in your abilities. You need to believe in yourself and God.

God Will Deliver You For A Good Purpose

Jeremiah 15:11 says, "The LORD said, "Surely I will deliver you for a good purpose; surely I will make your enemies plead with you in times of disaster and times of distress." The God we serve and worship is so generous. God is kind, compassionate and loving. In this Scripture, God is declaring that He is capable of delivering you and me for a good purpose. Have you ever wondered what happens to us is planned by God? God promises that even our enemies will become our friends and will not fight against us. If it is God's purpose, your enemies will become your friends and they will support you.

One day, I was watching National Geography channel on a cable TV and I saw a lion taking care of a young antelope. This was strange to me. I began to wonder how could this be. How come and why? Lions usually chase antelopes and eat them. As I pondered on those questions, I concluded that only God can make enemies come together. It is only God who can deliver the enemies to become your friends when disaster and crisis occur. God can do things that you are unable to do and God has no obligation to explain to you because God has ultimate authority and power.

God's Promises Are Made To Fulfil His Purpose, Not Man's Plans

Romans 8:28 is a powerful Scripture about God's promises, which many believers have confused or misinterpreted. This text states that, "And we know that all things work together for good to those who love God, to those who are called according to his purpose." Look at that. All things work if you love God and are called according to His purpose. You might even love God and never get all things working good for you. Why? This is because it is not according to His purpose. This also means that finding God's purpose is more important because all things will work or you will become successful when you know God's purpose.

Nobody Will Run Away
And Avoid Fulfilling God's Purpose

The purposes of God are forever and nobody created can run away and avoid doing the work of God. An example is the life and story of Jonah as recorded in Jonah chapters 1 and 2. God told Jonah to go to Nineveh and warn the people about their wickedness that had come before God. But Jonah decided to go in a different direction and place away from where God wanted. Jonah decided to go to Tarshish by way of a city called Joppa. He found a ship that was going to Tarshish, paid for the fare and was on his way. While in the ship, a storm came up that was so strong; passengers in the ship were terrified that the ship was going to sink. The crew in the ship wanted to know who was causing the storm. Were the gods angry at someone? Who was it? They cast lots and it fell to Jonah who was asleep in the bottom of the ship. They woke him up and interrogated him. He admitted that He was running away from God who made the heaven and Earth. Then Jonah told them to throw him in the sea and the storm became quiet. This story is powerful in the fact that when God gives some people an assignment, they want to run away from it.

I will put this to you: If you try to disobey God like Jonah did, you will receive a "storm." Or you will face challenges. There will be no peace or comfort. There will be instability and conditions of life will become chaotic. The waves of life will batter you up and down from all sides until you accept His will. The storms will take you under the water but God is with you in the water. Never run away when God gives you an assignment because God will never give up on you. If God choses to use you, you cannot run away from Him. Jonah tried to avoid doing God's business, but God followed him up.

Never run away when God gives you an assignment, because God will never give up on you.

Opposition Will Come Against You As You Are Fulfilling God's Purpose

The book of Nehemiah shows a story about a prayer for the Jews. Let me give some background here. Nehemiah the governor of Jerusalem who helped in re-building the wall of the city (Nehemiah 1:1; 8:9; 10:1; 12:26, 47). Nehemiah was a descendant of the Jewish population that had been taken captive to Babylon in 586 BC. In 539 BC, Cyrus the Persian gained control over all of Mesopotamia. He permitted the Jewish exiles to return to the city of Jerusalem. Nearly a century later, in Nehemiah's time, the Persian ruler was Artaxerxes I Longimanus (Who ruled between 465–424 BC). Nehemiah was his personal cupbearer (Nehemiah 1:11).

In 445 BC, Nehemiah learned of the deplorable condition of the returned exiles in Jerusalem. The wall of the city was broken down, the gates were burned, and the people were in distress. Upon hearing this, Nehemiah mourned for many days, fasting and praying to God. His prayer is one of the most moving in the Old Testament (Nehemiah1:5–11). Nehemiah then received permission from Artaxerxes to go to Judah to restore the fortunes of his people. He was appointed governor of the province with authority to rebuild the city walls. Nehemiah asked the people about the situation in Jerusalem. The people said that Jerusalem was in ruins and the walls were destroyed and broken down. This greatly distressed Nehemiah who cried to God because the problems of the people of Israel and walls of Jerusalem are broken down. God gave him the task to rebuild the walls.

Pray When People Attack You Or Your Dreams and Vision

When Nehemiah was attacked, he prayed to God as mentioned in Nehemiah 4:4: "Hear, O our God, for we are despised; turn their reproach on their own heads, and give them as plunder to a land of captivity." Never reply people who despise you, but pray to God. The two men even became unhappy when they heard that the walls were half way to completion. There will be moments in your life time when people will test you and even get at you because they want to stop or discourage you from working towards your goal. You must not bow to the pressure or the attacks that come to you. You will need to learn the way or strategy that Nehemiah applied when people planned to stop him. This will always be the situation. Never give up. Adversaries will plan to kill you, but press on and never give up.

Nehemiah 4:11 states, "And our adversaries said, 'They will neither know nor see anything, till we come into their midst and kill them and cause the work to 'cease." There was a desire to kill them and cause the work to cease. Imagine that! There are people in your circle right now who are against what you are and they want you to stop. They may be envious of you. There may be a number of reasons. I urge you to learn from Nehemiah. He never gave up. He also positioned men to guard the project from all corners against the physical threat from their enemies.

You must do that when you have a project of your own. Never leave the project because of negative comments of people. You have to keep going. Nehemiah gave clear instructions about what to do when there is an attack or problems. When you reach that situation in life or as you work to implement God's plans, you need to learn to send messages and avoid going to the territory where the enemies are located. Tell your enemies you have great project you are doing. Do not meet with them.

Furthermore, Tobias and Sanballat intensified their mission and schemes against Nehemiah (see Nehemiah 6). Another man, Geshem, joined Tobias and Sanballat in the attack. They sent a message to Nehemiah for a meeting (Nehemiah 6:2) and the plan was to harm him. But Nehemiah sent messengers to meet them with a message by saying, "I am doing a great work, so that I cannot come down. Why should the work cease while I leave it and go down with you?"

As you struggle to work on some important task there may be some people who plan to harm you. They may even invite you to negotiate with them. The men insisted and sent the messengers with threatening letters to Nehemiah five times. But Nehemiah did not agree or accept the invitation. Be careful and always send somebody in your place to represent you with your message and reasons why you can't join them. The project continued until it was completed. Nehemiah completed his purpose and fulfilled God's purpose of rebuilding the wall. The key secret in life is get involved in a great work or project without stopping doing the project that God grants you to accomplish. Idle people get into problems and are destroyed. In my own life, every time I complete a project, I start another new one almost immediately and this keeps me busy and away from wrong groups and associations. Learn to be competent and effective in accomplishing your tasks.

God's Purposes Are Different From Man's

Note that what happens on earth is determined by man because of the power God gave mankind. God gave each person a will, but God's purposes are totally different from the plans of man. When I was seeking admission into the university – a month before the admission lists were released – I prayed to God to help me get a "better" course. In those days, the Bachelor of Commerce was considered the best and everybody wanted the "better course." When the University released the admission lists, I was not considered for the course because of the increase in cut-off points. I was so discouraged and sad. I was not happy about the course of study to which I was admitted. To make matters worse, one of the students who was not admitted even teased me saying, "So what will you be?"

After graduation, my friends and I all went in different directions in pursuit of our own dreams and visions. God favored me and I found myself working in the United Nations, which is a dream job for most people in my country and most countries in the world. Ironically, my friends who did the "better courses" are still in Uganda and some are in their country of origin. What can explain that? I believe that only God knows what will happen to us. This story is a testimony that God's ways are not our ways, nor His thoughts are our thoughts and plans not His plans.

God's Thoughts Are Different From Man's Thoughts

You need to know that God's thoughts are different from yours and His ways are different from your ways. What God thinks about you is unknown and so are His plans. The secret to peace and confidence in life is what God thinks about you. God is not obliged to tell you his thoughts and the ways you will take in life. God can lead you in a way or a road you can think is bad for you, but in the end you will see it was right path.

In Isaiah 55:8-9, the Lord says,

> For My thoughts are not your thoughts, nor are your ways my ways," says the Lord. "For as the heavens are higher than the earth, so are my ways higher than your ways, and my thoughts than your thoughts.

This is what God thinks. He thinks differently from humans and His ways are so different from the ways that men take. We must learn from these words of Prophet Isaiah. Our ways are not God's ways and our thoughts are not God's thoughts. Let God Be God; we are human beings and not God.

Working In A Rural Village In Bugiri, Uganda

After completing my undergraduate studies in Makerere University, I started job hunting. I got a job in one of the remotest villages in Uganda. My first trip to this village was an experience I will not forget. I recall arriving in a bus to the district and riding a bicycle for over 80 km to the actual place where the office was located. I was smartly dressed in a nice light green suit and black shoes. I went to this remote area without electricity, water, and good roads.

After I returned to the city of Kampala, I did not want to go back to that remote village again. I was offered an appointment letter to do so. I was in a dilemma, so I sought answers in the Bible for answers and I recall reading Isaiah 55:8-9. I recall reading this Scripture and I said to myself, "I do not know what God thinks about me. I do not know which way He wants me to go. But God's ways are not my ways." So I decided to take that job. Taking this job has led me to work from a community-based organization to now the United Nations. I needed that experience first. I confess that God's thoughts and ways are different from ours. We need to believe God as His word requires us to obey Him.

A Person With God's Purpose Can't Be Killed Until The Fulfilment Of The Purpose

The whole story of Genesis 37 involves Joseph's dreams of greatness. Joseph was seventeen years old when he received the dreams. Joseph told his family about his dreams and his own brothers became unhappy with him. Just like Joseph, there will be people in your life that will oppose your dream. They will insult you. They will fight you. They will attack you. They will abuse you. They will try to malign you and antagonize you. They will speak evil of you. They will accuse you and reject you. They will do all manner of things that will cause you to abandon your dreams, plans, or visions. They will demotivate you. They will discourage you. They will demoralize you. They will even haunt you.

Many of them would tell you that you're not qualified but what they don't understand is that it is not about who is the best. I have been told almost these things and I just laughed each time they told me. I never gave up on my plans, dreams, and visions. Why? It was because the plans, dreams, and vision are given to me by God. The dreams are desires in my heart. God grant the desires of the heart. Psalms 37: 4 says, "Delight yourself in the Lord and He will give you the desires of your heart. The word delight means to please or honour. If you please God, you will receive what you desire.

God Gives The Desires Of Your Heart

This is one of my favorite Scripture, Psalm 20:4 says, "May he give you the desire of your heart and make all your plans succeed." This Scripture continues to inspire me. It is clear that when you believe God, He will give you the desires of your heart. The desire is not really in the heart alone but also in your mind. There is something you have always desired to accomplish or own. That thing is a desire. God grants people's desires and not what they want. Let me caution you that a desire is not an evil act that you are planning to do. God is not going to bless your desire to steal government funds to build a mansion and buy an expensive car. That is not a desire but a want. That may be your desire, but it is not from God.

A desire is something that is genuine and obtained with the help of God. God will help you to get the desire of your heart through taking steps of faith and then believing God to do it according to his time and ways. God will be responsible to fulfil the desire only if you believe in Him. Without belief in God, it is difficult to have the desire given or granted and "If it is not from the Lord, you do not want it anyway."

God Makes Your Plans Succeed, Not Man

The second part of the above Scripture states that He will make your plans succeed. Nobody has the plans to succeed except God. Put it in another way: God is the one who can make your plans succeed. It is in His hands. You might have a plan to run for a political office, build a house or take children to an international school or foreign university. Only God can make that plan succeed. You can do it your way and with your wisdom, but if God is not in it, it will not succeed. I would like to advise you on this and give you the secret. Before you make any plans, you need to seek and consult God. Go to the presence of God in prayer so that your plans will succeed.

When I wanted to build a house in Kampala, I began to plan for it. I got the land and commissioned the architect to draw the building plans. I recall before the start of the construction, I had no money, but I prayed to God. Two months after that prayer, the building plans were approved by engineers and town council. Two months after that approval, I went on a foreign trip and was paid a daily subsistence allowance that helped me start the foundation of the building. In addition to my savings, I used the allowances from the foreign trip to complete the building project. God was with me and today we have a house built in Kampala without loans or mortgage. God did it for me. God fulfilled the desires in my heart and made my plans succeed.

The Dreams You Have Will Attract Attacks

Genesis 37:8 says, "... Shall you indeed reign over us? Or shall you have dominion over us? Then in verse 9 Joseph says, "Look I had another dream. And this time, the sun, the moon and eleven stars bowed down before me." The brothers of Joseph turned against him; they conspired to kill him and said to one another, "Look the dreamer is coming!" When he arrived at his brothers at Dothan, they tried to kill him, but one of the brothers said,

> Let's put him in a pit and we shall say he was killed by wild animal." But Reuben pleaded, "Let's us not kill him," and they threw him in a pit. There was an argument among the brothers. What profit shall they get by killing him?

They decided to sell him to Midianite traders that passed by and Joseph was taken to Egypt. While in Egypt, Joseph became a slave (Genesis 39) and became a ruler. (Genesis 41: 37-57)

Rising From The Pit To The Palace

The principle here is that you can come from the pit to the palace because of your purpose. You may be enslaved, but if it is God's will, you can become a ruler. No matter how you were treated –as long as you are fighting a just cause – you will come out and become a prince. Joseph came out of the pit and became a ruler. The purpose of God is more powerful than any problems that we go through.

There is a reason why God allowed certain things to happen to us. God allowed Joseph to go to the pit, become a slave, and be imprisoned. God's purpose was that Joseph will go ahead of the family to be a planner and Disaster Officer to save the entire family of Abraham from famine. You could be in the pit right now in your personal life, but I want you to know that it will not last. You will come out of it stronger than you went in and you will get to the palace.

God is watching you as you stay in the pit or that situation. Only God knows how He will lift you up from the pit or situation. The secret to your lifting is to believe God even when you are in the pit and when you are in the palace. Believe God all the time in your life. Jesus never got killed by storm He died on the cross.

Another great example is in Luke 8:24-25. One day Jesus got into a boat together with his disciples and said to them,

Let us cross over to the other side of the lake." As they sailed in the boat, Jesus fell asleep and the windstorm came against them that the disciples were terrified and afraid. The boat begun to fill with water and they rushed to him and woke him up saying, "Master, Master, we are going to drown!" Jesus got up and rebuked the storm and the wind and the raging water became calm. Jesus asked a question, "Where is your faith. (Luke 8: 25)

In this analogy, the storm could not kill Jesus and His disciples because they had not accomplished their mission. When you have not completed your purpose, the storms of life may push and pull, it will not kill you. There are many of you who are experiencing storms, but I encourage you to have faith against any storm in your life. It is only by faith that you can rebuke the storm. Jesus taught His disciples about the power of faith that can overcome the storms of life and make them fulfil their purpose.

Purpose Eliminates Fear And Creates Confidence

2 Kings 6:16-17 says, "Do not be afraid," the prophet answered. "Those who are with us are more than those who with them." Then Elisha prayed, "O Lord, open his eyes so he may see." Then the Lord opened the servant's eyes, and he looked and saw the hills full of horses and chariots of fire all around Elisha. In the midst of fear, do not fear. In the midst of storms, do not be afraid of it, but use the storm as a stepping stone to greater height.

In the midst of the earthquake, do not fear, but wait for the voice. In the midst of fire, wait for the quiet voice. In the midst of problems, be stable and stand on the rock. Why? This is because these things in this world are not permanent but temporary.

Nowhere in the world has there been a perpetual earthquake, or floods, or outbreaks of fire.

Crisis, war, famine and storm are temporary. They have an ending date. The Tsunami that struck Indonesia in 2005 came and went. The earthquake that destroyed Haiti on 2 January 2010 came and passed. The Australian fire came and went. This teaches us lessons that nothing is permanent. Even a divorce from a spouse or a shameful condition is temporary.

Examples Of Leaders Who Accomplished Their Purpose

When you study the great men and women in history, you will find something interesting about their lives and why it is difficult to erase their names from the history books. One of the oldest book in the world is the Bible. This unique book gives an insight into history of God's redemptive works and His creations. The Bible details the story of men and women who accomplished purpose. These men and women were born, faced many challenges, problems, and were able to accomplish the purpose for which they were born. They were able to overcome their difficulties.

Abraham, Father Of All Nations

The story of Abraham is one that should teach many a lesson. Abraham was married to Sarah. They could not have a child of their own. They were frustrated because they had no child and were ridiculed by the people in their community. This is common even today when a man and woman get married; society expects the couple to produce children. When the couple fails to produce a child, you will start hearing comments from the people, in-laws, friends, and the entire village. The reproduction capacity of the man or woman comes under attack. This happens everywhere in world.

For the case of Abraham, he was 75 years old when God promised him that he will be the "father of many nations." God promised that his descendants would fill the Earth, but at that age he did not have any child. As a result, the wife became impatient, told the old man Abraham to sleep with the housemaid so she could beget a child for him. Abraham, because of pressure and not purpose, slept with the maid servant and they had a son named Ishmael. Sarah attempted to fulfil God's purpose, but it was not time and God took His time. When the right time had come, Sarah conceived and bore Abraham a son named Isaac. This is the son, who later became the grandfather of the twelve tribes of Israel through Jacob. Abraham accomplished his purpose and became a father to many nations. Dear reader, know that this principle also applies to you. God may allow you to accomplish your own plan, but ultimately, it is God's purpose that will be accomplished in your life if you believe Him with all your heart. It does not matter how long it will take even if it takes 25 years like Abraham, you will fulfil God's purpose.

Noah, Built The Ark That Saved God's Creatures From Floods

This man as you remember was the only man who was found perfect in the whole land where he lived. He had a family and God said, "He was blameless and righteous." God used him to save the people who were in right standing with God. He built the ark and when he finished building the ark, God sent rain for 40 days and 40 nights. In that time, God destroyed everything that was on the Earth. There are many lessons in this story. We must be in right standing with God if we are desirous of fulfilling our purpose.

Moses, The Leader And Deliverer Of Israel

This great giant of faith was born by a Jewish mother, but the early days after his birth, he was hidden by the mother until a daughter of Pharaoh in Egypt came to the place at the river where the young baby boy was hidden in a basket. The boy was taken to the palace and he grew up there. Years later, he saw an Egyptian beating up a Jew and he was upset and decided to kill the Egyptian. He buried the body, but it was later discovered. Out of fear, he ran to the wilderness and it was there that God met and called him. Moses was born, but never knew his purpose until God called him and told him he was going back to bring the people and deliver them from oppression from Pharaoh and the Egyptians. Moses did as God had commanded him, and delivered the people from Egypt and led them for forty years. He died after delivering the people when he was 120 years old.

Elijah, The Prophet And A Leadership Mentor

Elijah was one of the prophets of God in the Old Testament who delivered the message of repentance to his generation. He fulfilled part of his purpose, and was succeeded by Elisha. In the course of fulfilling purpose, Elijah gave up because he was afraid of what happened to the other prophets who were killed. This is instructive because many people give up easily because of scary stories of things happening to other people around them. Elijah heard the stories of other people and never gave up or surrendered to the situation. As human, Elijah was afraid just like any of us.

The story can be found in 1 King 19, it says:

And Ahab told Jezebel all that Elijah had done, also how he had executed all the prophets with the sword. Then Jezebel sent a messenger to Elijah, saying, "So let the gods do to me, and more also, if I do not make your life as the life of one of them by tomorrow about this time." And when he saw that, he arose and ran for his life, and went to Beersheba, which belongs to Judah, and left his servant there. But he himself went a day's journey into the wilderness, and came and sat down under a broom tree. And he prayed that he might die, and said, "It is enough! Now, Lord, take my life, for I am no better than my fathers!

You might have reached a phase where you are about to give up, but look to God. In 1 Kings 19:5, Elijah says, "… I have had enough. Lord he said takes my life…" Many times we can feel like this great man of God. We reach a point in life where we feel like giving up because life has beaten us down or we have met resistance and obstacles. Sometimes, people even want to kill you for the vision and purpose that you have. My advice is no matter what happens, believe in yourself and God but not situations, circumstances, or problems. Never be frightened by problems or situations. Believe in God always.

Elisha Succeeded Elijah

The next example is Elisha who succeeded Elijah. Elisha would complete the purpose of Elijah and succeed him as a prophet. Elisha got a double portion of the anointing power from the Lord. Purpose, therefore, is much bigger than the person who starts to pursue it. Do not worry when God gives you purpose for your life. If it is truly from God, He will assign someone with strength and courage to complete it. God promised Joshua that He was going to be with him as He was with Moses. God will give strength, resources, ideas, and faith to the next leader so that purpose is fulfilled.

Reasons Why People Never Fulfill Their Purpose

Many people do not fulfil their purpose for many reasons. These might have accounted for the failure and hopelessness that many are experiencing today. There are many reasons why people never accomplished God give purpose.

1. Abuse And Misuse Of Time

Ecclesiastes 3:1 says, "To everything there is a season, a time for every purpose under heaven." The management of time is an important principle. Time is not forever. Time is short. Time is important. A lot of people have not mastered how God works. God is a God of time. God has given each and everything a specified amount of time. When the time is over, nothing else, not even purpose can be accomplished on Earth. Every human has the same amount of time given by God. Everybody has 24 hours a day and 365 days in a year. Both the rich and the poor have the same amount of time. But why are some people successful whereas others fail? The answer is simple. They have not used their time and capacity to plan effectively. Why? Time is the most important resource that you have. You can make more money but you cannot make more time. When money is misused and mismanaged, it goes away. The same is with time. Wasted time cannot be recovered. Do not waste the time to do things that cause you to be unhappy, disorganized and unfocused. Focus on using your time wisely.

2. Fear And Giving Up The Struggle

I believe that the greatest enemy of you achieving Gods purpose is fear. There are questions that may run through your mind as you start to face or take the road to God's purpose for your life. Fear can cause you to surrender and give up. Fear is not from God but comes from the devil. You can give in to a situation and not confront it. There are some people whom I have seen who were on the way to a successful end who decided to surrender to challenging situation. I recall hearing the story of Nelson Mandela in South Africa. When He had spent over 25 years in prison, the government of South Africa offered him a deal to give up the struggle against apartheid in South Africa. And in return, he was promised a car, house, money, etc. The answer from Nelson Mandela was to throw away the key and lock the door. "I am staying in prison," he reportedly said. His captors could not believe he rejected the offer and preferred to be in prison. The lesson I want you to learn from this is that you should never give up once you start fulfilling your calling and purpose. The desires are your true reason for living. Without these reasons, you will be frustrated, disorganized, and never fulfil your purpose.

3. God's Anger

When God gets angry with the person who is given the purpose, the purpose will not be achieved. For example, in Numbers 20, God was angry with Moses because he struck the rock instead of speaking to it. Consequently, Moses never reached the Promised Land. God can promise you something, but if you annoy or disobey Him. He can stop the promise from being fulfilled. The most important thing to learn is that people should be consistent and responsible all the time. Therefore, to accomplish your purpose, you need to be consistent and responsible all the time as being inconsistent and irresponsible can cost you God's blessing and result into failure to fulfil the desires of your heart. Sometimes, God can show you the destiny where He is taking you, but your disobedience can cause God to stop you from reaching the final destination. As I study the Scriptures about Moses, I discovered that God had good plans that will enable Moses lead the Israelites to the Promised Land, but God cancelled the plan. Even though Moses was shown the Promised Land, God didn't allow him to get there because of disobedience. Take note; this is true with your life. God can show you things that you are dreaming about, but if you do not follow God's instructions, you will not see and experience them.

You also need to know that God could cancel his plans and purposes for your life because His anger is burning against you. You might have been doing well and you were destined to go to the "Promised Land" but now you are stuck along the way. The reason for being stranded might be because you disobeyed God. Hence, you need to go back and seek for God's forgiveness. God called Moses to deliver Israel to the Promised Land. God said the people were stiff necked and the wrath of God was to burn against them. Why? It was because of the worship of "The Golden Calf."

4. Disobedience To God's Instruction

The story of disobedience is evident in the book of Samuel. In 1 Samuel 15:3, God told Saul to attack and totally destroy everything that belonged to the Amalekites. Nothing was to be spared: men, women, children or infants, cattle, and sheep. God told Saul through his messenger, Samuel, to destroy everything, but Saul did not obey. The cost of disobedience was the throne. Saul lost the kingship, authority, and leadership of his people after disobeying God. In fact, God grieved that he made Saul King (1 Samuel 15:10-11). Saul never completed his purpose as planned by God, and as such, David was appointed to take Saul's place. God can fire you from a job he gave you to do and put another person who is anointed and full of the Holy Spirit to take that place.

5. Lack Of Knowledge And Wisdom

Another reason is the lack of knowledge and wisdom. Some of the people whom I have met just lack knowledge and wisdom. I remember working with two senior colleagues who were running the show so to speak. They had the opportunity to be confirmed in those high positions. According to rumors that made the rounds, they were to be appointed and confirmed. But the two of them had lots of character flaws. Their people leadership and management skills were poor. Most of the staff and partners complained about them and they were advised to change. But they did not. Hence, when it was time to be promoted to higher positions, they were passed over even though they had the experience and were academically qualified. They lost the opportunities to serve because they wanted to be great without serving the people. They were not "servant leaders." I also believe that a lack of or inadequate knowledge and wisdom must have led to the missing of the opportunity. 1 Kings 12:7 says. "And they spoke to him, saying, 'If you will be a servant to these people today, and serve them, and answer them, and speak good words to them, then they will be your servants forever.'"

In Hosea 4:6, the Lord says "...My people are destroyed by lack of knowledge". When you lack knowledge in life, it becomes difficult to make quality decisions. The decisions are made when information is available. When you have information knowledge will appear too. Most people do not want to look for knowledge and this is why they die and are destroyed. People are not destroyed because of the devil but because of the lack of knowledge. You can avoid being destroyed. When you get destroyed, your purpose will not be fulfilled.

Furthermore, Ecclesiastes 7:24-25 says, "Whatever wisdom may be, it is far off and most profound – who can discover it? So I turned my mind to understand, to investigate and to search out wisdom..."

Wisdom comes through discovery and search. Wisdom is hidden from people. It requires discovery and searching. Something that you search for is not readily seen in the space where you live or stay; it is hidden and takes energy to get it. It takes time to read books to get to know or acquire knowledge. Wisdom is a treasure, and when found, makes you successful in that area or specific field. Seek wisdom. That is why Steve Jobs was successful. Because he discovered something that other people could not have. He posed the wisdom to make and design Apple computers which eventually led to the iPhone and this made him very successful.

6. Your Mouth Could Destroy Your Purpose And Potential

"With his mouth the godless destroys his neighbour, but through knowledge the righteous escape" (Proverbs 11:9). The person with knowledge will never be destroyed but will escape. For example, if you know how HIV/AIDS is transmitted, then you will avoid things or situations that expose you to it.

Also, if you know that rat poison can kill you, you will never keep it near you or put it in your food. Why? It is because you have knowledge that once it is eaten, you will be destroyed. Knowledge is a source of wisdom. You cannot be wise or have wisdom unless you know something. The biggest challenge in today's world is that people are not interested in searching for knowledge but rather spend time watching TV, movies, and exchanging useless ideas on social media.

7. Pride and Arrogance

Luke 9:25 says, "For what profit is it to a man if he gains the whole world, and is himself destroyed and lost." Instead of pursuing the things of God that are eternal, many people are running after temporary things like money and popularity in the world. Do not pursue things that are not for God. You must do the things of God. Never become proud and arrogant. What shall it profit you to gain the whole world and lose your own soul? Humble yourself and remain human as you fulfil the purpose God has bestowed upon you.

Purpose May Be Fulfilled By Another Person

There are times when your God given purpose would be completed by people other than yourself. It is not automatic that God will allow you fully accomplish the purpose He has given you because the purpose may be bigger and requires other people to take over from you once you are dead or gone. In Joshua 1:1-9, we read the account of how Joshua succeeded Moses. The Lord approached Joshua and said, "Moses, my servant is dead. Now then, you and all these people, get ready to cross the Jordan River into the land I am about to give to them – to the Israelites" (Joshua 1:2). In this example, Joshua took over to fulfil the purpose of leading the Israelites into the Promised Land.

Moses started to fulfil the purpose of God and was succeeded by Joshua. This is true even for your business, company, organization, firm or political party. You might start it, but it will be taken to the next level by another person or group of people. In this example, there is a person next to you who will take over to fulfil the purpose of God and for your life.

Never Interfere With God's Purpose

Many times people, family members, friends and associations will fight each other when they are pursuing their dreams, plans, and visions. The end results are chaos, conflict and disagreement. If it is God's purpose through men and women, no amount of interference can stop the will of God. No amount of tribulations can inhibit God's plans. In this passage, Peter attempted to interfere, intrude, hamper and inhibit Jesus' vision and purpose, but Jesus rebuked him against making comments.

Let us study Matthew 16:22-23, it says,

> *Then Peter took him aside and begun to rebuke him saying; Far be it from you, Lord this shall not happen to you! But He turned and said to Peter; Get behind me, Satan, for you are an offence to me, for you are not mindful of the things of God, but the things of men.*

God's purpose cannot be stopped by man or any opposition. We can learn a great deal about how God will accomplish His purposes from the following passage in Acts 5. The passage is an account about the disciples of Jesus Christ after the ascension. The disciples were brought before the council and the high priest interrogated them with questions in a Jewish court. The disciples were being arraigned in court for spreading the Good News of Jesus Christ and preaching to the nation about the risen Lord. This was a crime according to the Jewish decree not to speak about Jesus and was punishable by death.

When they brought the disciples before the court they were asked to defend themselves. Peter the leader explained and defended their actions but the high priests were not willing to listen to him. Peter spoke about Jesus as the one who forgives sin. Peter said Jesus was a Prince and Savior. In those days, this was blasphemy, a capital offence. In the text, some people had been killed because they were preaching or doing things that were not permitted by Jewish law. The two people who had been killed are Theudas and Judas (not Iscariot) who were rebels. Sometimes, people can go to an extent of accusing you before the courts of law, but let this be an encouragement that you are on the right track.

Now when the time came for the disciples to be interrogated, one of elders, named Gamaliel, who was a council member and Pharisee, stood and told the council an interesting story. He said in past people like the disciples have been killed innocently. He went on to say this:

Therefore, in the present case I advise you: Leave these men alone! Let them go! For if their purpose or activity is of human origin, it will fail. But if it is from God, you will not be able to stop these men; you will only find yourselves fighting against God. Finally, the disciples were set free and they left with songs of joy. All this happened after they had been flogged as recorded in Acts 5:40.

Principles
- *When you find the purpose of God, nobody can stop you. You will become invisible and unstoppable.*
- *Nobody can stop the purposes of God.*

Purpose And Vision

Purpose comes in phases and sometimes it is not revealed at once. God will give you a vision. Joseph was a teenager when he saw the vision of feeding his family and helping them. His purpose was to save his family from starvation and famine. He never knew what he was going to face to achieve the vision and fulfil the purpose. If God had showed Joseph the process, I believe Joseph would have told God to stop.

Note: Write down your vision and purpose.

CHAPTER TWO

THE FUNDAMENTAL PRINCIPLE OF PASSION

"It is an ideal which I hope to live for and to achieve.
But if needs be, it is an ideal for which I am prepared to die."
~ Nelson Mandela

What Is Passion?

You have heard the saying; "love what you do". This is true. If your desire is become successful and effective, then you must have passion of doing what you. The word passion means desire, hunger, thirst, appetite, craving, lust, urge or ache. Passion is like a conviction in your heart. Passion is an internal strength. Millions of people who live on this planet have no passion about life and not bothered about what is happening in the world around them. In order to be successful, you need to develop an intense craving for success that you are willing to lose your life. This is because success will never be obtained on a silver plate that is handed to you. Passion is a strong commitment and conviction to a cause, goal and purpose and vision. The people that have affected history had a passion for what they were doing. Passion makes you willing to die for the cause or your purpose. People who have passion for something are not afraid of death.

Passion is an appetite to change the world and it comes with heavy price or cost. In my own life, one day I was praying and I was thanking God for the gift of life, job, car, house, family and sisters and brothers, I had a quiet voice tell me, "I cannot use you yet. When you find something to die for then I can do my work and business with your life for the next generation." These words are still fresh in my mind and I keep asking God to show me and guide me to that passion. I learned that passion is never impossible. Passion says it is possible; it says it can be done. Passion never takes no for an answer. But just wait and things will work out.

Passion is the highest form of desire that keeps you going towards your goal against all odds, obstacles and problems. It is the hunger, thirst, the lust and ache. Passion is like the rage, fury that comes within you to do something when you are about to surrender or give up. You are really passionate when you are willing to die for your convictions or ideas. Passion is confidence that you will overcome and gain victory after the struggle. Apostle Paul tells the Roman church in Romans 1:14, "I am obligated both to Greeks and non-Greeks, both to the wise and the foolish."

Paul was obligated to preach the gospel to Gentiles (non-Jews) and places around the world. The word "obligated" means compelled, forced, obliged, required or duty-bound to preach. Passion makes you compelled and obliged to do all you can to accomplish your cause. I have discovered that if you have no passion for something it means you will not have the commitment. I also discovered that millions of people have no passion or obligation to do what they are assigned to do. When you are passionate about something, it means you are very dedicated to it more than anything else. Nothing can hold you back nor stop you. When you have passion for something in life, it means you are willing to pursue it at the cost and expense of your life and personal safety. The life you have becomes public as opposed to private. You no longer are so selfishly protecting yourself.

One of the most important lessons and observations I have seen in life is that a person who finds his or her purpose for living never gives up to the challenges that come their way. These people never surrender to the crisis or obstacles. The people never surrender when calamity strikes. They do not let any predicament stop them, but are willing to forge ahead and until they reach a defining moment; they never give up. They keep fighting for what they believe in.

They face the crisis, manage it and come out with victory. The people with passion never take holidays or vacations. People with passion are willing to be crucified. These people are strange and are not interested in vacations, holidays and leisure. They have no time for holidays, parties or vacation. The questions that I am going to ask you: "Have you found your cause"? What is your reason for living? Why are you living on Earth? Why is it that you are still alive while others have left this "world"? The majority of people are interested in beer or food, but until you find something greater than that, you have no reason for existence.

You are wasting the time given to you by God. When a person finds his or her cause or passion, they behave a bit strange and unusual. People with purpose and passion for something have no working hours. When you look at the people who have affected history, they died pursuing their cause and purpose. They were ready to pay the ultimate price, including laying down their lives for their friends. I am not talking about suicide bombers but am talking of people like Nelson Mandela, Martin Luther King Jr. and others.

Examples Of Leaders Who Had Passion

Peter

Peter is the close friend of Jesus Christ, who became the leader of the early Christians. Peter was a fisherman when Jesus called him to follow Him and become His disciple. Peter was with Jesus throughout many events and occasions when Jesus performed many miracles and also taught His followers. Peter was Jesus' number one aide. Peter is quoted as having said he would never abandon Jesus even when he is arrested.

The story is an interesting one but Jesus prayed for his faith. Jesus said, "But I have prayed for you, Simon (Simon is another name for Peter): that your faith may not fail. And when you have turned back, strengthen your brothers" (Luke 22:32). Until Jesus sent the Holy Spirit, Peter had not received his purpose and passion.

After receiving the Holy Spirit as Jesus had promised His disciples, Peter began to preach and many of those with whom he spoke about the Kingdom of God thought he and his friends were drunk (Acts 2:13-15). But it was because they were so full of the Holy

Spirit. Peter discovered his purpose and passion. Peter took on a spirit that was stronger than death. Peter received his revelation for his passion and from then on he never feared anything – not even death.

Nelson Mandela

Another example of a person with passion was the late first black South African leader, Nelson Mandela. Mandela spent over 27 years or over 10,000 days in jail. Mandela was in prison for nothing that he did wrong. His sin was that he fought for the rights of black Africans. He and many South Africans suffered racial discrimination.

When South Africans were ruled by a white minority, Mandela was imprisoned and incarcerated for over a quarter of a century. He never gave in to the temptation to give up for a single day. He was willing to die for South Africans. The white minority government offered him freedom when he was in prison on condition to abandon the fight for freedom.

He never gave up until the minority white government was dismantled and apartheid destroyed. Upon his release and taking on the leadership of South Africa and in the inaugural address to the nation at Union Building in Pretoria, this is what Mandela said, "Never, never and never again shall it be that this beautiful land will experience the oppression of one man by another."

Mr. Nelson Mandela made this statement on the day he was sworn in as the first democratically-elected President of South Africa. Those words are words coming from passion and purpose. Mandela had a passion to fight against oppression of one man by another and oppression of black men by minority of whites. He was ready to die for his cause and purpose. Mandela had a passion for what he was doing and he was prepared to die for it.

He never accepted to go for short-term enjoyment or happiness as most of us do. The statement above is an indication of passion. He wanted freedom for all humans. He hated oppression and suppression. Mandela hated people who oppressed and suppressed others and fought equality between people of South Africa. What is your passion? Think about it. Write it down. Are you ready to pay the price for passion? These words to me show the passion in his eyes and as he spoke on that day he meant those words all over his body, soul and spirit. As part of the history and to put it on record, I was in Johannesburg for the first time the first week of December 2013 when Nelson Rolihlahla Madiba Mandela passed on. As we visited and delivered buckets of flowers to Nelson Mandela Square in Sandston City and his home in Houghton, the reality of what Mandela was passionate about hit me and my friends. Mandela had passion for equality among humans.

My personal conclusion is that unless you have a passion and great desire to sacrifice and die for your beliefs, you will never reach or get hold of your passion, purpose and vision. As we drove to Oliver Richard Tambo International Airport, we experienced the feeling that injustice is the worst form of human punishment. Nobody should be or ever be subjected to it because we are born free and born with innocence, and above all, born as sinners who need a Saviour in Jesus Christ to reconcile man back to God. Mandela was passionate and that is why oppression was defeated. When you are passionate about something, you will win. What is your passion?

Martin Luther King Jr.

In addition to that example is the life of a famous Civil Rights activist, Martin Luther King Jr. One of the greatest statements that a man can ever make is the one made by this man. Martin Luther King Jr. said,

> *I have a dream that one day this nation will rise up and live out the true meaning of its creed: 'We hold these truths to be self-evident: that all men are created equal. I have a dream that my four little children will one day live in a nation where they will not be judged by the color of their skin but by the content of their character.*

This speech was made on the steps of the Lincoln Memorial in Washington, D.C. on August 28, 1963. Before the *"I Have a Dream"* speech, Martin Luther King Jr, had travelled to many places in the United States giving speeches. He spoke at Mason Temple, a church in Memphis, Tennessee and gave a moving speech in reference to the bomb threat to his plane. He spoke of his own possible death. In fact, this is what he said:

> *And then I got to Memphis. And some began to say the threats, or talk about the threats that were out. What would happen to me from some of our sick white brothers? Well, I don't know what will happen now. We've got some difficult days ahead. But it doesn't matter with me now. Because I've been to the mountaintop.*
>
> *And I don't mind. Like anybody, I would like to live a long life. Longevity has its place. But I'm not concerned about that now. I just want to do God's will. And He's allowed me to go up to the mountain. And I've looked over. And*

I've seen the Promised Land. I may not get there with you. But I want you to know tonight, that we, as a people, will get to the Promised Land. So I'm happy, tonight. I'm not worried about anything. I'm not fearing any man. Mine eyes have seen the glory of the coming of the Lord.

By this time, the movement of the people fighting for social justice was growing and unstoppable. At that time, he knew that his life was coming to an end and was in danger. He knew that there were many people who never agreed with his beliefs, philosophy or ideas or ideology. There were people who had threatened to kill him. They had thought and planned to take away his life by assassination. They wanted him dead.

They wanted him to stop spreading his ideas and beliefs. To me what Martin Luther King Jr. said in this Temple was that it doesn't matter anymore. At that point He never cared anything anymore. I think He said, I do not care about what you want to do to me. When you find a passion for your life then there will be the spirit that will be upon you that is ignited inside of you. That spirit will never die. It is the beginning of doing what God created you to do. You will have the conviction and readiness to lay your life down your lives for your friends, for freedom and justice for others. There are many people who are afraid of doing something. They are interested in good life only. Do not be afraid of people but fear God only.

When a person says it does not matter anymore, it means that person has found a greater purpose and passion for their life and that is the beginning of leadership. In my own life, I have a conviction that the purpose for which I was born to accomplish is more important than threats and I am ready to die for it. I am ready to die for my beliefs and convictions. I believe I was born to impact my generation, **to equip and empower** aspiring leaders. I will work and do whatever it takes to see people equipped and empowered. Do you have passion for what you are doing? Do you have passion? Are you willing to sacrifice your life for others' sakes? For what are you ready to die for?

Daniel

Passion may cause your enemies to worship your God. Daniel was accused of disobeying the king and he was subjected to a harsh treatment, harassment and intimidation. Read about this in Daniel 6:10-23. Daniel never did anything wrong, but because of his faith, belief and convictions, he was an enemy to some people in the land. They wanted the lions to kill him. The plan was made to have him thrown into the den of lions. But Daniel was willing to die for his beliefs and convictions. He believed in God almighty. He declared before the king that he would not worship any other God except the God of Israel; He would not worship the king. He rejected the edict that everyone in the kingdom was to pray only to the king and just accepted what was coming to him. They seized him and threw him into the lions' den.

When Daniel arrived in the den, no harm or no lion attacked him. God had shut the mouth of the lions. God saved him. But in the story when the king saw what had happened, he commanded that Daniel be pulled out of the den. He then put the enemies of Daniel in the den and they were killed. The king then declared that the whole nation should worship the God of Daniel.

This can be true for you as well. Many times there are people who have done wrong towards you and have accused you falsely. Do not worry about them because the passion you have will always help you come out of the situations. In which you will be confronted. The secret is to put your trust in God and God will take care of every situation. God will protect you from the "lions' den." God will intervene and rescue you. God will not allow the lions to eat you. In fact, God will make your enemies become your friends. In the long run, you will win. Never give up when you have received that kind of passion. The passion you have is the key to your success when combined with convictions and belief in God. The passion is what wins the game. The passion is what determines victory. Passion overcomes the plans of the enemy and makes you come out strong.

Daniel had passion for God and He was willing to do things that he believed was more important than threats. He prayed and gave thanks to God three times every day. He was accused of praying to another God besides the king. This happens all of the time. People will attack you in what you are doing and turn against you, but if you believe what you are doing is what God told you, you never surrender. Daniel never surrendered to the pressure of authorities and people who fought him. He stood his ground, and at the end, even the king became a convert and declared that all people worship the God of Daniel. It is because of passion that people follow you, not because of the looks and beauty. Passion attracts people to follow you as you run towards your purpose and vision.

Stephen

Stephen was one of the faithful followers of Jesus Christ. He was converted and was taught by apostles. He received his faith and belief about Christ as the Lord and Saviour. He was chosen to be a leader among the early church because of his character, faith and integrity. Stephen was full of faith in God and this is what led him to trust God. Stephen had a passion to minister the message of Jesus's resurrection. He had a passion to serve Christ. He had a passion to go to the entire world to fulfil the Great Commission. The passion led him to accept death. God allowed him to be stoned to death. Stephen died, but before his death, Stephen saw the Glory of God and the Heavens were opened. Stephen's last words were, "God, forgive them for they do not know what they are doing."

Acts 7:54-60 is an account where Stephen becomes the first martyr as a result of his passion and dedication to the Great Commission. He died because of his passion for Christ.

For what are you willing to die for? We need to be willing to die for what we believe. We need to be willing to die for our purpose. We need to be ready to die to fulfil our purpose and calling. Passion makes you willing to sacrifice even to the point of death. When you find your purpose, your passion will help you stand against all odds because anything else in life no longer matters. Passion is the greatest sacrifice to fulfilling your purpose. Passion is self-sacrifice for public betterment and improvement.

As mentioned earlier, the God we serve does not protect us from challenges. God will allow you to pass through tests that can even lead to your death. Can you imagine a man full of faith in God being allowed by God to die? How about you? What challenges are you willing to face? What price are you willing to pay? God is concerned with people who are faithful and full of faith in Him than those who are after fame. It is more important to be faithful than be famous. Faith is more important than fame. Persistence is more admirable than popularity.

Passion Gives You Freedom

Passion is a key to happiness and will help in the achievement of purpose and vision. In Acts 16:25, the Bible says, "But at midnight Paul and Silas were praying and singing hymns to God and the prisoners were listening to them." Paul was passionate about what he was doing. When you have passion for something, you never get discouraged to the point of giving up on your purpose. It drives you to push harder and move forward.

Passion does give you the attitude of not surrendering and giving up. These two gentlemen were happy and motivated by what they were doing. Not even jail could stop them. Not even chains could stop them. When you become passionate about something in life, you will win and succeed in it because you will be driven and motivated to do it without feeling like they are forcing you. People who have passion about something do not need a clock to tell them to get up at 4am. Passion will make you get up at 3am after going to bed at 1am. Passion gives you energy, strength and life.

Passion Attracts God To Your Side

Acts 23: 11 says, "But the following night the Lord stood by him and said, 'Be of good cheer, Paul! For you have testified for me in Jerusalem, so you must also bear witness at Rome." Paul was passionate about what he was doing and willing go where God was leading him. Paul was prepared to die for his mission and calling. Paul was jailed because of the passion he had to preach to the Gentiles. Paul was hungry and thirsty to preach to all the Gentiles and this is what caused him to be jailed because he believed in what he was doing. Do you believe in what you are doing? Do you have passion for it? Or you are merely doing it to earn a living? When

Paul was in jail, the Lord visited and encouraged him. Times of discouragement is when God shows up. Be assured that God will come to your side if you are passionate about your purpose and vision.

Passion Enables You To Press On To The Goal

Paul is a typical example of a person who was passionate about what he was born to do. Paul was known as Saul until that fateful day when God intercepted him on his way to Damascus. Paul's assertions in Philippians 3:12-14 is very important. I think the statement is an indication of his passion. The statement is my favourite Scripture. I urge you to keep and master it when you are confronted by challenges and obstacles. Paul said,

> *Not that I have already attained or am already perfected, but I press on, that I may lay hold of that for which Christ Jesus has also laid hold of me. Brethren, I do not count myself to have apprehended; but one thing I do, forgetting those things which are behind and reaching forward to those things which are ahead. I press towards the goal for the prize of the upward call of God in Christ Jesus.*

When you observe the people who made an impact in the world, you will notice that these people had set themselves goals for which they willing to die. Paul had a goal that he was working to achieve. He was determined to achieve that goal and even when he was confronted with challenges, he was not mindful of the hard times but the goal. You should be like Paul. Do not be distracted by storms of life or your successes.

The bigger the goal, the greater the challenge and obstacles that you will encounter but never surrender to challenges or any difficult situation. You need to get bigger goal and work to reach it before you die. Many people whom I've met have not set goals. They have no goal. They wake up every morning without anything on paper or written goals and objectives. This is dangerous because goals give you energy and strength to move on amidst challenges or storms of life.

Without goals, you are rotating in cycles and may never attain desirable height in life. When you have set goals, they should become permanent. You should be clear in your goal setting. My goals keep me focused everyday. They make getting up each day with a smile and motivation easier because I know what I want to achieve for that day. Goals prevent me from gossiping or spending time with wrong groups and associations. Goals will keep you with the right people and right places.

Passion Gives Faith And Confidence To Endure Any Pain

Romans 1:16-17 says,

> *For I am not ashamed of the gospel of Christ, for it is the power of God to salvation for everyone who believes; for the Jews first and also the Greek. For in it the righteousness of God is revealed from faith to faith; as it is written, 'The just shall live by faith.*

Faith is the belief you have in God as the creator and owner of all things on Earth and heaven. Faith is belief in the unseen and unknown. Paul believed in God and His Kingdom. Paul heard the voice of God as he was on his way to Damascus. Paul's beliefs created his confidence. Paul became the greatest preacher and disciple of Jesus Christ after discovering his purpose and passion. Paul preached the gospel to the different cities and visited several places such as Philippi, Corinth, Galatia, Thessalonica, and others.

Paul was jailed for the sake of the gospel. Paul experienced shipwreck in the middle of the sea, which meant he could have drowned and lost his life. In spite of all this challenges and life threatening moments, Paul continued with purpose which was fueled by passion. Passion will propel you to overcome all obstacles and sustain you to carry forward the purpose because purpose is greater than challenges. Challenges are temporary events that check our mental state and test our level of maturity. Mature people are not afraid of challenges. They pursue their purpose and convictions. They are more concerned with conviction than conversations and gossips.

Challenges are temporary events that check our mental state and test our level of maturity.

Passion Delivers You From Past Behaviour

Romans 3:12 says, "Therefore, just as sin entered the world through one man, and death through sin, and in this way death came to all people, because all sinned." Paul made this statement as an encouragement to the believers in Rome. This is the greatest source of confidence where Paul says sin affected everyone. There is nobody or person who has not committed sin. Everybody has a dent in their life. Everybody fails and many people have sinned against God. Everyone makes mistakes. Nobody wins all the time. Nobody succeeds in everything.

The great people in history also did terrible things and made mistakes. Great people and leaders in history were not perfect individuals and some of them made mistakes and committed errors. They were not blameless and righteous. Nobody seems to achieve everything and have everything. The decided to forget about their past mistakes and errors to focus on their purpose. Your purpose is more important than problems or pressures of life. Therefore, be encouraged that your past behaviour will only haunt you if you keep reliving it and remembering it. Your past behaviour is not your whole life but a portion of it. You have a greater life ahead of you. Do not destroy your future because of what has already happened.

Your purpose is more important
than problems or pressures of life.

Passion Frees You
From The Bondage Of The System

Romans 7:1 says, "Do you not know, brothers—for I am speaking to men who know the law—that the law has authority over a man only as long as he lives?" Then in verse 6, it says "But now, by dying to what once bound us, we have been released from the law so that we serve in the new way of the Spirit, and not in the old way of the written code."

It is my personal belief that majority of the people are trapped by a system that has been put in place. The system could be government legislation. In South Africa, before the abolition of apartheid, the government of white minority had created the laws that oppressed black majority of people. The laws could not stop Mandela and his friends from fighting for equality and justice for all South Africans.

Mandela got his freedom because of his passion for equality and justice. Mandela never got freedom from people but from passion. The white minority who ruled South Africa had no choice but to accept all conditions put forward by Mandela that culminated in his release. His passion caused the white minority to release not only Mandela but also his friends who were also passionate for a noble cause.

Passion Will Make You See The Glory From A Bad Situation

Romans 8:18 says, "For I consider that the suffering of this present time are not worthy to be compared with the glory which shall be revealed in us." Paul was not concerned about what was happening at the time he spoke these words. He was obsessed by the glory that he had seen which was revealed to him. Most people who are unsuccessful or live miserable lives are always depressed because they have lost hope and never expect anything in life. Paul saw the glory, a vision of God which was revealed to him by God. Do you have a vision? The best counsel for you is to look at the bad situation that you are in right now and see the glory that could happen if you are willing to believe God. There is something that is bigger than even the bad times and situation that you are going through right away. This is why it is important not to focus on the situation but things that are positive and great. Paul was passionate about the glory that was revealed or shown to him by God and this enabled him to look and see bad situation as good one.

Passion Will Lead You To Victory And Success

Therefore, my dear brothers, stand firm. Let nothing move you. Always give yourselves fully to the work of the Lord, because you know that your labor in the Lord is not in vain. Death is swallowed up in victory (1 Corinthians 15:54)

Can you imagine how death is swallowed up in victory? When you are in Christ Jesus, death is powerless. It is swallowed up because Jesus overcome death when he himself defeated it on the cross then went to the grave and took the keys of death. Paul was confident that death was nothing that it was powerless because he was in Jesus Christ's mission who destroyed the power of death. As a Christian, when you are in Christ, death is nothing. It is powerless and that is why Jesus died on the cross so that you never die again. Instead, you have eternal life. I tell you friends, when you find your passion for living, you have found victory.

Without passion, you might end up a failure. Passion will take you from one level to the next and to the place of victory. Passion will keep you out of trouble knowing that you have victory. Passion in the long run will bring you to victory and a place of getting the prize from Jesus himself.

Passion In The End Leads To Reconciliation With God

2 Corinthians 5:20 says, "…We implore you on Christ behalf, be reconciled to God." Paul was originally known as Saul before his conversion. Paul after conversion got transformed and his mind was renewed. Paul discovered the power of the love of God, Who forgave his acts towards the church. Paul discovered that his old

education and ideology of the Romans were not right. Paul got a revelation that his sins were forgiven, and this revelation made Paul passionate about God that He wanted the Good News preached in every nation of the Earth. Paul was passionate and this in the end made him reconciled with God.

Passion Gives You Grace To Fight The Good Fight Of Faith

Paul says to Timothy in 1 Timothy 1:18 that, "This charge I commit to you ... having faith and a good conscience, which some having rejected, concerning the faith having suffered shipwreck."

Without passion, you will lose faith and with passion you can live through all conditions and situations that you encounter. Passion will give you the grace and stamina to carry on. Passion helps you to keep your faith and to fight the good fight. Only those who fight the good fight will be welcomed in heaven and given rewards for the fight. You need to fight hard to keep your faith through passion. Passion will keep you in the game of life and life of this world. Without passion, you have lost everything. Passion comes from conviction that Christ will give you the grace that is sufficient to take you to the level you have never been.

Passion Leads You To The Crown

James 1:12 says, "Blessed is a man who endures temptation; for when he has been approved, he will receive a crown of life which the Lord has promised to those who love him." Without passion, it is impossible to conceive and achieve a big dream in your heart. Without passion, it is not easy to keep moving when you are faced with opposition, criticism, or temptations. Passion gives you energy to endure the temptations, trials and pain. Passion motivates you to keep moving forward and keeps you going. Passion drives away fear and gives you progressive courage. Passion gives you the ability to resist and press on towards the goal.

When you have endured and overcome the temptations, challenges, ridicule and trials, then you will be awarded with a crown of life, which is a wonderful gift. Without passion in whatever you are dreaming of becoming you will not get a crown of life. Without passion, you will not get medals. People who win Olympics are passionate about sports and that is why they end up getting laurels and awards. Those without any passion will never be remembered by history. What temptation have you endured in life? Do you have an experience which has impacted your life? This temptation makes you better and a stronger person. It strengthens you and makes you a better person. The temptations and trials in my own life made me a better person. The temptations and trials made me stronger by preparing me to endure until the crown is rewarded and received.

Decide To Clarify Your Passion

It takes effort to know something you are passionate about. Passion is something that you love to do and brings joy to your life. It is more rewarding and exciting to do something that you love doing than forcing yourself to do something for which you have no passion for.

You need to search and research but also reflect on your life. What is that thing that you have been doing which gives you a smile, joy and brings an improvement for your life? It is important you do not waste time forcing yourself to do things that you do not love and enjoy. Also, ask yourself, what things are you passionate about? If you force yourself to do something for which you have no passion, you will not do it naturally and will lose steam very quickly.

What is your source of passion? How do we get passion to achieve our dreams and visions? When you clarify these questions, you will be in a better position to clarify your passion and fully understand your reason for living. Purpose and vision (preferred future) kicks in self-sacrifice, which makes leadership possible. True leaders have a vision that they are created to fulfil. Moses had a vision of leading Israelites to the Promised Land. Abraham had a vision of his descendants as countless as stars in heaven. Jesus saw us redeemed and reconciled back to God before the foundations of the Earth were formed. What is your vision? Do you see it? What preferred future are you seeing?

Throughout the years of research and study on vision, I have discovered that every vision always has only one believer first. That is why very few people always follow the leaders immediately when the leaders start to pursue their sense of purpose. Vision often makes leaders lonely. Moses was alone in the desert. Jesus was alone in the desert when Satan tempted him. Every person who begins to cultivate their leadership capabilities will often find their vision tested.

Time comes when all those who are always with you abandon you because they lose their belief and trust in you, but you must believe the vision. True leadership is always like this and leaders may find themselves lonely. It is how the leader utilize the period of loneliness this is what makes leaders to become leaders. Only God knows your purpose and will give you a vision motivated by passion for you to fulfil you sense of significance. The pursuit of vision will make you become a leader. Leaders are individuals who have decided that their vision is more important the present and pursue it.

You must therefore have a relationship with God so you can know why you were created and conceived by your parents. You are not a mistake and you might be wondering why you are on Earth. There is a big reason for your existence. If you want to know that purpose, you need to study the ultimate manual, the Bible. One of my favorite Scripture is Proverbs 19:21 which says, "Many are the plans in the man's heart, but the Lords purpose will prevail." Therefore, you need to get to know God for yourself.

Note: Have passion for your dreams.

CHAPTER THREE

THE FUNDAMENTAL PRINCIPLE OF PLANNING

"Plans are nothing. Planning is everything."
~ Dwight D. Eisenhower

What Is Planning?

Year in year out, numerous people, myself included make resolution lists of the things to achieve in life. We all write down these aspirations and dreams on paper and even in our minds. I have also heard people say, "I do not set goals." Others say, "I have my goals." All such actions can be considered as planning weather you like it or not. I believe that every human being carries out planning in some way. Even a drunkard is a planner.

Even a prostitute is a planner because she plans her activities for the day and night. Even a chain smoker is a planner because he or she plans to buy cigarettes as well as the times of smoking and where to smoke. A fisherman is a planner because he plans what equipment to use and when to use it. A hunter is a planner because he plans when to go hunting. A plumber is a planner because they plan what they want to do. Policemen, soldiers, teachers, students, etc., are planners. Indeed, everybody is a planner. Why? The answer to this question is that each of this people makes plans of what they will do every day. They are all planners. We are all planners. Both the people who fail and succeed are all planners. Everyone has a plan which can either succeed or fail. God requires every person to produce or prepare a plan (Proverbs 16).

However, planning is a process of making a plan for something. It is a process of identifying goals to be achieved over a period of time with given resources which include people, money, equipment and time. Plans are achieved when there is a strategy and resources. For the plans to succeed, goals must be defined clearly, strategies agreed, resources mobilized and activities implemented.

_____

He who fails to plan is planning to fail.
~ Winston Churchill

People Decide To Fail And Succeed

Those who fail decide to also fail. Remember, not making a decision is a decision. Likewise, those who succeed decide to succeed. Failure is predictable and success is also predictable. Failure is guaranteed and success is also guaranteed, but it depends on the actions that are taken. Every given year we have is an act of God. It is as if He hands the year itself a blank sheet of paper, as it were, to determine the next course of life. How will life be lived? How will the time be utilized?

Every person can decide what kind of life they want to live and what it will look like depending on the actions taken daily. I believe that many people are in the first chapter of their lives. Others in the third chapter; others in the fourth chapter; and others in the fifth chapter and so on so forth. To put it another way, some people are 10 years into their developing life, others 20, others 30, others are 40 years and so forth.

Furthermore, many people talk about plans and planning. Every time a year begins people talk about plans and planning. You hear of organizations talk about planning. So I thought I needed to give understanding of planning.

- Planning is concerned with the future or what you hope to do and accomplish.

- Planning is about preparation. Planning is organizing yourself before you embark on a journey to your destination.

- Planning is forecasting or forming projections about where you want to go in life.

- Planning is preparing or making arrangements to develop yourself for betterment. Without planning, there is no improvement, growth or development. Planning deals with the future and its expectations.

- Planning is concerned with desired change or preferred future. Planning is about accomplishing your dreams and achieving your goals. Planning is about reaching to the end of your goal.

- Planning is defined as the process of setting goals, developing strategies, outlining the implementation arrangements and allocating resources to achieve those goals. It is important to note that planning involves looking at a number of different processes. Planning is a decision to choose where you want to go with your life. Planning is necessary for success and without it, failure is guaranteed.

- Planning creates plans which are road maps to a desired end or destination. When a pilot is about to take off from one airport to another airport or destination, he or she receives a flight plan. The purpose of the plan is to guide the pilot to take a right direction.

Without proper planning and clear articulation of intended results, it is not clear what should be monitored and how to do it. Hence, monitoring cannot be done well. Without effective planning with a clear objective for good results in a set framework, the basis for evaluation is weak. Hence, evaluation cannot be done well. You need careful monitoring with the necessary data collected. Otherwise you cannot evaluate the results effectively.

Why Do Nations Or Organizations Have Plans?

To accomplish important goals and objectives, plans are developed. Planners in organizations or nations are always tasked to develop plans, so what will be achieved over a financial year is known. The planners will spend weeks putting ideas together through workshops, meetings and discussions. When all that is done, resources are allocated and a consolidated document is prepared and produced. That document is usually referred to as National Development Plan for most countries The document can span up to five, ten, twenty, or even fifty years. Look at the words "Development Plan." If nations can have plans, what about humans who are created by the master planner, God? Do you have a personal development plan? How many years does the plan cover? What strategies do you have to reach all the goals set in the plan? What resources have you allocated to achieve those goals? Who are your partners in implementing those plans? What are the threats, opportunities, strengths or weaknesses? When do you intend to review the plans? What will be the frequency?

The Benefits Of Planning

1. Planning enables implementation of activities and strategies for achieving mission and vision.

2. Planning aids proper setting of clear goals and objectives to be achieved.

3. Planning enables formulation of strategies that will be needed to achieve the vision.

4. Planning enables formulation of an implementation plan or activity calendar plan.

5. Planning enables allocation of resources (time, money, land, etc.).

6. Planning enables identification of stakeholders, partners and allies.

7. Planning facilitates development of monitoring and evaluation plans and also deters the critical success factors and indicators.

8. Planning enables effectiveness and efficiency in achieving results.

9. Planning enables prioritization and organization.

10. Planning enables planning for risk management and threats that affect plans.

11. Planning enables good control and ensures that targets and benchmarks and milestones are achieved.

12. Planning facilitates the coordination and systematic approach to accomplishing tasks and activities.

13. Planning facilitates division of labour and responsibilities.

14. Planning allows development of sustainability plans or succession plans.

15. Planning allows for effective use and allocation of scarce resources.

16. Planning allows development of contingency plans, what is normally called Plan B when Plan A fails or does not succeed.

God's Message About Planning And Plans

As a teenager, I used to read the Bible during devotions, and I got to know the great stories from 1 Samuel like David killing Goliath, Samson and Delilah. Then the and story of Samuel, and the son of Hannah. In one of those days during devotion, the Spirit of the Lord led me to the book of Proverbs. As I kept reading, I came to Proverbs 16 and it was an interesting reading and discovery. When I read this chapter, my life began to change and I realized that no matter how smart or powerful we are, if our plans are not in line with God's purpose, we cannot succeed. Proverbs 16:1, there is a statement which talks about plans. It says, "To man belongs the plans of the heart, but from the Lord comes the reply of the tongue."

This verse is a powerful statement that improved my life. I learned from this verse that man must have the plan first from his heart and mind and put it on paper and God will give the reply. The "reply" means an answer or account or response. This means that plans are man's responsibility and answer to plan or payment is God's responsibility. God is responsible for how your plans will be paid, costs will be achieved and how your plan will be funded. The word "responsibility" is two words in one: "response and ability" put together.

This means that man has the ability to respond and this is not the work of God. God has given man the greatest power — the will of the human or power of will. The power of will is the power that God expects humans to use to plan and change their lives for better or worse. Are you willing to wait for the answer from God? Are you willing to wait for the reply? Only God can give us answers to our plans. Without God's reply, we will always be unsuccessful.

Most People Never Take Planning Process Seriously

Inadequate planning has been a major challenge for the human race. Human beings, as result of conditioning or life experiences, are afraid to plan. The process of imagining the cost always paralyses the minds of a lot of people. How much will it cost? That's the question on the lips of many human beings. Many people have great plans and ideas but are afraid to take the step of faith forward to achieve the plans and the dreams in their hearts.

Planning Is Taking The Step Of Faith

If there is something you are planning to achieve or dreaming about you need to take a bold step of faith and write the plan down on a paper or note book so that you do not walk around with your ideas in your head. The reason is that God gives you ideas to remember. You need to write or draw those ideas on paper. You need to take time to carry out this plan. I realize that it is hard work to plan, but you have to sit down and plan. All your plans, ideas and dreams will evaporate from your mind or head unless you have written them down.

You need to document your plans and begin to see how the plans can be reached. In this book, there is a format for you to write your plans as a guide. I want to assure you that God is not asking for you to get a reply by yourself. God always asks you for the plan not for the money or resources. God says it's his responsibility. God is not a liar like most humans.

Please know that God's ways are not our ways. Over the years, I have understood that God's purposes are not meant for us to be comfortable. Our plans of living an ostentatious lifestyle is not

God's purpose. Helping humanity is the core of God's ordained purpose. If you have plans to get rich, God will not bless you with resources. However, if your plans are to help humanity, God will open great doors and windows of heaven to support you to help you achieve the plans. I urge you to begin developing a plan that is aimed at helping humanity; you will see how resources will be attracted to you. The resources that will come your ways include people, time, money and other opportunities.

I have a testimony about a project I wanted to do at home in Bukedea District in Uganda. One day, I was seated in the beautiful pool area of InterContinental Hotel in Nairobi waiting for a cup of coffee. As I waited, I decided to draw the ideas of the building I wanted. As I write this, I have finished building the house. I took the ideas in my mind, put them on paper and gave the architect my ideas as they appeared on paper and I started working on it. I cannot recall how and where the funds came but I believe God made it possible for the funds to be available to make the project a success.

You could be having ideas that you want to achieve like building a hospital, starting a piggery or poultry firm. To bring it to fulfillment, write all those ideas down or draw how the buildings will look like. This ideas or drawings will motivate you and commit them to God. You need to believe in God and your abilities and have unwavering faith in God. It works because it has worked for me and it will work for you.

Commit Your Plans To God

Proverbs 16:3 says, "Commit to the LORD whatever you do, and he will establish your plans." This means that when you commit to the Lord your plans, whatever you do, He will make them successful.

If you do not have anything on paper, in a notebook or diary then what shall you commit or bring before God to be blessed and in what do you want to succeed? This verse demands us all to have a plan and not live without it. When you have a plan, then you take it to God, and explain to Him; "This is the plan that I want to succeed."

In addition, when you have the plans, take the plans to God and make a commitment. A commitment means you forsake all the other things you want do and focus only on the plans. You must put the plans before the Lord God almighty. When God receives the plans, you will achieve the goals. God establishes the plans and actions that are brought and committed before Him. Anything you do without God will not be established. The secret is each time you want to do something and achieve it, begin by bringing it before God and commit it to the King of Kings.

In Proverbs 16:3 it says, "The LORD works out everything to its proper end even the wicked for a day of disaster." The Lord works everything for His Namesake - His ends. This text means that God will work with you to achieve the plan and bring it to an end. It means that you will succeed because God will work out the plans even if there will be challenges. As long as it is God's purpose for your life, God will make sure the plan is achieved. Proverbs 16: 5 says "The LORD detests all the proud of heart. Be sure of this: They will not go unpunished." The word "detests" implies hates, despises, and dislikes. When God is working with you to achieve the plan, do not be proud in your heart and under look people as God works in you and through you. In other words, do not become proud as you gain success or when God blesses you. God dislikes those individuals who are proud. This is a principle you must take to your heart.

The secret is that you need to maintain humility all the time in all places as you continue to fulfil your purpose for your life. In my own experience and short journey on this Earth, being humble all the time has kept me through life, enabling me to do the things God created me to do. I believe humility is the most difficult attitudes that people fail to apply. Humans like power and authority, which makes it difficult to stay humble.

People's pride is so high and exceeds the level of our shoulders. God hates those who are proud. God resists them. I advise you that you learn to be humble and remain humble despite all attacks that you will experience in your life. Humility will preserve your life. In essence, the lesson I want you to learn is that humility is important. Do not be proud.

Furthermore, in Proverbs 16: 6, it says, "Through love and faithfulness sin is atoned for; through the fear of the LORD evil is avoided." It is important to demonstrate love and faithfulness as you work with God to achieve your goals. Love the people that God has placed to work with you and be faithful to God who has approved the plans and given you resources.

When you show love to those that work with you, they will have commitment to work according to plan and support you to achieve the plan. But then if you dislike them, they might turn against you and your plan may fail. The secret to success is having unconditional love and being faithful all the time. God is looking for people who are faithful, not famous. Samson was a famous fellow who was feared by his enemies, but in his life, he messed up. He had pride, which destroyed him. Be full of love and be committed to faithfulness to God.

Besides, as you maintain your faith in God through faithfulness to Him and trusting in Him, He will open more doors of opportunities to help you achieve the plans. If you are faithful in the small project God gave you, he will give you a bigger project. Jesus said, "If you are faithful in small things then I will bless you with big things." God will never bless you with big things without checking how you managed small things. Do a good job with small things and you will be blessed to manage big things. Proverbs 16:7 says, "When the LORD takes pleasure in anyone's way, he causes their enemies to make peace with them." When your ways please God, your enemies will become your friends.

I love this because it teaches us that even those folks that criticize you will eventually start to follow you or become your friends and support you. God has the power to stop people who are against you and cause them to become partners in your dreams. This only happens if you are faithful, doing the right things that please God.

Better A Little With Righteousness

Proverbs 16:8 says, "Better a little with righteousness than much gain with injustice." "Better a little with righteousness" simply means do not steal or become corrupt in order to achieve your plans. "Injustice" simply means unfairness. As you work with God, be righteous and do the right thing. I recall the time in my life when I had not many things as everyone would love to have. I often felt inadequate and fear would afflict me, but this Scripture was a source of my strength. When I look at some of the people who had much at the time, I would wonder how they made their money. I would agonize about and wonder why I can't command such an amount of affluence. This happened on several occasions but my faith remained in God. I believed in God as the "Owner of everything." What He has given is better because it was gained through hard work, not corruption or abuse of office or illegal means.

As I look back, I see most of those people in my country are down and have lost everything that was gotten illegally with injustice. Some of the people I know spent several years in prison or jail. They lost the assets acquired because they had to be sold and their children were also affected by crisis of their parent being in jail. Do not engage in acts that are illegal such as corruption or abuse of office. When God gives you little, God is testing how you are managing the little things He has entrusted to you. Believe me if you remain faithful, God will bless you with big things. God is about to bless me with big things because I have been faithful in small things. What about you?

I recall meeting a lady who knew the family of a prominent politician in my country. At that time, the politician was more powerful because he had acquired illegal wealth. He was extravagant. Because of this, I felt the politician was without any challenge or worry. After probing further, I discovered that this politician had lost his marriage and his children all got messed up in life.

When you are faced with difficulty, I will encourage you not to panic and engage in things that are not right before God. Stay steady and believe me, your time of greatness will come and without struggle. You will see God's revelation and fulfil his purpose for your life. Do not be afraid of any test. You should not be afraid of the smoke. You will come out of every situation when you keep your faith. You should not allow your faith to fail. Do not lose your faith in the midst of trials and temptations. It is important that you aspire to be faithful rather than to be famous. Fame is like flame; it vanishes quickly.

God Will Direct The Plans You Have Prepared

Finally, in the same chapter, Proverbs 16:9 says, "In his heart, a man plans his course but the Lord directs and determines his plans." This means that God cannot direct you if there are no plans. You must have the plans and God will direct you what to do or who to contact to support you. God will give you ideas. I have seen most people spend a lot of time in church, praying for so many years. God will lead you in to your dreams.

I recall when I first bought a piece of land for a house in Kampala, I had no money. The land was bought using the loan from the bank. There was no extra money or resource except my job at that time. As I started to think about the building project, the first thing was design or getting the plans approved. I engaged the architect to make a plan and submit to the authorities. The plan was approved. As time went by, I prayed to God for the plans to succeed.

Now watch what happened. God began to move in ways that I cannot believe! God gave me an opportunity for international travel in which I was paid a daily subsistence allowance that was a huge sum of money. When I return back home, I used part of the money to start the building foundation. God determined the steps of how the house was going to be completed. Furthermore, as I continued to work, I cut my expenses and saved part of my salary. For over two years, I was doing all of these cost-cutting measures. When the time came for roofing, there was no money because roofing was to be done at once. I remember praying to God, and God told me to ask my friends.

140

At that time, I had friends from Sierra Leon, Baimakay Sanko and Moses Ojota; these two are still my close friends. When I asked them for money, they loaned me the money and I was able to roof the house. And today, my family lives in that house and I no longer pay house rent except bills such as water and electricity. The house was built through the guidance of God and his provision for the vision I had. God will provide for His vision; it does not matter what happens. God will lead you to the source of resources and dream in your heart will be fulfilled.

This is what God says to every person who has a dream or a vision:
1. Where is the plan?
2. Is the plan in line with God's plan?
3. Where do I lead you?
4. How should I bless you?

Therefore, each and every person with a desire to succeed needs to have a plan. A plan is a document that describes what you want to accomplish. It shows the goals to be achieved. It shows the timeline when activities will be completed and the responsible person or persons to carry it out. When you have a plan, God will lead you to achieve and fulfil it. When you are led by God, then you will be blessed. So make a plan and follow these steps that I have listed above. As someone with a vision, you must put a plan on paper and God will direct it. Then you will stop wasting time. If you want God to lead you, you must commit your plan to paper. Put it in writing.

The Significance Of Planning And Plan

In 2013, I was flying from South Africa to Kenya. As I was at Oliver Richard Tambo International Airport, I met a team of pilots who had been with us at the Holiday Inn International Hotel in Johannesburg. The pilot of our plane spoke to me and I asked about the departure. He was waiting for a flight plan. It is a global principle that you cannot leave the airport without one. This incidence taught me a big lesson that a plan guides and leads one to a final destination or goal.

Without a plan you will not have good control and direction. Before the pilots leave an airport to another destination, they see the destination in pictures (which I call vision) and they put a plan in place. A plan states how many workers will go on the trip, how much food is needed in the plane for passengers, how much water and how much time it will take to arrive at the final destination. Plans are prepared before actions are started and it serves as a guide for every aspect of life.

Another example where I believe planning has been effective in my life was in 2005. I had been having the desire to go back for further my studies and I was working in Northern Uganda in Kitgum District. It was very difficult to go back to school fulltime because I had other responsibilities that required me to work in order for me to meet my obligations. I decided to set aside some money for about two years and I was looking for ways of getting back to college.

But just as I was planning to go back for fulltime studies. an opportunity came my way where I was able to start my Masters studies by distance education online. The funds that I set aside is how I paid for the tuition, textbooks, and other materials. I kept my job and continued to study because I had to plan my work and accomplish all my tasks during the day while at night in my room I was studying and doing my assignments and coursework. I became so organized that I had to priorities my life and know what was important for me.

I reduced the time I socialize with friends. I cut off some pleasure activities and got committed to the plans I had set for myself. Within a period of three years, I successfully complete my master's degree program and graduated. I believe that if I could accomplish this with busy schedule that involved work and family, then anybody interested in achieving their dreams and plans can achieve it. It is possible. Through proper planning, you too can achieve your goals. People don't achieve their goals and plans because the plans and goals are easily forgotten. Success is possible when you plan and when you have the commitment. You must be committed, loyal, determined and dedicated to your plans. Do not plan and be interested in pleasure, frivolities and parties; you will fail. Plan your life and you will have an interesting and effective life.

God's Plan For You And Me

Another Scripture where planning is mentioned is Jeremiah 29:11, 'For I know the plans I have for you,' declares the Lord, 'plans to prosper you and not to harm you, plans to give you hope and a future.' The source of my confidence is that God knows the plans for my life even if I do not. So I should seek God's plan. God created you in His image and He knows what is best for you. God will not give you things that you are not ready to handle.

For instance, you might want to be a great leader, but God knows His own plans and will only give you what you have the maturity to handle. The secret to success is knowing that God has plans for you. You might have your own plans that are not in perfect line with

God. God has your future in his hands but things will not happen on their own; you must plan and seek God to bless whatever you are seeking.

God Can Decide To Answer Or Not

Many Christians know the content of Jeremiah 29:11 and they quote it all the time. What does this statement really mean? It means that God has a plan but you do not know about it. It means we have to seek God to know the plan that He has. It means we have to write a plan down and believe that it's in line with God's plan He has for us. The text also means that God Himself is a planner. God is a planner, because we are products of Him, God expects human to prepare their plans and commit them to the Lord.

Now if God is a planner and we came from Him according to Genesis 1:26, that means humans are inherently planners. The challenge is that most human beings do not take time to plan and write down their plans. If you want to be successful in life and move in life without an accident, then you must plan. It is important to mention here that if you are not moving towards your purpose and goal, God cannot help you. If you have no plan, God cannot help you. God can only help you reach your dreams and vision when you have a plan. God is a systematic God, who planned to achieve the vision He had before creating the universe.

In Habakkuk 2:2-3, God told the prophet to write the revelation given to him on paper. From this we can conclude that the Lord wants us to put His guidance on paper. Take the vision and put it on paper. A vision is a plan. It is a part of the planning process. It means seeing where God wants you to be at the end of your destination. In my life, I have believed and trusted God. There are times when I felt like giving up but when I recall what I put on paper, I get up to work and pursue the plans and think about it. I go back to God and seek His wisdom and guidance. The secret is that you must stop, sit down and plan if you are going to fulfil your vision and achieve the plans you have in your heart.

Call And Pray To God So He Can Listen To You

Furthermore, success is the orderly and organized movement towards the goal. God desires your success more than you do. God cannot listen to you when you have no plan. God only listens when you have a plan. In Jeremiah 29:12, it says, "Then you will call on me and come and pray to me, and I will listen to you." When you present a plan to God through commitment, then you can call on Him and He will answer you. The word "call" means cry, make sound, noise, appeal, request and plead with God.

The reason why people's prayers are not answered by God is because they have no plans and their purposes are not in line with God's will. God is always waiting for a plan from you of how you need to get out of your situation or circumstance. I have seen many people cry to God. I came to a conclusion that unless there is a plan, God cannot direct your steps. God gave you the capacity, ability and will to plan. This means you must use your capacity and ability to think and plan for your dreams and vision that you want to achieve.

Seek God And You Will Find Him

In the same Scripture, Jeremiah 29:13, it says, "You will seek me and find me when you seek me with all your heart." God requires that when we seek Him, we should have a plan. Then we shall find Him. When you find God, your plan succeeds. God demands us to make plans and goals that lead us to our vision. You have heard and known that he who fails to plans, plans to fail. But many people also fail to implement the plans or take action.

You have heard and known that he who fails to plans, plans to fail. But many people also fail to implement the plans or take action.

God requires the whole heart, not a divided heart. Some of us make plans, but we have divided attention and no commitment. The whole heart means no division of the heart. We cannot find God unless we have an undivided attention between the things of the world and things of God. We have to approach God without a divided heart, totally focused on Him.

God Will Deliver You From Your Situation Or Crisis

Jeremiah 29:14 says,

> "I will be found by you, 'declares the LORD, 'and will bring you back from captivity. I will gather you from all the nations and places where I have banished you,' declares the LORD, and will bring you back to the place from which I carried you into exile."

What does this text mean to contemporary followers of Christ? This text means there are people who are in bondage and captivity. The situation or circumstance that you are currently facing is a result of lack of planning or having no plan. In order to get out of bondage and captivity, you need a plan. The plan will provide a way for you to get out of those circumstances or problems. The key to getting out of the situation is planning and it will liberate you and set you free. The key to your future is planning.

Planning Is Faith And Faith Is Planning

During the course of my Bible study, I came to connect planning to faith. In my study and conclusion, planning is faith and faith is planning. Hebrews 11:1 says, "Now faith is the substance of things hoped for, the evidence of things not seen." In reading this, how can you speak of things you hope to accomplish and look to the evidence of the things that you cannot see physically? It seems contradictory. But this is only possible when they are contained and included in the work plan that you have.

Faith believes in God's promise. Faith is the evidence of putting substance to the things you have not seen yet, but you are hoping that they will be manifested. Faith is conviction of things we physically do not yet see, things regarding the future yet unknown to us. Faith talks about things that you hope to accomplish or achieve. Planning is also concerned about the things you hope to do and achieve. In this case, the two concepts of faith and planning are the same.

Have Faith In God, But Have A Plan As Well

Faith therefore demands a plan. When you plan, you are putting down things you want see happen. When you plan to build a house or public university, you are having the faith it will be seen, revealed and accomplished. When you are working with an organization, you usually have a plan to do something for the organization or target group; this means you have faith that the activity will be done. Planning simply means having faith in the unknown that you hope to achieve and complete.

One of the things I have discovered about some Christians is that they are lazy people, drifting along in life. They know how to quote the Bible and memorize the passage; they understand its meaning and application. But they will fail to plan. I have found something interesting about God. He has a plan for you but does not plan for you. Planning is the highest expression and application of faith in God. Planning is the act of capturing God's vision for your own life and the life of the next generation. Planning pulls promises of God from eternity into time where we live.

Planning Is the highest expression and application of faith In God.

Planning is the process of documenting vision. Your vision is nothing without a plan. Without a plan, life has no definition, meaning or self-control. If God tells you to do something, you document it, plan for it and prepare for. Planning is the act of capturing God's will for your life and your destiny. When God instructs you to do something, you should act on what He has told you to do. Plans without action is like faith without works is dead (James 2:17). Having faith without a plan is not good enough. You have to plan your way with an eye to heaven so the Lord will direct your steps. I would like to put it in another way: Planning without works is dead. When you have a plan and you do not work, that plan will remain just a plan. Planning is concerned with influencing your environment and changing your life. Planning is about creating a better future and taking hold of that future. Planning is one key for you to enjoy effective living.

Planning is the process of documenting after capturing the true vision from God.

148

Without A Vision, Faith And Plan, People Perish

When you plan, you are documenting after capturing the true vision from God. I have already said, planning is faith and faith is planning. Vision is, therefore, faith, or planning. The Word of God says, "Where there is no vision, the people perish" (Proverb 29:18). People perish because of lack of a vision, faith or plan. Without a plan, there is no way you can reach the vision that you have for your life. Planning without work is failure. Faith without action is dead. God is the greatest example of a planner. God is a planner; He planned the creation of the world.

God Chose You Before Anything Else

Ephesians 1:4 says, "According as he hath chosen us in him before the foundation of the world, that we should be holy and without blame before him in love." God conceived the plan of redemption before Jesus Christ was even born. God planned what was going to happen to you and me before he begun to create the universe. He says that He chose us before the foundation was laid. When you start the building of the house, you do not start with roof or walls but a foundation. The foundation is the most important part of the house. (Matthew 7:24-27)

The Weak Foundation

A weak foundation means, the house will not last long and a strong foundation means the house will last long. My challenge to everybody is that you should strive to build a strong foundation in your life. How strong is your foundation? Another secret in life for peace is the fact that God chose you before the foundations were laid. God knew you. This implies God knows the future of your life. God knows the end of your life. Whatever happens is God's will and not your will. There are things in your life that you have no control and you must not try to have control. When things happen in life do not try to condemn or blame yourself, but instead trust God. How strong is your foundation in God?

Imitate God When Your Plans Fail

I know that people are taught never to fail but strive to succeed. Failure does not just happen to one person. Everybody fails in something. God Himself failed even though you might not agree with me. To me God failed when He gave man instructions in the Garden of Eden. Man did not obey God's instructions but someone might say that that the failure of the Garden of Eden was actually in God's overall plan of redemption. People think failure is only one-sided but it is two-sided. When you send your child to college, and he fails to come with a good report, the cause could be the child or you never provided good guidance. So God gave instructions but perhaps He did not follow thought to make sure that the instructions were implemented.

What To Do When Plans Fail

If your plans failed from the past, you need to imitate God. God did not panic when man failed. If you do not have a plan, then there is nothing for you to change. Not fulfilling your plan does not mean you are out of God's will. People say God never fails, but God failed also even though God is sovereign and Almighty. God put Adam in the garden to rule, dominate and subdue it. But Adam messed up. The story of this act is found in Genesis 2.

God failed and developed the plan of redemption. Believe in the plan because it contains your goals and purpose. The purpose you have is more permanent and more powerful than problems. Plans may change but purpose remains permanent. I will accomplish the purpose even though the plans change. Failure is an opportunity to start again. You only lose when you quit. Make new plans when the plans do not succeed.

When you fail to plan that is when you will completely fail. When plans fail, it is not the planner who has failed; it is the plan because of many factors beyond you. You might have planned to save money (for example, $2,000 a month). In 12 months you will have $24,000. Along the way, you lose a job that gave you money to save; it is not you who failed, but your plan. You might have saved $40,000 for buying a house or an apartment in the city, but a financial crisis, or inflation cost of houses or apartments have gone up. You cannot afford to buy the house or apartment that you wanted; it is not your fault. It is the market or economic forces, but you could try to buy the property from another location. You might have wanted to go back to college for further studies, but unfortunately you get an accident and fail to go to college; do not blame yourself. It is beyond you. You might have planned to marry a lady that you loved so much, but the lady changes her mind; what do you do? Go back to the drawing board and look to God for another potential partner.

Life is that way, you always have to plan and when you have a setback, do not give up. You might have wanted to start a hair dresser business, restaurant, super market, clinic, transport, but for some unknown reason you have not been able to do it. Do not give up on your ideas; make another or alternative plan. It is important to remember: when the plans fail, it is not the person or the individual who has failed but the plans. Plans are changeable.

Plans are modifiable. Purposes are not changeable. If your plan is go to your city, and one road is blocked, what do you do? The answer is you take another route until you reach the city. Going to the city is the purpose. If your plan is to get a degree and there is a pregnancy in your family, do you drop your plans? No, you wait until after the baby is born and then study to get a degree. The degree becomes your purpose. This image of getting the degree is called vision. Vision is a glimpse of your destiny. The secret to life is that people do not fail. Instead, only the plans and strategy that fails. Do not blame yourself when the plans do not work out.

Review The Plans And Keep The Lessons Of Failure

If you work for a government or non-government organization, you will discover that when their plans failed, what these organizations do is to review the plans and develop another one. The secret to success is reviewing your plans constantly and learn the lessons of failure as you continue to chase the dreams of your life.

Jesus Christ Powerful Teaching On Planning

Jesus Christ taught His disciples about the power of planning. He gave a detailed process of planning and I believe you need to imitate this model if you are going to succeed in your life and impact the next generation. In Luke 14:26- 27, Jesus said to His disciples, "If anyone comes to me and does not hate his father and mother, his wife and children, his brothers and sisters – yes, even his own life – he cannot be my disciple." To be a disciple is to be a lifetime student. To become a student, Jesus said you must hate your relatives. What does "hate" mean in this context?

Furthermore, hate means that you need to make sacrifice and a decision to follow Him and this is always a personal decision and choice. If you want to achieve something, it is going to involve personal sacrifice, and the decisions are personal. Success comes when you decide to sacrifice everything for the sake of vision. It might mean abandoning sleep, parties or company of some good friends. Success requires following the instructions until you reach the destination. The key to success is planning and forsaking all things for the plan that you have developed.

Success comes when you decide to sacrifice everything for the sake of vision.

You must be willing to commit to the plans in your heart if you are to succeed. Commitment is important for success because it is possible to quit or give up in the middle of a project. Millions of people usually start things, but in the middle of it, they quit when the going gets rough and tough. Do not surrender when you have started something.

Planning Involves Sitting Down And Estimating The Costs

Jesus spoke about planning in Luke 14:27-28, "And anyone who does not carry his cross and follow me cannot be my disciple. 'Suppose one of you wants to build a tower. Will he not first sit down and estimate the cost to see if he has enough money to complete it?'" The text is full of principles that are related to planning.

1. We must carry our cross to be Jesus' disciple.
2. We must also sit down and plan before we build something like a tower.

This requires estimating the costs that you are going to incur: Your time, money, resources, friendships, and many other things. Sitting down might mean taking time to have a retreat or planning meeting and coming with a concrete work plan which reflects priorities and goals that must be achieved within a given time frame with resources available.

In these meetings, you will develop a plan of action, estimate the costs involved, resources needed and how long it will take to build. Planning is essential for success in any dream. Planning will produce a work plan. No one will do this planning for you. You must be the one to plan for your life, family, community and nation.

Another secret is sitting down, estimating the cost of the plans and working to achieve it. Without sitting down through retreat, seminars or workshops, it is not easy for organizations to develop plans. In order to come up with plans, or work plan, you might need to go to an isolated place or quiet place away from home or familiar environment. When you are in a far place, say a quiet place, there ideas will be revealed to you and this can be translated into a concrete plan. In addition, you will have an opportunity to reflect and meditate. Through this process, you will come up with incredible ideas and goals.

Start With A Foundation

I learned so many years ago that life has a foundation. Foundation is a principle. Every house or building usually starts with a foundation. Builders and engineers usually start any construction work with a foundation and they keep building on what they start. You cannot build a house or building in one day, it takes time and so it was with God, it took six days for God to finish creating everything that He wanted. How can we ensure success in building a house? To be successful, there needs to be a strong foundation right from start to finish.

Similarly, the key secret in life is establishing a foundation and continue building from there. Our failure in many areas of life including relationships or nations results from having weak foundation. The houses or buildings that collapse have weak foundations. How strong is your foundation? The houses that fall of have weak foundations. The building will give way when there is pressure or storms because of weak foundations. The marriages that fail have weak foundations. The relationships that are destined to fail have a weak foundation. How strong is your life's foundation? Are you built on a solid rock? Are you built on a weak sand? Who is your foundation? In my life, Jesus Christ is my foundation. I believe in Jesus Christ in everything I do and I commit whatever I want to do to Him. It is His will that matters and my personal relationship with Him. Do you have a personal relationship with Jesus Christ?

In Luke 14: 29 Jesus says, "For if you lay the foundation and are not able to finish it, everyone who sees it will ridicule you." In this Scripture, there is a great lesson that that as you start to fulfil your purpose and the plan that God has approved, you could lay a foundation and fail to complete it. This happens to everyone at some point and it is no surprise. This is natural. Do not be intimidated by people who might ridicule or even belittle you. You must keep moving and focusing on your goals.

Principles
- *If you start to lay a foundation and do not finish, you might expect some ridicule, but just keep going and build that foundation.*

- *There are people who will ridicule or belittle you; do not worry about them and do not stop because of what they say.*
- *Keep working hard on your dreams.*
  You will realize those dreams and plans will succeed.

Plan Before Going To War

There is no success in war without a plan and strategy. Any war that is started without a plan will end as a disaster.

Luke 14:31-32 says,

> *Or suppose a king is about to go to war against another king. Will he not first sit down and consider whether he is able with ten thousand men to oppose the one coming against him with twenty thousand. If he is not able, he will send a delegation while the other is still a long way off and will ask for terms of peace.*

In this text, the planner must never start a war without proper assessment and judgment of his or her capacity. Some situations in life will require direct or indirect negotiations with the oppositions groups. Another secret is not to be intimidated when you plan and there are no immediate results. People will talk more about your failure than your success. The secret is to keep going with your plans and guard your spirit.

Principles
- *No plan can be achieved without first sitting down and considering the resources that the planner has.*
- *There are some things which will require delegation and you must decide on that. You cannot do all things.*

156

Give Up Everything For The Sake Of The Plan And Dream In Your Heart

Luke 14: 33 says, "In the same way, those of you who do not give up everything you have cannot be my disciples." In other words, we must sit down and plan. Give up everything and focus on the plans and goals you want to achieve. It is important to sit down to produce your plan and have it on paper. Jesus says, sit down and plan. Most people do not sit but instead are busy doing things that are not related to their dreams and vision. Some people spend their lives without planning. It takes time to sit down, but it is of outmost importance to plan.

Principles
- *A planner with desire to achieve the plan must give up everything for the sake of the plan.*
- *A planner must abandon everything for the sake of the plan even if it costs him his life.*
- *Purpose is only achieved with great discipline, focus, passion, and commitment.*

Discard Old Ideas That No Longer Work And Get New Ones

Luke 14:34 says, "Salt is good, but if it loses its saltiness, how can it be made salty again?" During the planning process, there are things that you will need to throw away. This is because they are no longer good. Planning calls for a review of resources in your possession. There are things in your life that have affected your progress and some of them could be your company, friends, attitudes, and habits and acquired new behaviours. If you want to advance and progress, you need to assess what is best. If people, old habits and bad behaviour are dragging you down, then move away from them. Throw away what is obsolete. You need to search for new knowledge, ideas and information to fulfil the plans.

Principle
- *There are things that are no longer good for you, throw them away.*

Luke 14:35 says, "It is fit neither for the soil nor for the manure pile; it is thrown out." He who has ears to hear, let him hear. Here we see that there are people in the world today who never learn. This is an opportunity to learn from others. If you desire to achieve a plan, you must be willing to hear and take action. There is no person who does not have ears for hearing unless they are born with abnormalities. Many people have ears and have been told about planning and still they are stuck in their old ways. If you want your life to become better or improve, you need to hear this and heed this advice.

Principles
- *Anyone who is willing to hear and apply these principles let him do so and there will be no regret. Do not ignore these ideas because you claim you know it all. Nobody knows everything. What you know you learned from somewhere else besides yourself.*
- *Plan your life and you will be effective.*

God Cancels Man's Plan Because Of Wrong Motives

The first place where we encounter the concept of planning through God himself. In Genesis 11:6, The Lord said, "If as one people speaking the same language they have begun to do this, then nothing they plan to do will be impossible for them." This is the story of the Tower of Babel. God said when people come together in unity, then nothing they plan will fail. God had to come down himself to stop the project because the motive of the project was wrong. When you make the plan, check the motives. If the motive is to help humanity, then God will not stop it. Your motives will determine if God will bless it. God sees the hearts of men and women as man only sees the outside. Be careful of your motives and check your motives if they will please God. The reason why plans do not succeed is because of our motives which may be selfish ones.

In this story God Himself talks about planning. In this text, we read the story of men working to build the tower of Babel. The men and women set up to achieve their vision. They wanted a tower to go to heaven. They made arrangements and were working together. The Bible says God took a decision to stop the project. The endeavor was so great that God Himself was concerned and had to come down from the throne to cancel the work of these men and women.

Principle
- *To succeed in any work or goal, people must have one voice and understanding guided by unity and team work.*

Genesis 11:7 says, "Come, let us go down and confuse their language so they will not understand each other." God can decide to stop your selfish project by creating confusion in what you are doing. God can cause misunderstanding between you and your family, your church board, governing council or leadership team. God can stop you from implementing the plans that you have because of the motives that you have. Likewise, Genesis 11:8 says, "So the Lord scattered them from there over all the earth, and they stopped building the city." So, you need to understand that God is committed to plans that have the right motives and intentions. He can make your plans fail if He so desires.

Principles
- *Check your motives before you start working to achieve your goals and vision.*
- *God will bless what you do if the motives are right and benefit humanity.*

What Is The Lesson And Moral Of The Story?

The lesson to me here is that when men plan to do something and they are united, God will look at the motive behind their plans and actions. If the motive is approved by God, then the project or plan will be successful. If the motive is wrong, then God Himself will get involved to stop it. As you pursue your projects and plans, you need to consult God for approval. When God approves your plans and project, adequate funding and success are certain.

Joseph Was An Example Of A Successful Planner And Visionary

Planning is also mentioned in Genesis 41. As you all know, Joseph was a son of Jacob who was rejected by his family. Joseph was a dreamer. Joseph had a vision of feeding his family. Joseph was a planner. When Joseph was sold by his brothers to Egyptian merchants, he became a slave in Egypt. Now in Egypt, the pharaoh had a dream which could not be interpreted by anyone in the whole nation. Pharaoh gave an assignment to his people to interpret the dream and propose a solution. There was nobody who could do that until when pharaoh was informed of a young man who was in prison named Joseph. Joseph was given the task to explain the meaning of the dream. Joseph did the task with precision and perfection. He was able to give a proper plan which was approved by the pharaoh. This account is recorded in Genesis 41:33-36:

> *And now let Pharaoh look for a discerning and wise man and put him in charge of the land of Egypt. Let Pharaoh appoint commissioners over the land to take a fifth of the harvest of Egypt during the seven years of abundance. They should collect all the food of these good years that are coming and store up the grain under the authority of Pharaoh, to be kept in the cities for food. This food should be held in reserve for the country, to be used during the seven years of famine that will come upon Egypt, so that the country may not be ruined by the famine.*

Joseph was appointed to lead the project and execute the plan. Joseph had a plan for pharaoh and that is why he got promoted. Without a plan, there is no promotion. A planner will be promoted because a planner is visionary and self-motivated person with passion and purpose.

God Will Fulfil Your Desire

Psalms 20:4 says, "May He grant you according to your heart's desire, and fulfil all your purpose." There is a desire to succeed in the heart of man. A plan is what you have documented or a desire that is documented. A desire is different from what you want. A desire is related to your purpose and vision. A desire is a petition, an aspiration, a longing, a craving and yearning that you passionately want for your life. A desire is a purpose that God want you to accomplish.

God's Plans Stand Forever

In addition to this, Psalms 33:11 says, "The counsel of the LORD stands forever, the plans of His heart to all generations." When God has revealed your purpose, you are guaranteed that His advice will stand forever. The plans that God gives you to fulfil your purpose will benefit not only your generation but all generations. This implies that purpose is generational and when you are planning, you need to plan for generations. Isn't that amazing? People I have met only plan for themselves and this is what most politicians do most of the time. Politicians are concerned with today and next elections, titles, and positions and only few leaders do the opposite. I want you to believe this. You cannot change the plans of God. His plans will stand forever.

Good Plans Are From God

Proverbs 12:5 says, "The plans of the righteous are just, but the advice of the wicked is deceitful." The word "righteous" comes from the root word "right." It means correct, true, factual, accurate, and exact. Righteous means that God justifies your plans and approved by God. That also means that you are doing the correct things that God has desired to achieve to benefit generation of people after you. As you work to fulfil your purpose, you will need to keep your life on course with God and stay close to your principles. Principles will protect you and save you energy. Do not do things without justice and fairness. Do not seek advice from those who are deceitful or seeking to achieve personal glory.

Principle
- *Make just plans that benefit every human, not selfish plans.*

Follow Jesus if you want your plans to succeed. Then Jesus said to his disciples, "If anyone would come after Me, he must deny himself and take up his cross and follow Me" (Matthew. 16:24). This is what planners need to learn from to succeed. It means planners must be willing and ready to do it on their own even if people around you will not agree with you. There will be people around you who will not approve or agree with your plans. But Jesus gave the message: Carry your cross and carry out your plans. "Carry your cross" means that in spite of the challenges and setbacks you may encounter, you have to endure to the end. Carrying your cross will affect your relationships. You will encounter discouragement along the way.

Furthermore, there will be moments when you will be tired, emotionally affected and discouraged. When these happen, do not give up but keep carrying your cross (plans). When you do this, you will succeed. Jesus carried his cross from the time he was arrested and taken until that hour when He said, "It is finished" at the cross on Golgotha. In the same way, when you carry your cross or plans, you will reach the end, and you will rejoice and smile. Your words will also be, "It is finished. I made it. I succeeded. I am happy. I am relieved and I rejoice." Abraham Lincoln once said, *"A goal properly set is halfway reached."*

Principle
- *To succeed, you must be willing to be a disciple, a perpetual student of life. Learn everything that needs to be learnt so that the quality of your decisions is informed by the quality of information and knowledge that you have.*

Why Are People Poor And Unhappy In The World?

There are many reasons why this happens, but to me, other reasons are related to lack of goal setting. There are many opportunities in the world but most people are still poor and unhappy, not able to live abundantly because there are no clearly defined goals. The lack of goals leads to wandering in life without any aim. The person or people without goals end up at the wrong destination. A goal is a road map for you to get to a better and successful life. To succeed in life, you must first be sure and know exactly what you want and then go for it. If your goal is to become a millionaire, you need to set the goal that leads you to being a millionaire. The reverse is also true. In order to achieve something, you need to set the goal to achieve that thing, and then follow through by working to achieve it and finally realising it. The goal will give you a sense of direction, meaning and destination. Therefore, to succeed you need to set goals.

What Is A Goal?

A goal is something stated in clear terms which is a person's desire or ambition. A goal is a target that needs to be achieved. A goal is something that you really desire. A goal is reached or stated when you know what you want to achieve.

A wish is nothing but an unclear dream. An interest is something fantasied about. An inspiration is a dream that is vague which you might have interest in getting. Dreams or aspirations never help people but goals will lead you to the desired end. You become successful if you have a set of clear goals.

The Importance Of Goal Setting

1. Goals give you the first steps to begin the journey to your dreams and visions.
2. Goals are like road maps that guide you in your life's journey.
3. Goals state clearly what is desired and leads to known destination.
4. Goals will lead you where you are going and what you are truly looking to achieve.
5. Goals will give you confidence and faith.
6. Goals create a plan and generate plan of action.
7. Goals will drive and motivate you to work for the dreams in the heart.

Types of Goals:

- Long-term Goals: These are goals stated for a long term period of more than 5 years. This can be a life goal set which states what you want to achieve before you die.

- Intermediate Goals: These goals are linked to long-term goals, which contribute to achieve the long term goals.

- Short-term Goals: These goals lead to immediate goals. These goals must be simple, measureable, achievable, and realistic and time-bound.

Make A Plan For Achieving The Goals

For any goal that you want to achieve, you will need to come up with actions or activities that you must do to reach the goal. If your goal is to obtain a degree from the university that means you have to do all of the activities that the university will require so that after a period allotted for the course you will have finished the degree. Here are some of the activities that you must do:

1. You have to register, pay all the tuition fees and obtain clearance.
2. You have to attend classes and lectures.
3. You will need to do all the tests, assignments and course work offered by lecturers.
4. You will need to sit through all the exams set by the university.
5. You have to defend the projects before the lecturers.

For every goal, you need the action plan which is practical steps that must consistently followed to achieve good results.

God's Purpose Is Important Than Man's Plans

Look at this Holy Scripture again: "Many are the plans in the man's heart, but the Lords purpose will prevail" (Proverbs 19:21). What does this scripture teach us? Purpose of God is more important than the plans that you have. Purpose is the most important thing that God has focused on than plans made by man. Purpose comes first before the plans. Are your plans in line with God's purpose? Ask God for your purpose before you make your plans. God is more interested in His purpose for the life He has granted to you than the plans you have for your life. The word plan means the schemes, ideas or thoughts or devices that you have in your heart.

Sometimes people come up with their plans, what they want to do, or where they want build their homes. At times they decide where they want to go and live or whom they want to marry or where they want to spend their holidays, and God is watching and waiting. What God is interested in is His purpose. First, you must consult God for His purpose or go to God in prayer first. There are many people who decided to do things before going to God first. For instance, people want to study degree courses without seeking God's purpose. And later they run back to God. It is imperative to always consult God before anything is done.

Plans are created by man but God's purposes are permanent. When you ever discover your purpose, you will no longer remember the past mistakes you will become immune to the opposition that comes against you and you will overcome every obstacle in order to realize your vision. When the enemies conspire against you, your purpose will serve an anchor. And you will keep moving on. The purpose is your obligation and nothing can stop you. You are unstoppable.

Principles
- *God's purpose is more important than man's plans, ideas, and schemes.*
- *Consult God before you do anything so that it is aligned with His purpose.*
- *God's purpose for your life is better than your plans.*

Note: If you fail to plan, you will fail.

CHAPTER FOUR

THE FUNDAMENTAL PRINCIPLE OF PEOPLE

*"The Lord prefers common-looking people. That is why he made so many of them." ~ **Abraham Lincoln***

Jesus Fulfilled His Purpose With His Disciples

The story of how Jesus chose His disciples is the best example that I can cite in this chapter as we begin to talk about this from my heart. I will also give other examples to emphasize the importance of people. As a young Christian in the Protestant Church in the 1980s, I was baptized as an infant and got confirmed. During that journey as a Christian, my friends and I were taught about the twelve disciples of Jesus. As a young Christian, I always wondered why Jesus Christ, being the Son of God, would come to select people to work with. Why did Jesus recruit the disciples?

Why did Jesus choose those twelve men? These questions may or may not have answers, but I came to realize Jesus chose the disciples as a backup for Him to accomplish His purpose on Earth. Jesus needed men who could help Him reach His destiny and also to take over from Him once He was done and gone back to heaven. Jesus knew that people are important for accomplishing God's overall purpose. Let me also say here that God cannot do business on Earth with angels; He works with people. God will look for people whom He wants to use and work with them regardless of their status.

Think About The Twelve Disciples

Have you ever imagined the kind of people that Jesus selected to be in His group? He chose people who were considered as the least in the society. He chose fishermen, tax collectors, and other "ordinary people" who were willing to follow Him. If you are going to be successful, you need people who will obey and follow you without attacking your vision. The disciples went with Jesus Christ everywhere and saw Him perform miracles, pray, heal the sick and also experienced His sad moments and torments of life.

You need followers; but most importantly, you need those who are willing to leave behind their businesses, job opportunities or careers for the sake of your vision. When Jesus called the twelve, He told them, "come follow me and I will make you fishers of men." I wonder if the disciples understood this philosophical statement. To be effective in life, you need people who believe in you and your vision, those who are willing to follow you irrespective of what they stand to gain from you-people like Christ's disciples who gave up their businesses, families and careers to follow Jesus Christ.

The Right People

In the game of life, you need not have just good people, but the right people. I mean right people not good people. There is a difference between right and good. There are two types of people – the toxic and non-toxic people. Toxic people are negative people. Negative people are the ones who oppose you or criticize you all the time. Toxic people are poisonous. They are deadly and lethal. I strongly advise you to avoid or, better yet, run away from people like this. Toxic people will tell you, you cannot make it. Who do you think you are? This might shock you but sometimes even the closest people to you such as (siblings, spouse, family, friends, and colleagues) can become antagonistic to your vision and purpose.

This is because these people think they already know you, yet they don't. I believe that only God truly knows us completely. I live with my children but I still can't boast of having a complete knowledge of them. I do not know my brothers and sisters even though I grew up with them in one house. I have to admit I do not know anybody as it were. Negative people can cause a miscarriage of your dreams. Negative people can cause your ideas to die in your mind. Negative people can cause your plans to perish. Negative people can make you die with the treasure that the world is waiting to receive.

Do not pursue your purpose alone, but get the right people who can support you in the work that is required to reach fulfil purpose. I would like to emphasize that you should identify the right people. There are people who are good, but not right, for whatever you want to achieve. As you start to pursue your purpose, you will need to identify a team of people or mentees (with you being the mentor) who are loyal to the purpose. You do not need to get people who will be against you or negatively challenge you. You need people who will support you and your objective so that you are able to make the right decisions and choice that are in line with God's commandments and accomplishment of His purpose and your purpose.

Associate With People Who Encourage And Motivate You

The closest people to you are not necessarily the most encouraging people to be around. They may be unduly critical and can really discourage you. They may know you from decades past but they do not really know where you are headed. If by some means you strife to get encouraged from other available sources, they would be surprised to see you graduate from college and get a good job. Whatever you do, do not allow their negativity to drag you down. Not all relatives and friends are like this, but some are.

Associate with people who encourage and motivate you.

The Story Of Moses And His Father In-Law, Jethro

This great leader of the Israelites was assigned by God to get the people out of Egypt and lead them to the Promised Land after they had been oppressed and enslaved for over 400 years. The Promised Land was the dreamland that God promised the people of Israel. The Egyptians had colonized the land and had complete control over their lives.

The Israelites could not save themselves. God had to intervene by sending an outsider to save and lead them to the promised land of Israel. God chose Moses for this task. Moses was at first hesitant and actually argued with God as he felt he did not have the capacity and ability to execute the task but eventually took it after God assured Him of His full support. In the end, he did deliver his people.

When the people were delivered and led towards the Promised Land there were several conflicts, and disputes that were taken to Moses for adjudication. Moses worked as a judge. The challenge was the great number of people or Israelites that Moses delivered out of Egypt. Moses was leading about 2.5 million people. Moses was able to administer justice even though he couldn't get the complete support of the people. When Israel first left Egypt, they had exactly 603,550 armed men for war – if all of those men were living at the time (Numbers 1:46). This number composed of all able-bodied men from the age twenty (Numbers 1:45) to the age of retirement around fifty (Numbers 4:3) or sometimes sixty (Leviticus 27:7). Now, suppose all the women, children and people over fifty are included; the number of Israelites who left Egypt would be about two and a half million.

This is a large number of people going into a desert in the east of Egypt. Let us assume for a moment that all the men of the census were indeed living at the time and were not a part of the pedigree records that were mentioned by Moses that also included the dead and the living. Let us look at the difficulties if we reckon all the men as then living.

This entire people had to bring their cases and disputes to Moses to resolve and reconcile conflicting people. Moses' father-in-law advised Moses to appoint judges to support him in the work. He could not have managed this task alone, he needed other people to support him. This classic example reveals that people are essential factors in the fulfillment of purpose. Success is possible with people but it must be the right ones for the situation in which you are dealing. You will never be successful without the right people.

Peter and his colleagues

Romans 12:2 says, "Do not conform any longer to the pattern of this world, but be transformed by the renewing of your mind. Then you will be able to test and approve what God's will is – his good, pleasing and perfect will." The biggest challenge in the world is, people love things that are familiar and comfortable for them. People are hardly ever interested in re-learning and getting to know new things in life. This is a call for the renewal of your mind and transformation. Without change, there can be no progress. Without information, there is no transformation. Transformation brings about change that can lead to progress at personal or corporate level. Positive change leads to goodness and perfection.

Principles
- *Our mind-sets must be renewed and transformed by a consistent intake of new information.*
- *Leaders must constantly learn and inform followers with new knowledge in order to cause transformation.*

Paul and Silas

Acts 16:1-20 is the story of Paul and Silas, who were later joined by Timothy. Paul had a desire to go to Macedonia but he could not go alone. He decided to work with Silas. They worked the mission and executed the plans. Paul travelled with his team to Philippi where they planted a church of believers and preached the Good News of Jesus Christ. Paul baptized Lydia and many people became believers. People are very crucial for any success or progress. Paul mentored Silas as well as Timothy. Timothy became what he was meant to be by following Paul. The key is that you cannot be successful without people but the people must be those who believe in your vision.

There are people who will be attracted to you because of the charisma, gifts or resources that you have, but not your vision. I have observed this over the years. I have had opportunities to work with people to do great things for God. I found out that most of them were interested in the gifts that I offered; money, cars and opportunities. To succeed, you will need the people who are all together working for the common vision. The example above shows that Silas and Timothy did not work with Paul because of money or gifts but because of the vision they had.

The main point to keep in your heart is that you need people for you to succeed in life. I can't overemphasize that point. There is no success without people who are committed to your cause and purpose. Moses was successful in his leadership of The Israelites to the Promised Land but with the help of Joshua. Joshua believed in the purpose that God wanted him to achieve.

Principles
- *You need committed people to your dreams and vision.*
- *You need passionate people to your dreams and vision.*
- *You need people with right attitude towards your dreams and vision.*

CHAPTER FIVE

THE FUNDAMENTAL PRINCIPLE OF PERSISTENCE

"What lies behind us and what lies before us are tiny matters compared to what lies within us." **~ Ralph Waldo Emerson**

True Story Of Derek Redmond, 1992 Barcelona Olympics Athlete

As soon as I began to pen this, I remembered Derek Redmond's inspiring story. He was one of the 400 meters' athletes during the 1992 Barcelona Olympics. He was rated the best athlete and was expected to win the gold medal during that competition. The young athlete was the favourite of majority of the spectators but 250 meters into the 400 meters' race. Derek got hamstrung, which totally disorganized him and brought him down with pain as his co-sprinters left him behind.

177

Derek got up, and as he persisted, a man jumped from the crowd and ran towards Derek. Breaking through the security, he got hold of him on the shoulder and went limping towards the finish line with him. This man was his father. He told him, "You can't finish it alone, I will help you." He helped him for a while and let him finish the few meters to the cross line or finish line. As Derek crossed finish line, he received a standing ovation from the stadium with a spectator of over 65,000 people. Derek did not win the race but he did finish it. How amazing!

One thing I learned from the story is that if you do not give up, you will reach the finish line of your purpose and achieve the dreams and vision that you have in mind. It taught me that though your way will not be easy, but through hard work, you will succeed. People are waiting to cheer you on and give you a standing ovation if you do not give up. You can only get a standing ovation when you reach the end or complete your assignment. The same is true with God. God is not so concerned about the pain and failures or events in your journey but about you reaching the end of the assignment or purpose.

What lessons did you learn from Derek? Write what you have learnt down for yourself. Are there experiences where you gave up? Why? Suppose you had not given up; what could have happened?

Ecclesiastes 9:11 says,

> *I have seen something else under the sun: The race is not to the swift or the battle to the strong, nor does food come to the wise or wealth to the brilliant or favor to the learned; but time and chance happen to them all. The race*

or journey of life is not a sprint but rather a marathon. Most people want to succeed incredibly quickly in life without persevering.

The race or journey of life is not a sprint but rather a marathon. Most people want to succeed incredibly quickly in life without persevering.

Principle
- *When you do not give up, you will win and succeed.*

The Meaning Of Persistence

- Persistence simply means not willing to give up or surrender to the situation or challenges that come against you in the pursuit of your goal or vision.

- Persistence means being determined and willing to lose your life, sleep, and peace for the sake of your desired vision and purpose.

- Persistence is the tenacity to go against all odds to achieve your dreams or reach the end of your journey.

- Persistence means the consistent insistence towards your mission, goal, purpose and vision.

- Persistence is the steady pursuit and advancement towards your goal.

- Persistence also means the constant move towards your desire.

- Persistence is the unfailing movement toward the goal or dream. It means you take heart with tireless effort towards the goals you want in life. It means to forget everything and focus on to the goal.

- Persistence also means dedication to attain all that you desire without quitting. It means you dedicate all your efforts, thoughts, faith and confidence in the fact that what you are doing is right. Any opposition is not right and could be wrong. In order to achieve your purpose or desire in life you must dedicate all your abilities to get it and you will. It does not matter what happens, you have the capacity to achieve your goal.

- Persistence also means steadfastness with the quality of being stable. It means you maintain balance amidst the winds, storms, and dust you will meet.

- Persistence means you will stand against any opposition, hostility, disapproval, conflict, opponents, challenger or resistance.

- Persistence means you will cross over the humps or barricades of life.

- Persistence means you will sometimes irritate people who oppose you.

- Persistence means you will not accept obstruction. It means those who are your enemies will try to fight you, but you will not relent or give in.

Just remember during those times that nothing in this world lasts forever. I remembered the days of Noah in the Bible when God sent the rain for 40 days and 40 nights. One of the greatest sons of Africa, the former President of South Africa, Nelson Mandela, spent 27 years in prison. These examples are to show you that nothing lasts forever. His incarceration was not permanent. Your condition or state will change as new cool winds start blowing. This is called life.

The Persistent Widow

The story of the Persistent Widow is a good one to remember has always been my motivator towards my personal goals. Luke 18, records a wonderful story of a Persistent Widow.

> *Then Jesus told his disciples a parable to show them that they should always pray and not give up. He said: In a certain town there was a judge who neither feared God nor cared about men. And there was a widow in that town who kept coming to him with the plea, 'Grant me justice against my adversary.' "For some time he refused. But finally he said to himself, 'Even though I don't fear God or care about men, yet because this widow keeps bothering me, I will see that she gets justice, so that she won't eventually wear me out with her coming!'" And the Lord said, "Listen to what the unjust judge says. And will not God bring about justice for his chosen ones, who cry out to him day and night? Will he keep putting them off?*

I tell you, he will see that they get justice, and quickly. However, when the Son of Man comes, will he find faith on the earth?

The story is about persistence. Persistence also means you keep asking, keep knocking, and keep seeking. Persistence means you keep searching until you find what you want. Persistence means whatever you want will not be given to you for free especially regarding goals. Persistence means you are willing to pay the price or do what is necessary to achieve your goals.

This story gives an example of persistence. The widow kept following the judge until the unrighteous judge gave in to assist the widow. The work of judges is to help citizens enjoy their rights through administering of justice. As you can see, the judge was what you see today in the world. We have corrupt judges working in the judiciary. The widow kept pursuing the judge for what she believed was her right. The widow never gave up.

The lesson from this widow is to remain persistent until you win, like she eventually got what she wanted from the judge. The same is true for what you desire. If you keep pressing on you will get it. It will not come easy and it requires that you persist and never get distracted or discouraged by obstacles and challenges that you might meet along the way. Those challenges will test your determination, but when you overcome them, you will achieve your dream, desire, or vision. The people whom I have come to know as failures gave up too soon and missed the opportunity to write history. I encourage you to go after what you believe like that widow who persisted.

Putting it another way, persistence means you run after what you want. Being persistent means you never quit. There will be moments when you question yourself, your motives, and also your beliefs. There will be situations you feel like giving up, but when you reach those moments, go back to where you started. What I mean by this is go back to the vision that you originally saw. I mean go back to the purpose that started your desire. You will get inspiration and energy to run, walk, swim, and fly towards your dreams. The Bible says, "Let us not become weary in doing good, for at the proper time we will reap a harvest if we do not give up." (Galatians 6:9)

Keep Asking, Seeking, And Knocking

In Matthew 7:7, Jesus commands us to, ask and we shall be given, knock and the door will be opened and seek and you will find. Asking means that sometimes goes beyond verbal request. It will take hard work on your part. For instance, if you are applying for a job in government office, asking may mean writing an application, completing a curriculum vita, photocopying academic certificates and transcripts, delivering the application to government office concerned, preparing for interviews and waiting for their results. This is asking. Asking is a process, not an event.

In the same way, knocking means you knock on the "door." Whatever you want in life is usually locked inside a door and you have to knock at the door in order to get in. Sometimes when you knock, people who are inside might not respond as quickly as you expect, but if you persist and they hear you, they might open the door to you. Knocking once may not be enough to you to get inside. Seeking means to look everywhere for what you are looking for until you get it. Seeking also, means search for or to hunt for something that you desire until you can locate it. Suppose, you want a scholarship for master's studies. You have to look for it everywhere until you get yourself one and keep applying until you succeed.

If it is your vision, pursue it! Seeking means searching everywhere possible to get what you want. When Jesus talked about asking, seeking, and knocking, He really meant we have to work to get whatever we want in life including our salvation; even though we are not saved by our good actions, but God's grace saves us according to Ephesians 2:8-10.

Therefore, to be successful, we need to be persistent and apply this lesson in every area of our lives. The areas of our lives include family, relationships, friends, work, opportunities, dreams, and public missions. Without persistence, success will not be possible. You have to be persistent even though you will have lonely, dark, and painful moments as you pursue the goals and visions ahead of you. Through asking you receive; through seeking you find; and by knocking the door opens. Matthew 7:8 says, "For everyone who asks receives, and he who seeks finds, and to him who knocks it will be opened." The main point is that without asking there will be no receiving or getting what you want. Grants are available in life, but only those with a good proposal are funded. Only those people who go out to ask are "given unto."

Note that only those who are seeking what they believe will ever receive it. Only those who knock will be allowed inside. This knocking means that sometimes you have to continue knocking until you get inside. It takes a lot of courage to knock and ask, but anybody who continues to knock will finally find a door to enter. I believe that you have been in this situation for a very long time. You have asked and have not received; you have been seeking but not finding you have been knocking but deprived access so many times. Do not give up. I recall when I was looking for expatriate jobs with the United Nations. Some positions required a master's degree, which I did not have at that time but applied anyway. I never gave up. I kept working and preparing for the opportunity, preparing for interviews, researching and reading.

After I earned a Master's degree, I applied for the first position and I was not given the job. I did this repeatedly and it was not until the eighth application that I was successful and got the position. I joined the largest humanitarian and development organization in the world and finally fulfilled my dream of working as an international expatriate. Can you imagine what could have happened if I had only applied four times and given up? I wouldn't have fulfilled the desires of my heart. This is true even for you and the dreams in your heart. I applied for many positions, asking, knocking and seeking for what I wanted.

There could be some dream or plan that you want to see executed. You want that dream and you think you have done your best. Now you are about to fold your arms and believe what people have told you – that you cannot make it, that you are not going to succeed. May be you are chasing after your dream job, contract, or business but now you are frustrated and discouraged by all the many obstacles. You are worn out. But keep going. Keep doing the right thing and working towards the goal because in due time, you are going to achieve your dream. Keep asking, knocking and seeking until you get it. Never give up; persist.

---

*Keep asking, knocking and seeking
until you get it.
Never give up but persist.*

Obstacles And Challenges Cause Us To Fear

There comes a time when we might get challenged and our faith is tested. When you reach a point like that, you need to develop an attitude and remind yourself of your purpose. Why are you involved in this plan? Why are you chasing after your dreams? Why are you pursuing your vision? Jesus, even as the Greatest Leader ever, lived faced challenges. At one time, He said his heart was troubled. "Troubled" means worried, terrified or tensed. Here is the experience and statement of Jesus found in John 12:27: "Now is my soul troubled; and what shall I say? Father, save me from this hour: but for this cause came I unto this hour." This implies that as you work to achieve your purpose and vision, life will test you and you will get moments when you are downcast and discouraged. When this happens, you will need to remind yourself of the reason. The physical pressure and strain will affect you as you persist.

Do you have a cause for what you are doing? The best thing to do in life is to know why you are doing something. What is the reason that you want a car? What is the reason you want a job? What is the reason you want a house? What is the reason you want to be a politician? What is the reason you want to be a governor? What is the reason? What is the cause? Once you are able to know the reason for something, then you can endure anything and the conditions of life.

Jesus in the above text is troubled from the task ahead that he is about to give up. However, the source of his strength is the fact that He is able to remember why He came to the world. Jesus knew His cause for living and reason that brought Him to the earth and that strengthened him. What is your cause? What things do you want to change?

What reasons do you have when life becomes difficult? Why are reasons so important in the pursuit of a goal, dream, or vision? The reasons give you motivation to carry on with the struggle. Reasons give you energy to persist.

I remember listening to a story of an athlete who was running to win a gold medal because he wanted to dedicate it to his parents. I remember listening in South Africa to a hotel worker who said that Mandela persisted because he wanted South African to be free from apartheid. When you have a reason for something, you will endure the hardship because hardship or tough moments mostly come to make you stronger. Whenever you encounter obstacles, the reasons you have will remind you to continue with the fight. Remind yourself of the reason for pursuing your dreams, plans and visions. It does not matter what happens to you, keep going and never give up. Persistence is possible when you are focused or have focus, which is guided by a plan and conviction.

Motivational Quotes on Persistence:

- *"The key to success is to focus our conscious minds on the things we desire, but not on the things we fear."*
  ~ Brian Tracy

- *"A person who aims at nothing is sure to hit it every time." ~ Anonymous*

- *"I try to learn from the past, but I plan for the future by focusing exclusively on the present. That's where the fun is. And if it can't be fun, what's the point?"*
  ~ President Donald Trump

The Power Of Focus

What is focus? The word focus means to have a single concentration on something. Focus is the capacity to have a clear direction and an eye to the set goal and target without compromise. It is the ability to have single sight to a vision and purpose. It means to have special attention, effort, or emphasis on key things that are important in life. Focus is like having single sight or vision for a predetermined destiny.

The key to success is being focused on the things you want to achieve. Most people lose focus as the year begins. People lose focus when they set plans. People lose focus on their goals. If you want to be successful in life, you need to keep your eyes on the plans or goals. Stay focused on your dreams and visions all the time. Do not lose focus on the most important things that lead you to the vision in your heart.

Count It All Joy When You Go Through Trials

James 1:1-9 says,

> *Consider it pure joy, my brothers, whenever you face trials of many kinds, because you know that the testing of your faith develops perseverance. Perseverance must finish its work so that you may be mature and complete, not lacking anything. If any of you lacks wisdom, he should ask God, who gives generously to all without finding fault, and it*

will be given to him. But when he asks, he must believe and not doubt, because he who doubts is like a wave of the sea, blown and tossed by the wind. That man should not think he will receive anything from the Lord; he is a double-minded man, unstable in all he does.

James talks about counting it joy when you are tempted and go through many trails. How can you do this when you have lost a spouse, friend, house, a job, or got an accident? This is difficult especially for non-believers. The key to life is managing problems and challenges. The challenges will not destroy you but give you faith that overcomes the world.

The testing of the faith gives you traits that are rare in most people. One of such traits is patience. Patience is necessary for success. True success comes from being patient and accepting the will of God in your lives. In addition, it gives you wisdom and helps you make the right decisions in the future. Wrong decisions come from lack of wisdom and knowledge, but with wisdom, you are wise to make right decisions that will lead you to the right destination of your dreams and desires.

Note: You must persist even if there is resistance against you.

CHAPTER SIX

THE FUNDAMENTAL PRINCIPLE OF PERSEVERANCE

"If you are going through hell, keep going.
*Never, Never, Never, Give Up." ~ **Winston Churchill***

Jesus Christ Persevered On The Cross

To buttress the lessons from the earlier chapter let's revisit exemplary figures who demonstrated perseverance in the past. When I think of examples of people with an incredible attitude of perseverance, there is no greater one than that of Jesus Christ. Jesus was announced as the Christ and the Son of God, yet God allowed Him to endure the pain on the cross. In the book of Matthew, Jesus was struggling with the decision about His own crucifixion. The Scripture says, "Going a little farther, he fell with his face to the ground and prayed, "My Father, if it is possible, may this cup be taken from me." Yet not as I will, but as you will" (Matthew. 26:39) Jesus knew what was going to happen.

He was going to suffer on the cross. He saw and imagined the pain of the cross. This is because in those days, criminals would be arrested and nailed on the cross to serve as deterrent to others. Throughout the arrest and crucifixion of Christ, He endured the pain and this was the ultimate test of perseverance. Can you ask God's will to be done when you're going through challenges? Can you pray when the enemies are attacking you? Many times when you are being attacked by enemies, you reach a moment when you really want to give up. When you reach that situation, you need to surrender your will to God's will. God knows the end of your life.

Sir Winston Churchill On Persistence And Failure

Those who are persistent will always win. Sir Winston Churchill once said, "Success is stumbling from failure to failure with no loss of enthusiasm." It may take more than one swing to compose an efficient hit, so make sure you do not give up on the strike. And remember, a river cuts and passes through rocks and valleys, but not because of its power at a given moment. Continue with persistence and over time you will reach your final destination. Success is said to be a result of setbacks and overcoming challenges. You need to use failure as a motivator for you to become successful. Do not allow failure to cause you lose the game of life. Life is composed of both failure and success.

What reasons do you have to fight for your dreams?

Do you want to give up? What will happen when you give up?

Key To Persistence

The writer of the book of Hebrews said,

> *Therefore, since we are surrounded by such a great cloud of witnesses, let us throw off everything that hinders and the sin that so easily entangles, and let us run with perseverance the race marked out for us. Let us fix our eyes on Jesus, the author and perfecter of our faith.* (Hebrews 12:1-2a)

It does not matter who you are, whether a king, queen, or steward, whether you're rich or poor. Life is full of difficulties as well as opportunities. Keep your faith amidst all challenges of life. The most important weapon you have in the face of challenges and crisis and even tragedy is not money, but faith. Faith in God is so powerful that it gives you confidence to keep going to the end of your own purpose. When you are in the middle of the struggle for your dreams, you need to keep your eyes fixed on Jesus Christ. You will also need to abandon the things that can hinder you from achieving or attaining your goals. You might be doing bad things like smoking, stealing money from office or involved in bad groups. You need to stop all these things because they hinder your ability and potential.

Achieving Your Dreams

I was raised by my maternal grandmother. My grandmother was one of the most influential people in my life. As a teenager, she taught me the value of hard work. I recall the tough experience of waking up very early in the morning to go to weed the cassava, maize and groundnut gardens. This was a tough experience. We could wake up at 4 am in the morning to dig or weed. I recall we had to do this routinely before going to school in the morning. She would tell us, "If you do not want to work, then you should not eat." (2 Thessalonians 3:10) In those years, I learned a lesson you can only eat after you have worked. These teachings and messages from grandmother never left my head.

I still believe in this old teaching and I am convinced that work is the key to success in anything of lasting value. I also read in the Scriptures that lazy hands bring poverty to the house (Proverbs 10:4). The key to success is hard work. Hard work pays and it's nothing but the truth! Successful people are smart and hardworking people.

The inventor of the electric bulb, Thomas Edison, once said, "The three great essentials to achieve anything worthwhile are, first, hard work; second, stick-to-itiveness; third, common sense." Work is a must for those who want to better and change their lives. Work is a necessary and sufficient condition for you to attain and improve your life. Without work, you will become a poor person. In life, people do not want to be associated with poor or unsuccessful people. Work harder that you may become successful and impact your generation.

Power, Predestination And Purpose

I will begin with this story. I was once taking a shower when I recalled a Scripture reference that came to mind. I was curious as to why I was thinking of Ephesians 1:20. All of a sudden, I jumped out of the shower and rushed to my computer. Here is the full content of the passage:

I pray also that the eyes of your heart may be enlightened in order that you may know the hope to which he has called you, the riches of his glorious inheritance in the saints, and his incomparably great power for us who believe. That power is like the working of his mighty strength, which he exerted in Christ when he raised him from the dead and seated him at his right hand in the heavenly realms (Ephesians 1:18-20)

The Scripture talks about the power within us – the power that raised Jesus from the dead! What came into my mind was that the power is not external, but it is within me? The secret to success is that you have this resurrection power to succeed. The power to succeed is in you and you have to believe and trust God to do the rest. Another powerful passage in that same chapter is Ephesians 1:11: "In Him also we have obtained an inheritance, being predestined according to the purpose of Him who works all things according to the counsel of His will."

One of the key things in my life that keeps me in peace is that God predestined us before we began the journey of life. God knows the end of the journey before we even start it. God does this according to His purpose and not our plans. God does all things according to His will. You have no power to do things on your own. Sometimes, we want things in life, but God's will must be approved first. What is God's will for you? God has predestined everything about us and we cannot change it. We need to seek God for His will. How? Prayer and working hard all the time and doing the right things that bring glory to God.

Where is the power to succeed? Where does it come from? As I deeply thought about the above text, I came to a realization that the power to be successful never comes from outside of us, but within. We are conditioned to think that the power is in heaven, but God's power is actually working within us who believe. Our decisions will determine if we are going to be successful or not. On the one hand, success is not luck. Success comes as a result of right decisions that you make every day in your life over time.

Note that, failure is a result of decisions that are made by a person or corporate entity over time. Success happens when you continue to make the right decisions and actions. Then the reverse is true for failure. I want you to continue exploring the law of God's power in you by looking at some personal accomplishments that I have been able to get in my life. I am not trying to blow my trumpet or be proud, but using this as an example to confirm that the power is not really outside of me, but within. One of the examples I would like to share with you is when I obtained a position as an International Expatriate with the United Nations in Kenya, Somalia and others. I discovered we always want the best things in life. I wanted this position and it was my goal. People want to be successful. Nobody wants to fail in life. I have never met a parent who wants his or her child to fail in life. Everybody want the best for their children except with exception to some ridiculous cases.

To become an international professional expatriate and working outside of my home country Uganda was one of my major goals and desires in 2008. I wanted to gain exposure, knowledge and experience. I was hired as an officer and had to work with people from different cultural backgrounds and countries. Some of the people were my mentors and supervisors. My supervisors had periodic evaluations of my performance and each time this happened. I was always nervous. It's really tough to watch or listen to your superiors tell you about your strength and weakness.

This is a natural reaction, especially if people are going to give you a balanced score card or report about your performance. I had a performance evaluation that showed both strong and weak areas for improvement. As a National Officer, I never took the negative feedback personally. Instead, I used it to improve and develop myself.

This evaluation was conducted at the end of each performance cycle throughout the year. At the end of the evaluation, we were usually asked, "Where we would want to be in the next 5 years?" This question would always disturb my mind. It would keep lingering in my mind for days, weeks, and even months. As the year came to an end and the New Year approached, the question would pop up again in my mind. Once the question was asked again, I told the supervisors I wanted to become an International Expatriate. They said, "The power is in your hands." Two ladies got promoted and left Uganda for other assignments around the world. However, I remained in Uganda. My question to you; Where will you be in two years, five years, or ten years? Do you know where you are going? Do you have a plan? Are you ready to persist? Are you prepared to persist? What is your destination? Where are you going?

In the years that followed, I came under the leadership of another respected senior officer. He asked the same question and gave the same reply. Then, I had decided to update my curriculum vitae and followed the instructions of the recruitment systems in order to apply for the jobs that I was qualified for with the large humanitarian organizations. Disappointed to say the least "I did not get the first job." In fact, I applied for eight positions and was able to choose from three that were offered to me. I look back today and I can conclude that if I had not taken the initiative myself, I would not have gotten what I wanted to be successful in. My dream would not have become a reality.

As you read this book, just know that the power is in you for everything that you want, but you have to work to get it. It will never be handed to you on a silver platter. If you don't use the power that God has given you, nothing will happen. But I properly and effectively harness the power in you, I can guarantee you will get to your desired result.

Another example of putting this power to work was when I was going to build a house for my family in Kampala as I mentioned before. This is probably one of the things I did that I think made me realize the potential and power that operates within me. There were many demands on the household income but we needed our own home. It was both wasteful and embarrassing to keep renting apartments and moving from place to place.

For A Limited Time, Only

We have only a limited time on earth and we should not abuse it. Towards the end of his life, Steve Jobs, the brain behind Apple technologies had this to say:

> *Your time is limited; don't waste it living someone else's life. Don't be trapped by dogma - living the result of other people's thinking. Don't let the noise of other's opinions drown your own inner voice. The most important of all is to have the courage to follow your heart and intuition. They somehow already know what you truly want to become. Everything else is secondary.*

Are you willing to pay the price? You have the power within you, but you must be willing to pay the price and overcome fear.

How To Overcome Fear Of The Unknown

I have always wondered how great people have managed to overcome fear. Here are some of their secrets that serve as motivational quotes:

- *"I learned that courage was not the absence of fear, but the triumph over it. The brave man is not he who does not feel afraid, but he who conquers that fear."*
  ~ Nelson Mandela

- *"Price is what you pay. Value is what you get."*
  ~ Warren Buffett.

- *"Let every nation know, whether it wishes us well or ill, that we shall pay any price, bear any burden, meet any hardship, support any friend, oppose any foe, in order to assure the survival and the success of liberty"*
  ~ John F. Kennedy

- *"If you are determined enough and willing to pay the price, you will get it done." ~ **Mike Dikta***

The Price You Might Pay For Success in Your Dreams and Vision

I believe that there is nothing that will come easy. There is a cost to everything in life. There are few things in life that you will get for free. But the price you pay for success is rejection, criticism, isolation, and loneliness.

1. Rejection

As you attempt to move in the direction of your goals and work on your goals, you may be rejected by your family, friends, or even the state. I remember the story of Joseph. This young man received a revelation of his life and what he was meant to become. He was excited and shared his vision with his family, parents, and siblings. Joseph got a shock. His own family rejected him to the extent of doing evil against him. He was sold by his brothers to Egyptian traders and he was among the survivors of slave trade (see the story in Genesis 37:28). He paid the price of rejection.

2. Criticism

In addition to rejection, sometimes, you will face a lot of criticism where people who claim to love you will turn against you. An example is Moses, who was criticized by Aaron and Miriam, his siblings. This is the same even today. Your own family will criticize you. Do not be discouraged when you have been criticized. It will not kill you, it would instead strengthen you.

In life, I have learned as you pursue your dreams, you are going to come across several waves of life. You will be faced with criticism. There will be people who will disapprove, comment, critique and condemn you. Those who are willing to go over their critics and comments will become winners. Criticism is a great price that is paid by successful people, thinkers and dreamers.

If the person cannot handle criticism, it is a sign of immaturity. One of the things I noted in my life is that those people who spoke against me or made negative comments helped me the most. It was hard to take the comments and swallow them. The only way to know about your life is to get the opinion of others and their feedbacks. It is always better for people to talk against you and give you their thoughts than cover up your flaws.

This will help you improve and advance to your goals. You can always learn something true from what they say. Look for that kernel of truth and it could help you avoid some unnecessary mistakes or at least learn from them. Genuine success comes as a result of facing our weaknesses, shortcomings; our defects, flaws and faults not shying away from them. This is a price of a dreamer due to the fact that when you start to become what you were meant to be, you attract attention and start getting enemies. In other words, you expose yourself to the world. Let me say it this way: The most valuable lesson about criticism I have learned as a worker, motivator or teacher or leader is when you are criticized; don't just ignore it or feel like a persecuted martyr. Learn from it! There has to be something God is trying to tell you! What is it? Maybe you need to change!

3. Isolation, Loneliness And Aloneness

In your attempt to dream big and achieve your purpose and vision, you might find yourself alone – isolated from the crowd or even close family and friends. Do not be scared when these moments occur. They are expected and need to be planned. You need to prepare and expect to be by yourself and face the challenges on your own. The challenges will not kill you but will give you character. Most of those who have succeeded in history found themselves when they were alone, away from the crowd.

4. Torture And Insults

There are times when you will be physically tortured and insulted. Jesus Christ is an example of one who went through such things. That He was prepared for it is evident in His words, commonly described as the Beatitude in Matthew 5:10 it says: "Blessed are they which are persecuted for righteousness' sake: for theirs is the kingdom of heaven." Persecution is one of the prices to be paid to accomplish our set goals or dreams.

5. Fatigue And Exhaustion

This is the second and most difficult thing that you will encounter as you attempt to go after your goal. Just imagine an athlete running a 10,000-meter race. As you run towards the finish line to receive the gold, silver, or bronze medal, you will get tired. You will experience exhaustion, tiredness, weariness, and low energy. If you want to win, you have to persevere and never give up because the finish line is near and when you cross it you enter the history books. You could receive a gold medal! When you experience fatigue in life, you need to find balance between work and rest. You have to have rest or you will become fatigued.

6. Time To Think, Reason, Meditate And Contemplate

Another price that successful people pay is the time to think, meditate, reflect, and dream. You may not think that this is a price, but it is necessary to have this time of contemplation. The quiet moments when a dreamer is alone being a difficult time. To be successful, you must have time to think. I have heard people say, "The solution is not to work harder, but work smarter." Most successful projects and ideas become reality after several hours of deep thinking and thorough analysis.

7. Loneliness, Solitude And Seclusion

I recall the time when I was writing this book in Garowe, the capital of Puntland state of Somalia. I was lonely. I could not talk with anyone. I believe with all my heart that loneliness is a price to achieve something that can change history. In order to become what you want in life, you must be willing to be alone and lose your freedom. To succeed, the dreamer must be able to walk away from the masses and be alone in a solitary environment. One of the greatest examples is Jesus Christ in the desert. After the baptism, the Holy Spirit led Jesus to the desert and this was not a simple experience.

Mandela also was alone in that prison for 27 years. It is difficult to be alone, but if you manage to use your time well, the medals will be yours. In order to be able to stand alone or endure loneliness, you have to develop courage, conviction, maturity, and inner strength to stand against any opposition. For example, Elijah was alone and he became successful after the experience of solitude. The price to pay is having to make unpleasant or unfriendly decisions.

Sometimes you might be in a company, a group, a family and team and time comes to make a decision and take action. Someone once said there are three kinds of people: those who watch things happen, those who do not know what is happening and those who make things happen. Successful leaders make things happen by sometimes making unpleasant decisions and actions against the will of others around them. So be willing to make a decision even if it will go against the norm or your culture.

8. Overcoming Culture And Tradition

The greatest tragedy is being hindered by your culture, custom, habit, and tradition as you endeavor to go for the dreams and achieve the vision in your heart. These things from the past can be of benefit but also can weaken you as you attempt to move forward. You may pay the price of countering these demands as you face the expectations of family and friends. But to be successful, you may have to shed some of the past in order to forge the future.There are several examples of these people who paid the price.

Moses In The Wilderness Of Sinai

Moses spent so many years in the desert of Sinai in Egypt without his childhood friends, mother or father or close relatives. He found himself in that desert with new friends and even married a woman from a foreign land. If you want to become successful, sometimes you must be willing to leave the familiar environment and be alone. You will get a better understanding of who you are as a person.

David, A Shepherd Boy

This young hero was a shepherd and looked after his parents' flock. He was the youngest of the 12 sons, but that experience prepared him for success as a king. He learned a great deal during that time in the pasture, even learning to sling stones to defend the sheep against wild animals. He became such a good shot that he was confident of going up against the Philistine giant Goliath and took him down with a stone that hit Goliath's forehead. Then he could conquer the enemies of Israel.

Jesus Christ In The Wilderness

The Scripture has it that Jesus went to the Jordan River to be baptized by John the Baptist. As soon as He was lifted up from immersion, a voice accompanied the Holy Spirit in form of a dove from heaven "This is my beloved Son, obey Him" The Scripture has it that after baptism, the Spirit of God led him to the wilderness to be tempted. During the time in the wilderness, Jesus was by himself for forty days and nights. None of His family was with Him to help – not His mother, earthly father Joseph, step brothers, sisters, or cousins. He was by Himself. But let's examine what happened after the wilderness experience. Jesus returned to begin His ministry and it was a total fulfillment proven by numerous signs and wonders. He succeeded. Sometimes, we need to make a decision to be alone and believe in ourselves to achieve our goals, dreams, mission, and purpose.

A Story Of Two Friends Locked In Prison

There was once a friend of mine from my hometown. We attended the same primary school. While I was in the university, he gained employment with the local government administration. We had similar backgrounds as regards deceased parents, position in the family and leadership role. He was about 15 years older than I was and a successful role model to many of us in the community. He worked hard and upgraded his education up to a post graduate diploma level. He also pursued a master's degree from one of the leading Institutes in Uganda. He was promoted in the district local government to a senior position.

He acquired property and other assets. All these made people in the community consider him a success. It is almost customary in our community to measure success by physical possession. I believe this is wrong. To me, as I have already said, success is the fulfilment of God's purpose. To be successful in God's purpose, you need character. A person whose character is wanting will collapse through the weight of irresponsibility and inconsistency.

Something Good Might Come Out Of Something Bad

One day I went to a government prison area to make arrangement at the carpentry workshop so I could order door frames and shutters for my house. On entering the prison, I saw several people in yellow uniforms. My host officer explained that those were prisoners with minor crimes. They were different from those on death row or getting a life sentence. We greeted the prisoners and made our way to the carpentry workshop. We discussed the type, sizes, and quantity of the doors that I wanted for the house project. Among other things, I noticed the prisoners were the ones who made the doors, frames, and shutters. They were learning life and social skills and undergoing a correction program to live with obedience to law and order. It was part of their responsibility and rehabilitation program before they were released. As I walked past the prison building where they slept, I saw different categories of young, middle, and elderly prisoners. They were not allowed to talk to outsiders or visitors except after the approval the prison authorities.

I noticed something strange in their eyes. They had a yearning for freedom because life there was not easy. They had lost it to the crimes they committed or whatever brought them there at first. They were sleeping on the floor in a large hall. They were under the mercy of the prison staff manning all the gates. There were roll calls throughout the day. They went into their cells for the evening after 4pm. The living condition there was horrible.

As we made our way out of the carpentry workshop, I saw this respected man from my village who was now a prisoner. He told me that he had been accused of embezzling money, but was appealing the sentence. He was sure he would be released and I wished him well. But when I returned three months later, I found out that this man had been sentenced to a year in prison.

This man would serve out his 36-month sentence and be done. There is yet another story of a prisoner who had been a friend of mine. He got into trouble. He was working for a non-governmental organization. He holds a master's degree. When he was going for further studies, I admired him a lot and wish I could do so too. He got a successful job upon his return, but then got into a "get-rich-quick" scheme that landed him in jail. We visited him and he was optimistic that he would be released after serving his time. Now, he has been released and back to work. These two friends of mine had to learn the hard way and are different people now as a result. Mr. Mandela also paid his way to success. In the game of life, everything has a price. In order to be successful, you must be willing to pay the price.

This price can be in monetary terms, costs to relationships, associations and friends. There can be disappointments, sacrifice, sorrow, loneliness, isolation, confusion, and sometimes even your own life. I mentioned Nelson Mandela earlier in this book and his name comes up repeatedly because I have learned a great deal from this giant. He was the first black President of South Africa. He spent 27 years in prison. His eventual death shook the whole world. His funeral on December 10, 2013, was graced by 91 Heads of State and 10 former Heads of States. People all over the world who couldn't attend in person tuned in or streamed online to watch the world give him a befitting burial.

Persecuted For Righteousness

Matthew 5:10 says, "Blessed are those who are persecuted for righteousness sake, for theirs is the kingdom of heaven." Mandela is one of those who, I believe, were persecuted for righteousness. He endured and persevered. He fought for what was obviously right. Even though I can't claim to have absolute knowledge of the life and times of "Madiba" as he is fondly called in South Africa and the rest of the world, there are so many reliable sources that confirm these facts. And as a matter of fact, I discovered that Madiba's prison number was "46664." I got to know this when I visited Nelson Mandela Square in Sandton City, in a Johannesburg mall. This great man spent over a quarter of a century fighting for the rights of all humanity not only South Africans. Mandela was a man of great faith, conviction, belief and integrity. You might not agree with me but the point is he was prepared to die for what he believed. He was asked in court to abandon the quest for freedom for his fellow countrymen but he refused; reiterating his mission: *"It is an ideal for which I hope to live and to see realized. But, My Lord, if it needs be, it is an ideal for which I am prepared to die."*

He endured countless struggles, including the death of his mother while he was imprisoned. He was not allowed to even attend the funeral. Can you imagine the pain? What if that had happened to you?

When my uncle, Samuel William Odeke, passed away in January 2012, I was so depressed because I had just arrived in Somalia on an official assignment and was unable to attend the funeral. But the joy in my heart was I knew I was busy working to save the lives of people affected by conflict and natural disaster. It would be another month before I could return to Uganda to pay my respects and comfort my family. But think about Mandela not being able to leave prison for years to pay respects to his mother's grave. What price are you willing to pay?

Another incident was when Mandela's 10-year-old son died in a car crash and still was not allowed to attend the funeral. Nobody knows the pain he felt except God. It was surely beyond our comprehension. In spite of this however, Mr. Mandela kept fighting for what was right. He was persecuted for righteousness sake. He did not do anything wrong, but the government of the white minority was dominating South Africans and they were longing for freedom. In South Africa at that time of apartheid, black people were not considered equal to humans they were equated to animals.

One of my greatest desires was to meet Nelson Mandela, but God never allowed it. However, those who did meet him described him as a man who was all at once a lion, a king, prince, and a leader – a true leader. I was told of the time when Mr. Mandela went to a hall packed with people and buzzing conversations. When he arrived the whole place went silent. His presence was so powerful that everyone kept quiet in the presence of one of the world's greatest men. In South Africa and other parts of the world, Mandela was revered and honoured for his firm convictions and belief about freedom. He wanted freedom for everybody, black and white alike.

In one of Mr. Mandela's interviews, he spoke about his rough or rocky-like hands. Mandela said,

For 27 years he had held an axe in his hands and that his job was to crack the rock on Robben Islands. At first his hands became blistered and bloody, but they had to crack the rocks to escape the punishment. The blister turned into scabs and callouses. Then, there was no more feeling in them. He concluded the story by saying, "This was the price I paid for freedom.

How many of us are willing to pay this price? Is there a price you are willing to pay for the sake of making people better? Are you only concerned about your personal wellbeing? What price are you willing to pay?

During the last interviews of Nelson Mandela with BBC, Mandela was asked, "Do you have any regrets about your life? His answered No. I believe when he said that, he meant that in the same way Apostle Paul looked back over his own life and said, "I have fought the good fight, I have finished the race, I have kept the faith" (2 Timothy 4:7). In other words, he had completed what he was sent to do on Earth and his life didn't matter much anymore as it were. From the mid-1960s through 1991, the island served as a maximum-security prison, mostly housing offenders of political offenses. Mandela spent 18 of his 27 years in prison on Robben Island. From 1964 to 1982, Mandela was incarcerated there, but in 1990, he was freed. What is your final message? What are your final words in this Earth? Mandela said, "When a man has done what he considers his duty to his people and country, he can rest in peace."

Cancel Out Other People's Opinion In Your Mind

One of the things that changed my life was a statement told by a friend. He said, "Somebody's opinion of you does not have to become the gospel truth and reality set in stone." They may or may not be right. It does not have to become the conclusion of who you are or what you will become and what you believe. This statement gave me new seeds of thought and changed me. I started working on my dreams. Sometimes people fear success. They are not worried about failure but what to do with success. How will they manage the success? You need to control your emotions when you face criticism. Emotions are controlled by understanding regardless of what people tell you or say about you. Have self-control.

Stop Being Comfortable, But Get Up And Work

Most people get comfortable, stop growing, stop searching, and stop enjoying the moment. They stop pushing themselves and end up becoming cynical about life. They throw in the towel on their dreams and just fold their arms. Others do not feel worthy of their dreams and are scared to pursue them. Get out of the comfort zone and work.

Some people do not believe in themselves and will allow other people's opinions, weaknesses, and failures to hold them back. This keeps them from reaching their destiny. In order to reach your destiny, you have to believe in yourself rather than the opinion of people around you.

Take Life As A Challenge To Overcome

Life is about stretching and challenging challenges, looking for ways to improve yourself. As you go along the way, you will notice that it is possible. Your dreams are not far away. It is in the realm of possibility! It is important that you believe in your dreams because nobody is going to do it for you! It is you at the forefront. It is necessary that you do the work. You develop yourself. You must align yourself with people who are hungry, willing to stretch and give up comfort.

People who are unstoppable become change agents. It is necessary that you get the losers out of your life. You will see that not everyone will join you or support you, but you keep going. Be creative when you are working on your dreams. It is easy to get discouraged considering setbacks and obstacles but you shouldn't give up on your dreams. You should be flexible because this is a service-driven economy. It is necessary that you keep your word, maintain commitment, model integrity, and exemplify morality.

It Is Up To You To Decide And Succeed

No one is going to do it for you; it is totally up to you. It is you. You are the one who will face the disappointment, problems, and challenges. It is you who will experience the setbacks. It is you who will get bruised. It goes with the territory – you. You need to have this kind of attitude, "It's not over until I win." All of us need this attitude when we face rejection, disappointment, and setbacks. Even if nobody believes in you anymore and people have rejected you. Keep it in mind, "It's not over until I win."

You have to tell yourself this; it is not over. Life will yield to you and you will get what you desire. It is also important to keep these words in mind, "It is possible and I can achieve my dreams. I will work myself. It is me. I have to make it happen. It is not over until I win." You need to write the goals and think constantly on your goals. Find ways to pull yourself up when everyone thinks you are defeated. It is your responsibility. Sometimes nobody will get you out of the pit or problem unless you take action.

It will always be hard. It is not easy to become successful. It is hard changing life and character. It will always be hard when you are going through hard times. You will meet people who would not like you. Bad times will come, but it will not be like that always. Time will change and things change. It was hard writing this book while I was also working, reading for a doctoral degree, coordinating a business in Uganda, managing a family, and managing siblings – it was hard. There were financial difficulties. It was very difficult to get up each day believing I will make it. There were times when I doubted myself.

For those of you who have experienced hardship, do not give up on your dreams, goals, and vision for they are your life. It is the soul that keeps you alive. You have to keep running forward, pushing forward and one day, you will reach that goal and be free. It is a long shot getting there. You may be called all sorts of names and feel like a failure, but what keeps you going is your dreams and passion. Do not stop and never give up. Do not stop as you go toward your dreams. It is very important that you do not stop because there are moments that you will doubt yourself. Rough times will come, but they have not come to stay. They have come to pass. A day is coming when the storm will calm down. You are writing history and people will read it.

I remember one time when I failed at something. I was feeling within myself that I was a loser or a failure; I was down and negative. I went to listen to a church pastor and as he was teaching I realized that his message was not meant for anyone but me. His message emphasized that God is able. To buttress his points, the pastor quoted, "If we are thrown into the blazing furnace, the God we serve is able to deliver us from it, and He will deliver us from Your Majesty's hand" (Daniel 3:17). It changed my life. As he talked my heart was beating very fast and I cried. He said I want you to know you are blessed and highly favoured. As you go toward the future begin to know that you have greatness within you. Start to envision yourself being favoured; you can make people proud of you and change the world to never be the same again.

It is always possible. In every pit, it is possible to get out. It is not going to be easy. You are lying on the floor; you are sleeping in the house alone; you are day dreaming. You can do this! See yourself as being on top. Do not let anybody steal your dreams. I am the one to make it happen. God will make this happen. God is working through me! There is nothing we cannot do!" It takes personal responsibility. It will be hard. It will be difficult. At the end of the day, you will sing the song of victory.

You Have To Be Hungry For Success

If you are trying to do anything worthwhile, it is better to be prepared for the opportunities that would come your way. As you wait for opportunities, prepare yourself for them. If vacancy is announced for that job you want eventually, would you qualify for it? Your own personal organization helps achieve success. The people that are running after their dreams are relentless, restless, focused, willing to die, give up everything, and pay the price. They are creative; they have a winner's mindset; and they live out their plans. They say to themselves, "It's not over until I win. It is going happen. I am going to make it. I am going to succeed." Choosing the future, you want is more important than going to sleep at night and it is better to lose your life in order to make an affirmation successful. It is going to be hard, but you have to find out what it takes to make it happen. You need to write down reasons for your dreams. These will make you unstoppable – an uncommon person. What are those goals? If you know the reasons, then you can endure almost everything. If you know why you are doing something, you can endure because hard times are going to come and you will feel like giving up. Disappointments and rejections will come your way by the truck loads! Your reason will be the rod and staff to comfort you and get you running the next morning. If life knocks you down, your plan should be to lie on your back or fall by your side so you can look up and see why you fell down; you can get up and still push towards your dreams. Let the reasons get you up.

If you want to be successful, you have to give up your time, peace, sleep, money, everything. You have to think about your dreams, visions and everything that it is going to take to achieve them. When life feels useless, you have to be hungry for your goals and keep struggling. Think, "I will succeed this year." God places the future of everything in itself. Only those who dare to fail will achieve whatever they desire.

You have to think about your dreams, visions and everything that it is going to take to achieve them.

Motivational Quote
- *"There is no easy walk to freedom anywhere and many of us will pass through the valley of the shadow of death again and again before we reach the mountaintop of our desires." ~ **Nelson Mandela***

Forget The Past; Forge And Move To Your Future

One of the greatest things I have ever discovered and established in life is that the past can never be changed and what has happened can never be changed or undone. The past is actually just a portion of the life lived and not the whole. The past can be the greatest challenge to deal with because God promises to forget our past, but we have to live by the consequences of the decisions we made. It has caused many people to crumble in life as they view this spectre of the "past."

I remember as a teenager we had hundreds of cows in our hometown like most Iteso families, an ethnic group in Eastern Uganda and Western Kenya had during the 1970s and 1980s. These cows were the economic lifeblood of the people and we depended on them for our livelihood. I recall one day that cattle rustlers came and raided all the animals. We lost everything in a single day. Life became horrible and miserable for most of our families. My parents were not used to digging the soil and now it was time to dig without oxen. One of the things that I mentioned to my father was that we needed to forget about the cattle because they were no more. We could never recover any even though we prayed a million times.

Another thing that I told my siblings was to forget about the death of our mother. Several years my siblings would worry about her absence. I kept telling them that they needed to forget the past because it was not helping us move forward. It was restricting and frustrating us. The lesson I learned about the past is that the past is always not good. The past shows your weaknesses. The past shows areas where you failed. The past shows your short comings. The past reveals your mistakes.

In my own life when I look back to my past, I get depressed. I get concerned and affected by it, but I have learned how to forget about the past. It reminds me of the mistakes I made as a child and teenager. The past also reminds me about the mistakes I have made in my own adult life and this always puzzles me. But to succeed, you must forget the past.

What lies behind is what has happened. It is not your future. The future is still ahead of you. We must forget what is behind and go ahead to our future. There are things in life that must be forgotten. They are your failures, comments made by people, disappointments, and areas where you fell down. When you fall down, you should get up. Do you continue lying down when you fall? No, you rise up and move on. You might have fallen or failed; get up and move.

I remember after doing a national exam in math and realized I had made a simple mistake on the test that affected my grade. I was so disappointed in myself. I was hurt and thought about this experience for about three hours. Then I realized that I needed to forget about this and not let it ruin my preparation for the physics exam. That strategy worked and it was the best thing to do instead of worrying about the mathematics exam.

How Do You Forget The Past?

1. Rejoice At All Times

I have been researching for the ways, approaches, and strategies to forget the past. As I mentioned earlier, it is very tough and difficult to forget the past. In my life I have applied consistent daily planning of the activities and tasks to do every day that God gives. In the book of Psalms 118:24, it says, "This is the day the Lord has made. Let us rejoice and be glad in it." It is important to look at each day with great expectations. I want to encourage you to consider this an important approach to save you from dwelling upon your past. Some people's past may be good, but for others, it may be full of tragedy and mistakes. In order to effectively live your future, it requires that you plan your day and ensure priorities are in line with your goals.

2. Make A Deliberate Effort And Correct Decision(s)

The second strategy that you should employ about forgetting the past is to make a deliberate decision. We are all what we are because of the decisions that have been made in the past. Every day human beings under the planet make decisions. These include what time you will wake up in the morning, what you wear, what you eat, what you will do during the day, and what time you will go to bed at night. I discovered every human being has to make the decisions either consciously or unconsciously.

This means that what we decide is what will happen. Our decisions are important and they all have an impact on us. Our decisions control and affect us positively or negatively. My advice to you reading this book is to decide today not to look back at the past. When you make that decision, you are miles away from your past and miles closer to your destiny.

3. Focus On Goals, Purpose, And Vision

The third strategy for forgetting the past is what Apostle Paul said in the book of Philippians 3:10-13. Paul as we all know him was known as Saul before his life became interrupted by God on his way to Damascus. Saul's mission as a Jewish leader was to persecute the church of Jesus Christ. The word persecute means to oppress, pursue torture, torment, intimidate, hunt, and harass the church. Paul was notorious for these horrible acts. Paul was a murderer of the Christians of the early church. He mastered his game and was a professional in doing evil, one of the great things that God ever revealed to him was this message about forgetting the past. He was advising believers that they need to forget the past and pursue the purpose that God created them to do. This comes in the context of knowing Christ and the power of His resurrection life in us.

Philippians 3: 10-13 says,

> *I want to know Christ and the power of his resurrection and the fellowship of sharing in his sufferings, becoming like him in his death, and so, somehow, to attain to the resurrection from the dead. Not that I have already obtained all this, or have already been made perfect, but I press on to take hold of that for which Christ Jesus took hold of me. Brothers, I do not consider myself yet to have taken hold of it. But one thing I do: Forgetting what is behind and straining toward what is ahead, I press on toward the goal to win the prize for which God has called me heavenward in Christ Jesus.*

The above text is a powerful message that I want you to fix in your mind and never forget this text for the rest of your life. Forgetting what lies behind is about forgetting what is past. Paul was a clever fellow. He knew what he had done against the church but decided to forget the past. One may ask the question, "Why?" In my own interpretation, I noticed that Paul was more concerned about his future than his past. Paul was concerned about the goal ahead of him. Paul was concerned about a prize that God was waiting to award him. In one of my life's experiences I failed many times as a person, but I decided to forget the past. When you keep resurrecting the past, there is something that you will miss and this could be a prize. It could be a gold medal or an award. Are you mature?

Paul then said,

> *All of us who are mature should take such a view of things. And if on some point you think differently, that too God will make clear to you. Only let us live up to what we have already attained* . (Philippians. 3:15-16)

What I love about this passage is that only mature people think like this. A majority of people today are still immature even though they are adults. They are living according to the past. The word of God says mature people should not focus on the past, but focus on the great future that is yet to be lived.

The key to reaching your destiny is forgetting the past or your past life; past mistakes, past failures, even past success, and everything that is behind. Why? This is because your past mistakes will cause you to be depressed and frustrated. The past failures will remind you that you might fail again. The past success might make you reluctant and complacent. The past success might make you feel you have made it and now you can go to the beach or spend holidays in the Caribbean or Mombasa. You might think you can just rest on your laurels, so to speak. As a matter of fact, the past can become a weight in your pursuit for new successes and stop you from progressing and straining towards your new high goals and vision. You must apply this key to each and every day of your life. This is a law and when you break it, you will never reach the end of your destiny. You need to forget your past successes and go on to achieve more and do more because God is waiting to give you a prize and decorate you. Your future is more important than the past. The past is dead except the life we give it. The past cannot be changed but we could change the future.

4. Use The Power Of Foresight and Learn lessons From Failure

I will like to say this about the past: I am convinced that everybody has the capacity to reflect upon as well as to think about the past. The past gives you a review of your life and you can use the lessons you have learned to propel your life to the future. Never use the past to blame yourself but use it as a benefit by applying the lessons to life and its daily challenges. The secret is using the past as a vehicle to take you to the next level of life or a desired future. In this way, your past mistakes can help you to do better in the future because you learn from them.

Further, Paul was concerned about the future. He was moving towards a goal. When you have no goal to pursue, you will always get distracted and messed up. Goals create a path and lead us to our destination. God creates us with all the abilities including foresight. Each human has the capacity to think that could help in predicting and preparing for the future. To be successful in life requires you to prepare ahead of time for your future.

5. Do Not Be Afraid Of The Past And People

Isaiah 54:4 says,

> Do not be afraid; you will not suffer shame. Do not fear disgrace; you will not be humiliated. You will forget the shame of your youth and remember no more the reproach of your widowhood." Stop fearing people. Stop fearing failure because success is a result of series of failures. Be willing to fail because that is when you learn your lessons. What lessons can we learn from the past that can help us for the future? That is what is important.

I encourage you to forget the past; forget it and move on. Let's focus and achieve greatness and our dreams. There are more who are for us than those who are against us. If God is for us who can be against us? (Roman 8:31). If you want to make it in life and become successful, you have to learn and apply this law to your life. If you have failed in a relationship, forget about it. If you have failed in class, you need to forget it. If you got involved in an accident, you need to forget it. If somebody died some time ago, forget it. If you were divorced from your spouse, forget the pain and move on. If you lost money to robbery or burglary, forget what you lost. If somebody disappointed you, forget them and move on to achieve your dreams. The point I am trying to make you understand is to forget the past and think of new things. You need to concentrate on your future instead of the past.

6. Use The Power Of Focus

Another important secret to become successful is being focused on the dreams, plans, and vision that you want. If you have a divided mindset, you will not fulfil the dreams that you have. Failure is sometimes necessary for you to succeed. Don't wake up at sixty years sighing over what you should have tried and done but didn't do because you were afraid to fail. Just do it and be willing to fail. You can learn along the way as you try everything that needs done. Very few people get it right the first time. In fact, most people fail to get it right after the first five times. If what you did today did not turn out as you hoped, tomorrow will be a new opportunity to do it differently or in a different way. Interpret each failure as a lesson on the road to success and fulfillment of your dreams.

7. Develop A Positive Attitude For Life

Thoughts and ideas are like the steering wheel that moves life in the right direction, right time, and right place. Success comes from positive energy and positive thinking. You can choose to get caught up in the negatives that surround you, or you can decide to do something positive about your situation. You always have a choice and control of your mind. Remember, happiness is an element of success, and the happiest people don't necessarily have the best of everything. But they use positive energy to make the best of what they have. You must believe you can succeed. You must find the place inside yourself where anything is possible and not impossible. It starts with a dream, an imagination, vision in pictures.

When you become persuaded that you can do it, then confidence takes over, and it becomes a belief. The next element is becoming committed, and it becomes a goal in sight. When you decide to take action towards the actualization of your dream through determination and focus, with time, your dream would become a reality. Helping other people is a big part of being successful. Successful people constantly come up with new ideas, new projects, and new and innovative ways of helping others. This means that your aims and objectives don't just benefit you but also others as well. Your long-term success is directly tied to how well you serve your community.

Instant Success Will Evaporate Or Melt Like Ice

Success is a journey of countless steps and attempts. It is a constant process of growth. If you want to be successful, you must continue to hold yourself to a higher standard than anyone else, and strive to improve and get better. Oftentimes a person or organization will be successful, but then it drops off.

A person may become lazy, and an organization may succumb to weaknesses or competition. Sustained success means continually improving even if others may not see a need for it. Remember, the great thing in the world is not so much where we stand at any given time as in the direction we are moving.

A Personal Story About Power
And Persistence In High School

I recall my senior year in high school. I found a place to stay through family connections. I was obligated to clean the compound each day before going to school to attend classes. I did it with willingness. Something happened after three months. We went home to the village from town for holidays. But then, after the term break, as I returned to school, I found that my belongings had been put in the corridor and we were told to leave the house as we were no longer needed.

My friend left for the village immediately to join his parents but I stayed until eleven o'clock in the night thinking of my next course of action. I was befuddled as what to do and ended up going to my aunt's house nearby at midnight. Can you imagine carrying a suit case and a mattress at midnight for 2kms because you have no alternative in life? I went to my auntie's house in Mbale nurse's quarters to seek for accommodation so I could finish my advanced level studies. My aunt was taking care of 12 orphans in a single room. Because of my humility and stable character, the nurses who lived in Mbale hospital nurses hostel liked me and they allowed me to stay in their rooms while they were on duty at night. I lived like this for about 10 months until I finished my advanced level examinations that led me to Makerere University.

When I completed my examinations I went back to the nurses and thanked them for supporting me by accommodating me for over 10 months in different rooms. When the national examinations result was released by the Ministry of Education and Sports, I won a government scholarship to pursue a degree that was the turning point in my life. My persistence and perseverance and the decision changed my destiny. Today I am a doctorate degree graduate from Regent University, United States of America. I also won a scholarship from Regent University. What a miracle and favour from God.

Meanwhile, the relative, who was with me when we were ordered to vacate the house located at Indian quarters in Mbale town in Uganda, decided to return to the village and even quit studying after that incident. He gave up so easily. It is possible to quit like that, but if you know what you need in life, you do not make such wrong decisions. When he left was where he ended as far as academics was concerned. I came to the realization that without persistence, you cannot achieve your goals in life. There are moments when you have a big plan and goal that sleeping is not important. Leisure is not important but necessary. If you are going to become successful, you will have to persist. A tree will not produce fruits without enduring sunshine. There must be endurance. There must be persistence and patience. You must have an attitude that never gives up but continues to persist for the sake of the bigger goal and vision. If you study all men and women in history who were successful, they risked their own lives and gave up everything in order to get what they desired in their hearts and fulfil their dreams. Get ready to persist and it will make you stronger and successful.

Note: Never give up.

CHAPTER SEVEN

THE FUNDAMENTAL PRINCIPLE OF PRAYER

*"The Christian life is not a constant high. I have moments of deep discouragements. I have to go to God with tears in my eye, and say, 'O God forgive me. Help me." ~ **Billy Graham***

What Is Prayer?

In many religious movements, you will always hear about prayer. Prayer is an important aspect of a believer's life to a Super Natural Being. For me, I believe in God. God will not keep silent to those who cry honestly to Him. God will answer and fulfil his word. God answers prayers. God answered the prayer of Hannah for a son and other people who prayed honestly to them.

- Prayer is a constant connection, communion, network, and relationship with Abba Father our God.
- Prayer means an appeal, a plea, a request, desire, wish that you want fulfilled, petition, and supplication.

God answered the prayers of the Israelites when they were oppressed by the Egyptians. Humans came from God and to be connected means you stay attached to God. The connection is only possible with prayers. Let us begin this chapter by sharing what I learned and read about the Lord's Prayer. One of the interesting and instructive things I read in the book of Matthew is that the disciples kept watching the behavior of Jesus Christ each and every day as He interacted with them.

One day after watching Him, they came to Him and they asked Him to teach them how to pray. Jesus agreed to the request made by His disciples and began to teach them.

Matthew 6: 9-12 gives us how we must pray:

Our Father in Heaven hallowed be your name, Your Kingdom come Your will be done on earth as it is in heaven Give us today our daily bread. Forgive us our debts as we also have forgiven our debtors and lead us not into temptation but deliver us from the evil one.

Always Pray For God's Kingdom To Come On Earth

In the above teaching, we can see that Jesus told the disciples to pray for the Kingdom of God to come to earth and that the will of

God to be done in the same way it is done in heaven. Then, Jesus said we should pray for our daily bread. Why daily bread? It is because we need bread to survive daily. Jesus did not have us ask for power, wealth or authority, but daily bread. Many Christians are concerned about power, wealth and authority. They seem to take the daily bread for granted.

Ask God To Forgive You As You Forgive Others

Also, Jesus told the disciples to ask for forgiveness from sin. God is waiting to forgive your sins and mistakes but you must ask Him. Furthermore, Jesus asked to be delivered from the evil one or lead us away from temptation. The key is that we must pray for what gives us life. Bread gives us life. We need to pray to be away from sin or temptation. Sin destroys and disturbs us from achieving our purpose. Sin can cause us to fail to get to our destination. Sin can discourage us. There is need for you to believe that you are going to succeed and get what you want. When you pray, believe that God's Kingdom will come, you will receive your daily bread and God will keep you away from the evil one. You need to be positive in that you are going to get what you are praying for. In God's Kingdom, there is everything that you need because God is the owner of everything.

Jesus Lived And Was Motivated By Prayer

One of the secrets of Jesus was prayer. He prayed alone, seeking the will of the Father. Then having done that, He would go about His work in various places. One of the key factors we need to study is the term "will." What does "will" mean? Jesus said the will of God should be done on Earth as it done in heaven. The will of God is His purpose. God's will or purpose is more important that your plans or problems. When you pray, you need to seek the will of God. When you have God's purpose for your life, it will be done. God will make sure what happens in heaven is done on Earth.

Praise, worship and studying to know God better are really effective instruments I used in my life during the most difficult and challenging times. Prayer is the time you enter into a conversation with God in His presence: communicating, praising and worshiping Him. One popular chorus is "Blessed Be the Name of the Lord," which has been a great blessing during times of crisis.

If you are a Christian and sing this song it will change your life. Your attitude will change and you will develop a sense of peace. Key lines from this song quote the Psalmist: "Blessed be the name of the Lord, the most high. The name of Lord is a strong tower, the righteous run into it, and they are saved."

Another wonderful song you can sing in time of crisis is by the Gaithers, entitled, "Because He Lives." Another great song is, "My God is Able" by Tracey and Eloise Philips. When you sing these songs, you bring heaven to Earth. You shake heaven and God responds. There is also a song, "How Great is Our God" by Chris Tomlin and many more. When you are faced with challenges, you need to praise God. When you enter into praise and worship, be it alone or in a group, the devil trembles. The devil loses the battle and victory comes your way. God begins to reveal His great love and secrets to you. I remember one time I was so sad, frustrated and disappointed by some friends. I began to praise and worship God and He told me, "Fear not. I am with you. If I am, why do you worry?" As I mentioned when you come before the presence of God, He will act. It is like a child praising his father, showing thanks and appreciation. Do you expect the father to chase away the child singing praise to him?

Worship And Pray To God; Forget Everything Else

One day I was worshiping and praying to God for my major accomplishments so far: academic degrees, money, cars and houses. I recall praying to be in the presence of God. Do you know what I was praying? I was praying for God to make me a sweeper in His Temple court in His Kingdom. As I was praying, God said, "Your degrees, wealth and everything is nothing, but what is important is your connection and relationship with Me."

Then the Word of God came to my mind: "What good will it be for a man if he gains the whole world, yet forfeits his soul? Or what can a man give in exchange for his soul?" (Matthew.16:26) God said, "Come to me as you are and I will save your soul." I was telling God that I want to speak to millions of people, sharing with them about His love for me. God gave His Only Son to the world to save the world. This is an amazing story. God gave up His Son for the world to save a sinner like me. What love is that one, that God did not spare His Only Son? The lesson I learned in life is that loving God is more important than loving the things of the world. Worldly things are disappearing fast and you will lose everything that you treasure today. Also, God and His love lasts forever.

In God's Presence There Is No Guilt, Just Freedom

One of the biggest secrets that I have discovered is when you are in the presence of God, there is no guilt. There is fullness of joy and peace. There is no condemnation. There is no disappointment. In the presence of God, there is life. There is favour. There is mercy. There is rejoicing. "Rejoicing" means having joy come back again, having the peace you lost come back again, having the confidence that you lost returned, having broken relationships restored, having lost money returned or having your esteem restored. In the presence of God, there is restoration, reconciliation, redemption, recovery, renewal, revival and repentance.

Do you remember the powerful conversation between Peter and Jesus where Jesus asked him, "Do you love me?" Three times, Jesus asked the same question. Then Jesus said, "Feed my sheep. Feed my sheep. Feed my lambs" (John 21:15-17). God wants us to feed his sheep. In the presence of God there is rejoicing.

My advice to you reading this book is to seek and strive to be in the presence of God. The presence of God attracts His promises and blessings. It is important to be in God's presence than keeping company with the wicked people. When we walk away from the presence of God we lose these blessings! I remember when I did walk away, I was restless and had to return through prayer of repentance. Peter tried it and you know the outcome. When you walk away from God Who is Life, you go meet the devil and he kills you. Do you understand what I mean? The key is being in the presence of God. It helps you attract His blessings.

God Hears The Prayers Of Believers

Luke 1:13 states, But the angel said to him: "Do not be afraid, Zechariah; your prayer has been heard." God is a good God. He gives angels the information for His people concerning answers to prayer. In this case, the angel assured Zechariah that the prayers were answered and there was no more need to be afraid. Our problem is that we are always afraid when things do not work out as we would like. I would like to argue that you should fight against fear while believing God and His word completely. The reason I have been able to overcome challenges is that I have so much confidence that God knows the plans He has for me and He declares that in Jeremiah 29:11. God's plans are not to harm us but give us a future we desire.

Call on God and He will answer

Jeremiah was certain that the Miracle-working God, from Whom nothing is hidden, means business when he said, "Call to me and I will answer you and tell you great and unsearchable things you do not know" (Jeremiah 33:3). There is no God like our God. God is waiting for us as children to call on Him and like the Father, He will answer us. There are very few parents who will not respond when their children call. God created us and loves us. God wants to have fellowship with us and we must be ready to call.

God Answers Prayer

In the story centered about the birth of Christ, the events that took place were more of surprises; only Zechariah had his prayer answered. Whether it is Mary or Joseph or wise men or the shepherds, none of them seems to have been praying. However, God who sends rain and sunlight to all his people irrespective of their behaviour (Matthew 5:45), is the One who takes note of every cry of the heart. "Tired" prayers are those prayers that have been repeated over and over again, and yet deep within, you know you cannot give up. One of the challenges is to distinguish between lack of trust in God's ability and maintaining perseverance.

It is easy to give up and assume God has said, "No," and so when the answer comes, you cannot recognize it and remember that you prayed. Many times people wonder how long and how else one can pray over lingering problems. After much prayer and fasting over an issue, you are claiming God's promises yet you cannot see any sign of an answer that you desire. God alone will give justice. Do not look to your government. Jesus said, "And will not God bring about justice for his chosen ones, who cry out to him day and night? Will he keep putting them off?" (Luke 18:7). Take courage, arise, wipe your tears and call Him "Who is able to do immeasurably more than all we ask or imagine, according to his power that is at work within us" (Ephesians 3:20). How many times had Hannah prayed for a baby? You are not alone; other saints that lived before you have called on the Lord, over and over again on the same issue and they have realized: "Surely the arm of the LORD is not too short to save, nor his ear too dull to hear" (Isaiah 59:1).

Prayer Is Warfare

There are actions called prayers that Jesus described as babbling. Repeating words, using accents considered "spiritual" and other gimmicks that are meant to make God act according to the will of people. Saying prayers for image preservation so that others consider one Godly is hypocritical, self-deceiving and evil.

Struggling to preserve one's reputation as strong and in charge is the test that faces every believer particularly when aware that others are watching you. It is easier to pray for others, than to be seen as the one in need. That makes it difficult to open up, even to God because we would rather take care of our needs. How do you pray? How often do you pray?

God Heard Abraham's Prayer

There comes an inner struggle when a Christian has a burden yet wants to maintain an image of being in charge, wearing an "all-is-fine" façade. Deep inside one is wrestling with fear, shame, unfairness, and life is just not making sense.

Just what Abraham was struggling with when asked to pray for the barren women in the household of Abimelek, yet his own wife was barren? Genesis 20: 17 says, "Then Abraham prayed to God, and God healed Abimelek, his wife and his female slaves so they could have children again." Prayer is a time to be authentic and acknowledge that God is sovereign and He is almighty. Can you imitate Abraham by praying to God?"

God Sees Our Secrets

God sees inside and knows a genuine cry to Him. The life of Abraham as he struggled with disconnecting edges of his life is a testimony that God answers prayers.

Genesis 15:2-3 says,

> *But Abram said, 'Sovereign Lord, what can you give me since I remain childless and the one who will inherit my estate is Eliezer of Damascus' And Abram said, 'You have given me no children; so a servant in my household will be my heir. Are you struggling with what you knew was God's promise, but you now cannot see how it will be fulfilled?*

You do not have to seek sympathy from people or attempt to aid God. Are there moments when you feel childless? Do you feel discouraged? Pray to God Who sees what you do when nobody sees it. Believe me, God will consider your heart and motives. If you have correct motives and in line with God's will, God will give you an answer whether it is yes, no, not yet or wait. Waiting on God to do things is when faith gets tested. Can you wait for God for years to do one thing? Look at Abraham, a man who waited for 25 years to be blessed by God with a son.

Pray To God Sincerely In Your Private Room And God Will Answer You

Matthew 6:6 says,

> *But when you pray, go into your room, close the door and pray to your Father, who is unseen. Then your Father, who sees what is done in secret, will reward you." Is it not encouraging knowing our heavenly Father who is unseen, sees what is done in secret? Take courage, you who are praying over an issue and sometimes wonder what people who know you think of you.*

It is not about image and public opinion; it is secret business with an unseen Father. Petty issues dissolve as one gains perspective on what matters in life. A Christian who is a disciple and follower of Jesus Christ must make right decisions around meaningful priorities that relate to the kingdom of God. Abraham was told that his servant was not to be his heir but his own son. Even as you think about your situation, listen to what God told Abraham. He took him outside and said, "Look up at the sky and count the stars – if indeed you can count them. 'Then he said to him, So shall your offspring be'" (Genesis 15:5). God took Abraham and showed him. Then Abraham believed.

Think about these quotes:

- *When truth is known and not acted upon, it always, on every level of life, in any area of human knowledge, has this peculiar quality: It hardens, so the heart is not able to believe what it refuses to act on."~ **Ray Stedman***

236

- *Education is the great engine of personal development. It is through education that the daughter of a peasant can become a doctor, that a son of a mineworker can become the head of the mine, that a child of farm workers can become the president.* ~ **Nelson Mandela**

People Need Prayer To Be Successful

When you study all the great people in the Holy Scripture who were able to overcome difficult situations in their lives, they all cried and prayed to God. They believed in God not their situations. Think about these examples:

David was successful because he did not rely on his own strength and wisdom. He believed in God. In the book of Psalms, you will see the different moments where David cried and rejoiced with God.

- Daniel prayed when he was amongst people who never believed in the God he served and worshiped.
- Stephen prayed before and saw God's glory.
- Elijah prayed and God took him away and he did not suffer death.
- Hannah prayed for a son and God answered her prayers.
- Peter and apostles all prayed in one accord and God sent in the Holy Ghost.
- Paul and Silas prayed and God opened the prison gates.
- Abraham believed in God and he was blessed with a son.
- Jesus Christ before His arrest and crucifixion spent the last hours praying to God and God gave him the Spirit to stand strong and endure the cross.

No matter what your situation or circumstances, pray to God with faithfulness and do not worry about what people will say about you. God will answer your prayers. And even if God decides not to answer, He knows and is not obligated to answer all your prayers. God is sovereign. God does not need us to be God but we need God to be alive. God can decide to answer or not answer our prayers. If He does not answer, it is okay. Let God decide everything about your life. Your only duty and obligation is to believe in God and have faith in His word.

Never Worry About The Outcome Of Your Life

Jesus gave a warning against worrying in Matthew 6: 25-27, He said,

> *Therefore, I tell you do not worry about your life, what you will eat or drink; or about your body, what you will wear. Is life not more important than food, and the body more important than clothes? Look at the birds of the air; they do not sow or reap or store away in barns, and yet the heavenly Father feeds them. Are you not much more valuable than they? Who of you by worrying can add a single hour to his life?*

The majority of people whom I have met in life are worried people. People worry, weep, and wail when life becomes hard and things are not going on as expected. People worry about money, wealth, and daily challenges. The key to success is being relaxed and trusting God for your future. In my life even during very difficult moments, I have never worried about things or circumstances, but what I do is trusting in God Who knows the end of my life. My peace comes from knowing that God knows everything. That sounds so simple, but a familiar statement, "God knows everything", has kept me at peace.

Ask God To Bless You With Wealth

The Word of God in John 14:14, Jesus promised: "You may ask for anything in my name and I will do it." God is a generous giver. He answers prayers. If you want wealth, ask God and you will receive it. God through His Son has promised that whatever you want, you can ask anything.

But the condition is that it must be in His name, in His will and it shall be done. Furthermore; 1 John 5:14-15 says: This is the confidence we have in approaching God: that if we ask anything according to his will, he hears us. And if we know that he hears us – whatever we ask – we know that we have what we asked of him." Jesus said that: "Thy will be done on earth as it is in heaven.

Asking God With Faith

I believe the reason we never have things that we desire is due to our lack of faith. Jesus, teaching his disciples in Matthew 17: 20-21, says, "I tell you the truth, if you have faith as small as a mustard seed, you can say to this mountain, 'Move from here to there, and it will move. Nothing will be impossible for you.'" Moving a mountain is something we imagine is so impossible but God says it is possible. The truth is that nothing is impossible with God. The things you think are impossible about your dreams; purpose and vision are possible with God because God has ultimate authority.

Stop Doubting God

Jesus says, I tell you the truth, if anyone says to this mountain, "'Go, throw yourself into the sea' and does not doubt in his heart but believes that what he says will happen, it will be done for him." The enemy for the success is doubt which keeps people from achieving their dreams. If you ask for something, you must not doubt. Doubt comes as a result of little faith or no faith. Often times we believe in our abilities instead of God. God owns everything and created everything.

God needs you to believe and trust in Him. Never doubt God in any situation on several occasions, Jesus said, "I tell you the truth." Why did Jesus start His sentences that way? Because we have been told lies and Jesus wanted to correct those wrong messages and information that we have received and has kept us in the horrible place. That is why He said, "I am the way, the truth and the life..." (John 3). Jesus said in such a powerful way, that if you want the right way, it is through Him. If you want the truth, He is the only truth. And if you want life, He is the source of life. The truth in the world is found only in one man, who is Jesus Christ. If you want to know about your life, go to Jesus Christ and ask Him the truth about you.

Ask Anything You Desire

Sometimes, you want God to give you money, but God decides to give you a job. This means God wants you to keep the job and work so you have continued source of income that you need to generate greater wealth. Wealth is accumulated money to be invested. God is not an "instant" God. He gives us things we desire but expects us to work. Jesus says, "Therefore I tell you, whatever you ask for in prayer, believe that you have received it, and it will be yours." (Mark 11: 24)

I want to challenge you to seek God and ask Him anything. I recall praying for a job in July 2007 when I was working for the

World Food Programme. At that time, I was struggling to pay school fees for my siblings who were all doing undergraduate degrees, my own kids, my fees when I was doing my Post Graduate Studies and domestic expenses like rent, transport and feeding among other. Life was very hard and the cost of living was high. I used to go work in the office and take tea for lunch and one meal a day. I recall that one day I went before the Lord asking Him to intervene in my situation.

Things went completely upside down in my family and life was challenging. The times were tough times. As I began to seek God, I asked God to help me with a job that would yield enough salary to cater for the severely pressing family needs. On one particular day as I went to my office, I opened my e-mails and I saw several vacancy announcements from the largest humanitarian organizations that I always wanted to join. In my heart I knew God had answered my prayers so I went ahead and applied for the job which God gave me after taking part in the written and oral interviews. It took about four months to recruit and I received my appointment letter in November 2007. By February 2008, I transferred from one organization to another and took up a higher and better post and God answered my prayer and kept His word. This is a true testimony. God gives people what they ask for in prayer and when they believe as being their gift.

Another time in 2011, one of my close friends told me I was poor and there was no need to keep company with me. I felt so bad because it was not my choice to be poor. I did not choose to be born into a poor family or in a region that experienced war. I did not have any control when my parents passed on their situation, which became a problem for me. I recall going to God in prayer and

I saying, "God you created me to be poor and other people rich? God you have to do something." After praying and believing God I decided to complete an online application for an international expatriate position with the largest humanitarian organization.

This was in April 2011. It took another three months by July when I received a message that I had been shortlisted for an interview. I prepared myself by reading and researching and when the interview was conducted I waited for about a month without any feedback. Within that time, two more invitations were sent to me for interviews from the organizations I had submitted the applications. While I was waiting, I resumed to my office one morning in November 2011 and opening my e-mail, I saw an offer letter of employment from Human Resources division of the organization that I wanted to work as an expatriate. When I opened it, I saw the amount and other benefits that I was going to earn and I remembered saying to myself, "It is over," I went to the bathroom and couldn't stop crying. I cried and it confirmed to me that God answers prayers. That job took me to different places and helped me achieve the vision that I always wanted for the people in my community. The job opportunity helped me to achieve part of the dreams that I always wanted and wrote down to achieve in life. God's vision was being fulfilled. God answers prayers. Truly!

God's Timing Is The Best

This is the confidence that I have; God's time is the best. If God had blessed me with money when I was young, I would have messed up my life and distorted God's plans and purpose for my life. Do not panic when your friends turn against you and mock you about your unpleasant situation. You are not alone. Many people have gone through those sorts of things. Job was taunted by his friends

(Job 2, 42). Jesus Christ was betrayed by His best friend whom he shared meals with in the same plate. You need to go to God in trust and ask Him to make a way and provision. You have the power to choose your friends.

Principle
- *Choose your friends carefully and wisely.*

Note: Commit your plans to God every day to achieve your dreams. He will direct yours steps.

CHAPTER EIGHT

THE FUNDAMENTAL PRINCIPLE OF POTENTIAL

*"Continuous effort, not strength and intelligence, is the key to unlocking your potential." slo~ **Winston Churchill***

Genesis Of Everything

The beginning of everything is described in the story of creation by God. It is found in Genesis 1:1. It says, "In the beginning God created the heaven and the earth." This statement gives an indication that God had full potential to do everything. Everything was in God before the heaven and Earth came into existence. And when God began to speak in Genesis 1, everything started to appear and come into existence. The whole text in Genesis 1 gives an indication of the ability that was inside of God. It got revealed and appeared.

The Seed Is In Itself;
The Potential Is Inside The Product

Genesis 1:11 states,

> *And God said, 'Let the earth bring forth grass, the herb yielding seed, and the fruit tree yielding fruit after his kind, whose seed is in itself, upon the earth: and it was so.'" In this Scripture, we notice that God created fruits of different kinds but God did one thing which was wonderful. God put the seed inside itself, which gives us an indication of potency and potential. God put the future of seeds that produce fruits and seeds inside themselves.*

God put the potential inside the seed itself. That is why a seed has the capacity or ability to reproduce itself. Seed is inside the seed. Even scientists will agree with this analysis. As if to confirm that there is a seed in every seed or potential in everything He created, God created man in His image.

God blessed the humans He created and gave them an assignment. The Scripture above is loaded with key principles in that the potential of everything is inside. The seed is loaded with power to bring forth more seeds, trees and fruits, but if it is not in the right environment, it will not produce the trees. The same is with you, there are so many ideas that you are pregnant with, but unless you work them out, those ideas will die or you produce lousy ones.

Genesis 1:26 says, God blessed them and said to them, "Be fruitful and increase in number; fill the earth and subdue it." How can the man who has been created from nothing be told to do all these tasks and responsibilities? My own answer is that God placed the capacity inside man – the responsibility and accountability. God knew that man had the capacity to perform all that He wanted. Man had inherent capacity. He would not have told them to do this if they couldn't. This applies to all humans. God has placed in every human being the ability to dominate the Earth. You can overcome habits because God knows you can. God will never demand anything without giving potential and provision.

Whatever God calls for, He sees to it that it can be done and you can do it because there is potential from Him. God told the man to become fruitful, multiply and fill the Earth. God knew that man had that capacity. God does not talk much but everything He says happens because God had everything in Himself. This is the potential power of God. Everything God created was inside Himself. When God wanted man, He spoke to Himself by saying let us make man in Our Image. When God wanted trees, etc., He spoke to the soil and when God wanted fish and other sea creatures, He spoke to the waters. Everything came from somewhere and therefore must stay connected to that source.

All potential is in God. If God has potential, then everything that God created has potential like Him. Hebrews 11:3 says, "By faith we understand that the universe was formed at God's command, so that what is seen was not made out of what was visible." Everything that man has done or accomplished was invisible first before they became visible. Everything began as ideas which were invisible. The buildings you see today were once invisible. The cars that you drive in your city were once invisible in the mind of the manufacturer before they came to be. The same is true for humans. Everything starts in an invisible state before it becomes visible and physical.

The key to understanding life is not in life itself but in the source of life. In order to understand what a product can do, it is required that you ask the manufacturer.

How To Develop Potential?

The potential can be developed in several ways. It can be developed by working and being in the right environment. For example, a seed planted where all conditions of growth are satisfied will produce more seeds and over time and generate more trees and fruits. Furthermore, a child can be raised to become an adult, which means potential is being developed. An idea is a concept or a thought. An idea has to move into a reality, which manifests as potential. Ideas are potentials that attempt to become reality. Imagination is when an idea becomes a plan of action. But this needs to be documented on paper. The majority of people who talk never do anything. They are, at best, dreamers. People who make things happen are visionary. But a vision needs to manifest itself in action. Faith without works is dead. Vision without work is dead.

Ephesian 3:20 says,

> *Now to him who is able to do immeasurably more than all we ask or imagine, according to his power that is at work within us, to him be glory in the church and in Christ Jesus throughout all generations, for ever and ever! Amen.*

Before the foundations of the Earth were laid, God did something. This statement gives us an indication about God's potential. It also means we have the power to do all things that we can imagine. The word "imagine" is about visions, dreams or thoughts and ideas that run through the mind. Anything that you can imagine, God says you can do it through Him.

God Wants Us To Develop Our Imagination

God somehow wants us to have plans according to this statement. People have problems, but not plans. They are confused, disillusioned or discouraged with life because they have no plans. If you have no goal in front of you or no vision to pull you, you will be dragged down by the past. If you do not have a clear plan for your life, you will be disorganized and misguided. In addition, the statement in the above Scripture shows that there is potential in God. Pay attention to the words "imagine", "immeasurable", "more than we can ask." What do these mean?

Examples Of Potential Trapped Inside

Moses, Leader Of Israelites

Moses was born in Egypt. He grew up in a palace as a prince. When he turned 40 years, he started revealing his potential as a deliverer and leader of God's people. Moses wrote the first five books of the Bible as we know today. God had placed the potential ability to write books inside of Moses but nobody knew it. Also, when God called Moses to lead the people out of oppression and slavery in Egypt to the Promised Land, God had hidden the leadership potential inside Moses. It was trapped in there but needed time to manifest. God placed the ability to lead in him when he created him but nobody knew this.

David, Second King Of Israel

This young boy was assigned to look after his father's flock. His brothers never knew that the young David would be the next king after Saul. Nobody knew this boy would become a king. Inside him was the potential for leadership and kingship. The same David wrote the longest book in the Bible – the Psalms. Nobody knows you except God Who made you.

Abraham, The Father Of Isaac And Nations Of Israel

This great "father of faith" was not able to have a son until he was 100 years old. At 75, God told him that he would have a son. Can you picture a 75-year-old man today having a kid? Abraham was already old when God made a declaration of the future. No one would have believed Abraham could still have a child because his wife, Sarah, was barren. His neighbours must have laughed about his situation. But only God knew the full potential in Abraham. He knows your potentials also.

Never confuse your current challenges with your potential. Maybe people have said your dreams might not come to pass. You may have had people discourage you against keeping on to achieve your dream. Do not believe those people. Believe the God who deposited the dreams into your heart. God knows when the dreams will be actualized.

Paul, An Apostle, Preacher and Author

With so much of the New Testament credited to his name as author and a preacher, Paul was a social mobilizer and planner who participated in persecuting the early church and followers of Jesus Christ (Acts 1). But God interrupted his life. He became a preacher and wrote three quarters of the New Testament. God placed potential inside him. Paul wrote and preached the Gospel in all these places. This example of Paul teaches us that you can make a turn in your life and become a global leader or a world changer. God has placed potentials in you and you should begin to release them.

Potential Is Released When Demand Is Made

Potential is released when demands are made on it. You can tell how much potential a thing or product has by the demand placed on it. That means the minute you place a demand on something, it releases its potential to meet up the demand. Remember what God told Adam in Genesis? Adam had no parents and no education, but God had him name all the animals. How could God give someone without an education a task like that? It means he placed a potential in Adam. God also told Adam to have dominion over the Earth, to rule it and subdue it. But where was Adam's potential? Whatever God demands, God provides potential for it to succeed.

Whatever God creates, God provides potential for it to succeed.

Jesus told us, "Love your enemies." He would not have said it if there was no potential to do so. When God told Adam and Eve to be fruitful and multiply, there was the potential for this to happen. When you drive a car from point A to point B, you may choose to drive at a speed of 60km per hour. However, you can also increase the acceleration to 120km per hour. That means you are placing a demand on the car to release the potential that the manufacturer placed inside the car. Potential is released when a demand has been made on it.

Think And That Is What You Become

Proverbs 23:7 says: "As a man thinks in his heart, so is he." This can be interpreted as whatever a person conceives in his heart, he can do it. If you can think it, you can do it. It does not matter if it has not been done before. It is still possible. Jesus said if you believe, then it is possible. That is talking about our potential. God says if you can think it, you can do it. The problem with humans is that they do not think but expect their lives to change instantly – waiting for miracles. A lot of humans are lazy. It is common to many to not want to do anything. Many are too lazy to think. Even thinking is hard work. If you think it, you can do it. You become what you think. If you believe you can become a different person you can change your life.

Many look but few see; humans look but God sees. Moses was seen by many people in Egypt as a murderer and yet God saw a deliverer of Israelites. David was seen by his family as a shepherd boy, but God saw him as the king of a great nation. Saul was a murderer, but God saw a great preacher, an ambassador and an evangelist. 1 Corinthians 2:7 says, "No, we speak of God's secret wisdom, a wisdom that has been hidden and that God destined for our glory before time began." Destiny means God has a finished plan for your life before time began. God is the one who began time. God reveals His plan to us through His Holy Spirit. God saw you before the beginning.

Psalm 139:13 says,

For you created my inmost being; you knit me together in my mother's womb. I praise you because I am fearfully and wonderfully made; your works are wonderful; I know that full well. My frame was not hidden from you when I was made in the secret place. When I was woven together in the depths of the earth, your eyes saw my unformed body. All the days ordained for me were written in your book before one of them came to be. How precious to me are your thoughts, O God! How vast is the sum of them!

These thoughts blow my mind. God's original plan was to show his nature, to show his potency. This is what God sees. God's thoughts are not like ours: "For my thoughts are not your thoughts, neither are your ways my ways," declares the Lord. 'As the heavens are higher than the earth, so are my ways higher than your ways and my thoughts than your thoughts'" (Isaiah 55:8-9). God wants us to have a mind like His. God says for us to be transformed by the renewing of our minds. (Roman 12:2) Change your attitude toward yourself today. There is a book on you written by God. "Potential", means something which is latent, possible, likely, impending, would-be, imaginable, thinkable and having ability, existing in capacity and possibility, or aptitude and capability.

Potential Permits Us To Accomplish Our Purpose

I believe that potential is a powerful principle that every person needs to know. Without potential, purpose cannot be accomplished and God's purpose cannot be achieved also. I also believe no one knows you or me. Do you know yourself? There is an ancient Greek philosophy that states: "Know thyself" (an inscription on the Temple of Apollo at Delphi). The reason I have great respect for people is that I do not know them and the potential God has deposited in them. We write people out because we think we know them, yet in actual fact do not know them. A place we shall all go to one day is the cemetery. To me the cemetery is the "richest" place in the world. Why? The cemetery is richer than diamond mines of South Africa.

A Place Full Of Wealth

The cemetery is full of buried dreams, ideas, and visions that were never achieved or attained. The dreams, ideas, visions, or projects of dead men and women are all potentials that were never manifested and released. Every day, millions of people are dying with their dreams, ideas, books, industries, businesses, and projects. They are going to the grave without giving releasing their potential to the world. The greatest tragedy is not death itself, but the unachieved lives in the graveyard marked by mere stones.

The dreams, ideas, visions, or projects of dead men and women are all potentials that were never manifested and released.

Jesus' life is an example of life fulfilled. Paul is another example. Paul spoke words like, "I fought a good fight and finished my race." As I continue to study the word of God, I have come to a simple conclusion: No desire to have a monument in my cemetery, but instead I should do something that will make people remember that it was good that I lived on Earth and I built people and institutions that builds people's minds. I do not know much about my great grandparents, but I am interested in sharing my potential with the next generation so they do not lose out on my gift to them. The potential I have must be released for the benefit of the next generation. There is so much that has not been tapped and exploited. God is calling us to do something higher and so let's believe that God has given us the potential. If we are irresponsible and not accountable, the potential will be destroyed and cancelled.

I believe that the saddest things in life are the safety experts and people who are afraid to fail and do not want to takes risks.

Whenever you keep company with God you become secure and confident because you become just like him. When you keep company with God, you have to become like Him and you begin to think like Him. You have to have faith and believe that God told you to do it. When you see people behaving in a certain manner it means they know something.

Unless you do something you have never done, you will never grow and you will never know what you could achieve. Those who dare to fail greatly ever achieve greatly. Do not perceive your limitations to cause your limitations. Potency is the ability that is unused and you have all the potential to change your life. Every human being has been birthed with gifts, talents, ideas, and visions. All these are examples of potentials.

What is the meaning of the word potential?

- Potential means dormant ability, dormant energy
- Potential is the dormant or used seeds, ideas, talents, skills, or knowledge.
- Potential means unused strength, reserved energy or unused power.
- Potential is also unused success.
- Potential is everything you could do but have not done yet.
- Potential is what you could become, but not yet achieved.
- Potential is your vision of the preferred future, that has not be achieved.
- Potential is how far you can go but are not yet there and you have the capacity inside you.
- Potential is ability to perform better than what you did last.

How Can You Describe God?

- God is described as Omnipotent, right? This means all potential.
- God is also described as Omniscient? This means all knowing.
- Omnipotent is a word that describes God. All potential is found in God.

When you study and look at Psalm 90:1. It says, "Lord, you have been our dwelling place throughout all generations." Where was everything? In this sentence, David said, "You have been our dwelling place throughout all generations." It means everything was in God and all things were dwelling in Him. God is all potential and all potential is in God. In Him was everything. God created things with potential and that is why He told two humans to fill the Earth. He told Adam to name all the animals and plants that He created. Why? It is because God created and placed potential inside everything. Let me give you an analogy when you buy a phone, you will notice it can perform many functions. Why? To me the simple answer is it that has the potential. When you buy a car, it will have the power to perform, and that power is the potential placed by manufacturer inside it.

Things Too Difficult For Me

Is it difficult to discuss God? David said, "Such knowledge is too wonderful for me, too lofty for me to attain" (Psalm. 139:6). Potential has nothing to do with what you have done, but everything to do with what you can do. Potential has nothing to do with things that do exist, but things not yet seen. That means you do not know what is inside the people around you. One of the things that make me afraid is that people die with their potential. Paul said in 2 Timothy. 4:7, "I have finished my course", which means you finish everything.

The Bible says if you can imagine it, you can do it. Question: Do you know your children? Do you know your wife? Suppose Michelangelo died before finishing the Sistine Chapel? Suppose Mary had an abortion? This is why you should not abort or kill unborn children. You never know your neighbours, friends, and children. That is why God says that you should love your enemies because the potential to love your enemies is trapped inside you. You will never know their potential if you do not love. God is the author of potential, so he created man with potential. All things created by God were inside God. When something is in you, God brings it the same way he brought the universe it to being. I have reached a point where I have too much faith in God. Because if I think something, I believe it is possible and it is equivalent to saying that I can do it. God designed everything with potential. God created everything at once.

Every Seed Has Seeds, Trees And Fruits

In Genesis 1:11, God put the seed of everything in itself, as I have previously said. We like plenty, but God likes potency. Who could think five loaves would become twelve baskets of loaves in Jesus' miracle (John 6:13)? Who would think that two fish could feed 5,000 people? If you have a seed in your hand, you have an orchard; you have sacks of seeds, etc.

In every fish, there is a school of fish. In every horse, there are many horses. God thinks in the potential and not in the plenty. God sees but does not look. If you live by looking you will be depressed, but when you live by what you see with the mind's eye of God's potential, you will not be depressed. Instead of creating Adam and then Eve from him, why didn't God say, "Let the Earth be filled with 7.5 billion people?" God does not think that way. His thoughts are not our thoughts and His ways not our ways. Genesis 1:28 says that the Lord blessed them. To be blessed means that God has endowed you with potential.

Can we look at another practical example? Look at Abraham whom God said would be a "father of many nations" yet he had no son. But then came Isaac in his old age born to him and Sarah. God declared that these two people would fill the Earth. Whatever God calls for he provides for. God has built into you everything he calls for. When the Lord approaches you, tells you to do something, it is equal to "I can." There was potential in Abraham and Sarah to have a baby! The baby was a vision they could see but not physically until when the baby was born.

Every human has been created and born with hidden ability, talent, greatness, and competency from the inside by God the creator. The biggest problem is that most of the humans die with all that potential that God put inside of them. The Bible is packed with great examples of men and women who had their potential revealed and purpose fulfilled. The following examples are just a few and it is an indicator that you and I have potential just like these people.

Moses, The Murderer, Deliverer, Author And Leader

Look at Moses. A murderer who wrote five books of the Bible and these books are the first books that you find in the Bible. Suppose Moses had not written those five books; how would you know your origin? You never know who you have in your company. That is why you need to treat people with respect. God places potential in all creation and if the creation is in the right environment it will flourish and become that entire thing God intended it to become.

The key in life is being humble and kind in the way you treat people because God placed inside them a treasure. That treasure is potential. Potential is not what you have done, but what you can do. The education or degrees that you already completed are no longer your potential any more. If you built a house, that house is no longer your potential. If you have competed at a national athletic event, that is no longer your potential. If you have a written an article in a journal and it has been published, that is no longer your potential. If you have published a book, it means you have the potential to publish more books. If you are a leader of a football club, it means you have the potential to lead a bigger team. Do not celebrate your successes. If you have been leader in the department, it means you have the potential to lead the whole organization. The power is inbuilt by God and it is in you.

When you keep company with God, it means you have greater work to do because God is full of potential. God has put something in you that require eternity to bring it out. Sometimes you can become a stranger to some people because of the things you see and those around you cannot. You have so much to do in such a short time because you are full of potential. I want to say something that might shock you. Do you know that the time people have spent looking for boyfriends, girlfriends, quarrelling, and wasting time will make God unhappy and will make us cry when we get to heaven because we will have performed poorly? God is disappointed when we never believe Him in the things we need to do because God is pregnant God with potentials.

The Concept Of Intelligence Quotient (IQ)

I believe the concept of measuring people's IQ is inimical to the full release of the potentials in man. Humans have come up with worldly standards to determine things. Measuring IQ has been used to cancel people's destinies. History books are replete with people who were considered not intelligent enough using their IQ scores, but those people went ahead to become successful and effective in life. How can you explain that? The IQ has destroyed and limited the potentials of so many people because they are considered average students. Do you know that there are also many people who have been told they cannot amount to anything, but they refuse to believe? And then they become somebody in life. There are many people who have become what they were meant to because they believed in their potential.

Slavery Kills Potential And Purpose

Slavery is the worst form of human dehumanization and punishment. Slavery destroys potential and leads to the delay or cancellation of the fulfillment of people's purpose for living and attainment of personal dreams and plans. Slavery is a system under which people are treated as commodities to be bought and sold in the market and are forced to work. Slaves can be held against their will from the time of their capture, purchase or birth, and deprived of the right to live, work, or demand compensation. Historically, slavery was institutionally recognized by most societies. Similarly, oppression of people destroys human potential and causes them fail to fulfil their purpose in life.

But in more recent times, slavery has been outlawed in all countries. It continues through the practices of debt bondage, servitude, and serfdom. People are sometimes held as domestic servants and kept in captivity. There are certain adoptions in which children are forced to work as slaves and become child soldiers.

They are forced into early marriages as well. In the Bible, Joseph suffered a great deal, but in the end he became a ruler. Dear reader, please know that God's purpose is bigger than the suffering that we get or meet in life. In my own life, growing up as an orphan, meant hard work and I believe there was a reason all that had to happen. The principle is that purpose overcomes hardships.

Nobody Knew Us

When I was young, I had held a wrong definition of wealth, but as I grew older, I began to read the Bible and I discovered important principles about God and how he works. I discovered things like with God all things are possible. As I continued, I began to think with God all things are possible, then I decided to start believing God. I recall that my mother and grandmother always tell us to read the Bible. They taught us to read in Ateso (which is an Eastern Nilotic language spoken by the Iteso people of Uganda and Kenya) and also the Good News Bible. Today as I look back, I see the works of God in our family.

God has kept His word alive and we have been an example to many people in the community. People talk about me and think that am successful, but in fact am not successful; all am doing is fulfilling God's purpose and plans for my life. Whatever I do is connected to my personal purpose. Every day I do things related to my vision for humanity. My encouragement to you is that you should do something that is so big that people will remember you. Do something that makes people talk good about you. You need to do things for God and you will see what will happen in your life. If you want to become successful, work for God.

Note: Everyone has the potential. Exploit it consistently and your dreams will be reached.

CHAPTER NINE

THE FUNDAMENTAL PRINCIPLE OF FAITH

"God will not look you over for medals,
degrees or diplomas but for scars."
- Elbert Hubbard

What Is Faith?

In this section, I intend to share with you the power of faith in God. This is the most important principle of life. Faith is the only thing that will keep you strong when every you trust disappears. You will need it all the time to achieve your purpose and vision. When you are disappointed, demoralized or about to stop the fight, you need it. No matter the situation you find yourself, always know that God is good all the time. We should not worry because God is God. I was reading my Bible. In Philippians 1:6, the Bible says,

"He who began a good work in you will bring it the completion and to the end." Whatever God gave us to do, His purpose will be completed. God will give you the strength to complete the work that he gave you. God will give you resources.

God will give you the ability and potential. The word faith is from the Greek word "Pistis," which means "belief." I am always interested in getting knowledge and understanding so I can be wise with wisdom and make effective decisions. I have always met people who have names such as Faith, Hope, Peace, Grace, or Mercy. I always wondered if the parents who named their children faith really had an idea of what it means to have faith. Faith is the most important thing if you are going to go through life and overcome crises. There are no guarantees in life. If you are doing well today without any problems, there are no guarantees in this world. If you are employed and your job is doing well, let me say there are no guarantees that it will stay that way. If you are healthy today as you read this book, I am not sure whether things will stay that way and your health will not fail you.

Through my search for meaning of words (such as planning, accountability, goals, redemption, belief and others) I set out to get what faith means and why faith is the most important thing in life. During that journey, I came to my Bible and found in the book of Hebrews a statement which I believe gives the definition for the word "faith."

Hebrews 11:1 says, Now faith is the assurance of things hoped for, the conviction of things not seen." In Hebrews 12:4 , "...looking to Jesus, the founder and perfector of our faith, who for the joy that was set before him endured the cross, despising the shame, and is seated at the right hand of the throne of God. When we come through the storms, we shall receive a reward and God will seat us in His presence on His right. That is what I believe!

The Just Shall Live By Faith not Fear

Faith is so important that the word of God says, "The just shall live by faith" (Roman 1:17) and also, "We live by faith, not by sight" (2 Corinthians.5:7). In this statement, it means people were never designed and created by God to live according to what they see every day, but rather life is lived according to faith. When people live by sight or by what they see every day, they will be depressed, frustrated, disorganized, confused, and bewildered. Why? This is because every day, you will be confronted by bad information from the media showing disasters, people in crises, poverty, problems and this can discourage you from what you want to accomplish. Each day in the media, particularly broadcasting corporations such as, BBC, CNN, CCTV and Aljazeera, there are stories in the world about conflict, violence and persecution. The stories are horrible and scary.

The secret to life is living by hope and faith not by sight and what you see every day; because when you see challenges, setbacks or meet resistance or problems, you will be affected emotionally, physically, economically or psychologically. When you live by sight you will always be depressed and frustrated. Faith is belief and conviction that creates confidence in life. When a person loses hope, you lose direction for life and forces of life will run over you. Life will test you and you must have a secret to dealing with challenges, problems and obstacles that you will encounter.

I believe that most of the humanity on Earth are living by sight and not faith or vision. God always gives every one of us two eyes but these are to be used for seeing – not for life. We have to live by the pictures or the dreams that we have in our minds. I want to put it another way: Live by purpose and vision. Purpose is why everything exists. It is the reason for existence. People need to live by the purpose that God created and without purpose, there is no effective living and focus in life. Have you found your purpose? Do you know why you are alive at this moment? Have you ever thought about your assignment on Earth? Or you think you are here to pass the time? Most people are interested in attending parties, celebrations, discos, going on holidays in beaches, or visiting places. They call it exploring. Holidays are fine and rest is important, yet God did not create us to do all of that all the time. He gave us a day to rest which is the Sabbath. He created us to have a meaning for our lives.

Faith is Needed in Pursuit of Dreams

Faith is one ingredient that helps you to accomplish your dreams and plans for life. It sustains you even when the life gets rough and tough. When you lose your faith, you become like Jesus' close friend and disciple named Judas Iscariot. Matthew 27:5 is a statement of lost faith. It says, "So Judas threw the money into the temple and left. Then he went away and hanged himself." Judas Iscariot lost faith. Judas applied a permanent solution to a temporary problem. If Judas had not hanged himself, Jesus would have forgiven and restored him as he did for Peter as reported in John 21:15. Loss of faith causes crises and affects life profoundly. Judas lost his life because of loss of faith. I would like to advise people who might be considering hanging, killing, or attempting suicide that problems are seasonal and temporary; they will come and go. There is no permanent problem.

Here is a simple statement that has kept me: Do not apply a permanent solution to a temporary problem. In the case of Judas as we have seen, he applied a permanent solution to a problem that was temporary. Jesus could have forgiven him. You also need to note that you can always be forgiven or pardoned. If Judas had not killed or destroyed himself, you never know we could have gotten a Gospel according to Judas. Do not think you are the only one going through problems; there are millions of people who might actually be in a worse state than what you are going through right now. You will actually come out of it. The key in life is not make decisions that cannot be reversed.

Principles
- *Do not apply a permanent solution to a temporary problem.*
- *Keep the faith as you pursue the dreams and vision in your heart.*

Why is faith so important in life? Faith is the most important power you have in life and when you lose it you cannot be confident.
- Faith creates confidence and eliminates fear.
- Faith produces courage.
- Faith generates conviction.
- Faith turns hopeless situation to hopeful one.
- Faith gives meaning to life.
- Faith gives focus to life.
- Faith bring purpose to life.
- Faith is a source of strength in the face of challenges and crisis.
- Faith is power to pursue purpose and vision.

Let me say something. In your time of crisis, there is no need to fear anything. You need to keep your faith because you believe in God Who is bigger than the problems you are facing.

The Mysteries and Questions Of Life

Nobody can answer all questions and nobody knows what life is all about except God. As a teenager, I lost my mother and grandparents before I became an adult. In those years, I could go to the graveyard and would cry so that my mother and grandparents would be resurrected. This did not happen. During those traumatic years, I learnt important lessons and discovered the secret of keeping smiles on my face every day.

1. There are questions in life we cannot find answer or never answer. This means you must settle this and stop having frustrations or mood swings or emotions.

2. There are things in life we cannot explain when they happen to us. You must settle down and stop disturbing your mind. When search for explanations for everything in life you will always find yourself depressed, oppressed, worried, and continuously wailing.

3. There are things in life we cannot do and only God can do them. Only God can bring humans to life, and when someone dies, just know you cannot do anything about it.

4. There are things in life we cannot control or change. If someone decides to leave your organization, company, your life or marriage, there is little you can do to control or even change the personal decisions people make. You can pray a million times (for days, weeks, month or years or even fast for a long time) but if she or he decides to leave you,

you will try and fail. Let people move on and focus on your purpose. Your attitude must be to focus on working, fulfilling and maximizing your potential.

5. There are things in life for which we are not responsible (for instance, your child decides to engage in "bad" activities without your permission as a parent). You cannot take responsibility for the actions of others, even including your own children. You only take responsibility for your own personal decisions. Everyone must take responsibility for their actions and personal decisions. Life is full of decisions and every minute we make decisions that can either take us up or bring us down. The choice is yours and it is in your hands.

6. There are things in life we cannot stop. For instance, things like accidents, hurricanes or death cannot be stopped. If you cannot stop certain things, let them pass you; otherwise you will be destroyed because it will still proceed or go where it is going.

7. There are things in life we cannot exceed or go beyond. For instance, Hitler attempted to become the President of the World and he could not achieve this foolish ambition. There are people who think they can exceed things. If God wants, let it be.

We cannot do or have all things in life. Only God can do or have all things.

What You Need to Know About God

You need to know some secrets in life that will enable you to respond to crisis and turmoil. There are things you need to know about God. If you want to avoid depression, high blood pressure, stress and daily challenges and problems that we face, you must find ways to exercise your faith. You need to understand these things that I call "secrets." I discovered these things 20 years ago and have applied them in my life ever since. When you do this, you will never get depressed and you will not worry about your outcomes in life.

1. Know that only God can do certain things. Only God can raise the dead. Nobody except Him can do that. Only God did raise the dead. His Son, Jesus, was able to raise Lazarus from death. (John 11) Most of us worry when someone dies. When I lost my mother several years ago, I used to imagine she would come back to life but this has not happened. Remember that only God can raise the dead dead. There are things only God can change. If you cannot change something, leave that business to God. It is only God who changes people. One example is Saul when he was on the road to Damascus. God stopped him and changed him. God asked him a question that I believe blew Saul's mind: "Why are you persecuting Me.?" (See Acts 9:1-6) Saul had no answer!

2. Know that only God knows certain things. You will never know what God knows and if He wants you to know, He will tell you or He may not. That is God's business. There are things only God can explain. It is only God who can explain when someone dies. Sometimes you do your best to save the life of someone, pay medical bills, and take

270

care of the person but finally the person dies. You have tried your best and you have reached your limit. Only God can explain this scenario.

3. Know that only God can stop certain things. In the Old Testament, when God wanted to stop Saul from being the king of Israel, he sent Samuel to anoint David, son of Jesse. Once David was anointed, Saul was on his way out of the office of being king of Israel. (1 Samuel 15 and 16) Only God can do that and in His own time. God has the power to stop something in our lives. God can cancel your destiny and your dreams. God can make another person take over from you and dismiss you. God can also allow something to happen to us even when we have faith and belief in Him. God allowed His Son, Jesus to go to the Cross, yet He could have saved him. God allowed Stephen to be stoned to death. God can allow what you never expect to happen.

4. Know that only God understands certain things. The pain you are going through or you went through, it is only God who understands. Sometimes, people may have sympathy for you, but only God knows the pain we go through in life. God knows the pain and struggles you are going through. He will help you come out of them if He wants you to come clean.

5. Know that only God can answer the questions in life that we can never answer in our lifetime. For instance, when God asked Saul why he was persecuting Him, Saul had no answer. Another example is about Moses in the wilderness. Moses asked God, "Who are you?" God said, "I Am who I Am." Only God can answer these questions. No human can answer these questions in life.

6. Know that only God is responsible for certain things: There are things for which only God is responsible. For instance, it is God who created the universe and we did not bring anything to the world. If we want to do things, let us do things that we are responsible for and leave what is for God to God.

7. Know that only God can make us exceed certain things in life or go beyond the limits of our imaginations. This is because it is not our business; only God can make us overcome them. God made Daniel overcome the lion's den and Jesus overcome death on cross.

Can You Argue With God?

In the Bible, it was recorded that Job attempted to argue with God and God asked, "Where were you when I laid the foundations of the Earth?" Job could not answer this question. Attempting to be God is one of the biggest mistakes in life. Most of us humans think we know so much. Some of us think we are gods. But Almighty God knows everything, including much we do not know. As a teenager when my mother passed on, I was asking God why He allowed my mother to die. I remember getting thoughts that would later change my life. God said He too allowed His son to die without anything bad He had done on Earth.

Principle
- *Never argue with God. Let God Be God.*
  You cannot fight God.

Consequences Of Lost Faith

In Matthew 27: 5, we read a stinging account about loss of trust and faith. Judas threw away the money and went away; he hanged himself and died. He lost faith and that is the reason he killed in himself. Peter and Judas both denied Jesus. Judas lost faith as Peter did, but Judas applied a permanent solution to solve a temporary problem or daily challenges of life. Most people are frustrated and discouraged in life because they have little or no faith. The greatest power any human must possess is faith.

How To Face Life With Confidence And Determination

How do you face life with all the challenges and problems you encounter daily? There are five ways which are::

1. Know your limitations and what you are capable of doing. Some people are not wise because they do not know their strengths and weaknesses; they cannot tell their limitations. This statement means there are things you cannot do. Just accept that fact and settle down.

2. Know that you are responsible for your choices, decisions and actions. You must know your responsibility and what is not your responsibility. There are things I discovered for which God cannot take responsibility. For instance, when Jesus came to the Earth, He went to the cross on our behalf, went to the grave, rose again and declared to be our Saviour. Jesus does not save us without our permission and decision. Jesus will not save us without our will. Jesus knows His limitation. He does not violate our will.

3. Know what you can and cannot do. Do what you are capable of doing and leave the rest to God.

4. Know that everything will change. Change will happen and you can't stop it when it comes. Change is inevitable. Change is a necessity of life. Change is constant. Life is something you cannot explain. Everything will change and God promised this to us.

5. Know that God is God. Have Faith in God, because whatever we have is what God gave us. Even when life is hard or becomes hard – have faith only in GOD. Read the Bible every day and understand the Word of God, the mind of God and God's purpose for your life.

Personal Experience And The Mysteries Of Life On Earth

I have seen so many things in my short journey of life on Earth what about you? I have been poor and among even the poorest people with nothing to boast about. I have seen people born, die, and buried, personally buried my mother, grandparents and father and even friends. I have had much money, no money and lost money in the course of life. I have been attacked and criticized, misunderstood and abused; depressed and have cried in anguish.

I have been happy and laughed but also unhappy and gone through terrible pain. I have slept hungry without food for days and just living with tea or struggling with life. I have seen and experienced conflict, war, disaster or calamity. I have seen my friends turn their backs on me. I have seen my enemies come back to me. I have seen people being prayed for in church after God healed them; they gave testimonies how God healed or helped them but those they prayed for still died. I have seen families fall apart and families uniting again. I have seen sons turn against their parents and I have seen people turn against each other. In all this things, what has kept me going is not my wisdom, money, friends or jobs. What has kept me going, rather, has been my faith in God.

I believe most us have gone through these experiences and this is a key lesson in life. I am saying this and encourage you all to have great faith in God because God does not change; He is the same yesterday, today, tomorrow and forever. One thing I want to advise is that the way you want to live in life is for you to expect the best and prepare for the worst; that means do not be stupid and careless. Do all; that you can in your lifetime and leave the rest or everything to God. While growing up, I was taught in Sunday school: "Let God Be God. Have faith in God." This statement sounded so simple, but it has kept me through this journey of mystery. God remains God whether you agree with me or not, God exists.

What Is God Up To? What Motivates God?

What does God want when dealing with mankind? God is only concerned about the way we live and how we live on Earth. God is concerned about our strong and stable faith. The Bible says it is impossible to please God without faith. Hebrews 11:6 says, "And without faith it is impossible to please God, because anyone who comes to him must believe that he exists and that he rewards those who earnestly seek him." How stable is your faith in God? Your faith is as strong as the test it survives. How strong are you? How strong is your faith? Your strength is only equal to what you can physically lift up with your hands. What about your spiritual strength? What is your goal, objective or motive for following Jesus Christ? Why did you get saved?

Principles
- *God exists; you cannot change that fact.*
- *God is pleased when you have faith in Him.*

- *God wants you to believe He exists.*
- *God rewards those who seek Him earnestly.*

Why Are You A Christian?

Let me share with you the message in John 6:24-60 as a way of examining our motives for following Jesus. John 6:24 says, "Once the crowd realized that neither Jesus nor his disciples were there, they got into the boats and went to Capernaum in search of Jesus." They were looking for Jesus. The word seeking means looking everywhere until they found Him.

John 6:25-26 says,

> *When they found him on the other side of the lake, they asked him, 'Rabbi, when did you get here?' Jesus answered, "'I tell you the truth, you are looking for me, not because you saw miraculous signs but because you ate the loaves and had your fill.*

Jesus answered perfectly and wonderfully when He said this. The day before the people had experienced the miracle of the feeding of the 5,000 where the loaves and fishes multiplied; the sick were healed and Jesus preached the good news of the Kingdom of God. The crowds were looking for Jesus after this event. Jesus said that people were looking for him because they wanted more of these blessings, the free fish and bread as well as more miracles.

Sometimes, we follow God because of the blessings, gifts, and things God does for us. What if God does not give blessings, gifts or things? Will you still trust God? Will you still believe in God? Then Jesus said in John 6:27: "Do not work for food that spoils, but for food that endures to eternal life, which the Son of Man will give you. On him God the Father has placed his seal of approval". Do not put your faith on things that can disappear. Instead, put your faith in God who changes not. Jesus had spoken of working for food, so in John 6:28 they naturally asked, "What must we do to do the works God requires?" You can read the entire chapter of John 6.

So, instead of seeking the physical bread their work should be to believe in the true bread from heaven who was Jesus Himself. The miracles were temporary; Jesus is forever. Do you know God can give you a car and take it away? Do you think the car came from Nissan or Toyota Corporation in Japan? Who really gave you the car? I have gone through the tests in life and you are only as strong as the tests that you survive. When you survive the tests then you can be counted as strong. What tests have you survived?

Principle
- *People are always looking for gifts and miracles but not seeking to know the truth and God's vision for their lives. Look for the truth from the Source of truth.*

Where Is Your Faith?

The faith that believers must and should have, must be in God. Faith should not be in things, blessings and gifts or even miracles of God. All of these things, blessings, gifts and miracles are temporary in the eyes of God and will disappear. Kingdoms will fail. Monarchs will crumble. Dictators who suppress people in their countries will die. Jesus gave an answer to that question of "Where is your faith?" by saying, "Have faith in God" (Mark 11:22). Have belief in God. There are two types of bread in John 6 – the physical that is represented by the manna given to Moses and the bread Jesus multiplied. The other type is the true and living bread, Jesus Christ. For me, it has been 27 years of struggle without parents. "Where is your faith?" That is the question that emerged from this struggle. The answer is that Jesus said he that comes to me and eats of me shall never hunger. If we feed on Christ Himself spiritually, we will never be hungry again.

As I was writing this book, I remembered the story of Jesus and His disciples on the boat and the storms. I started to think God could have set it up to check how they would react or respond through the storm. The Bible says when the disciples woke Jesus up, He did immediately stop the storm, but asked a question: "Where is your faith?" He did not stop the storm immediately but checked the reaction of his disciples. Are you reacting to the storms of life or having faith in the Messiah? Whatever you are going through in life is allowed by God. The Bible says God allows tests to come against us. If the test is big, then by its size God is saying, "I believe in you." The bigger the test, the bigger the belief and faith that God has in you. You do not follow God because of the things He gives to you. Follow Him out of faith. It means God has more trust in you.

The whole discussion about eating the flesh of the Son of Man Jesus and drinking His blood was revolting to the Jews. Clearly, this has reference to the Lord's Supper from our vantage point of reading the gospel of John and understanding the big picture. But in the context of the passage, what were the Jews to think? Did He mean this in a physical sense? Of course not. But somehow Jesus would not explain it all to them then and even allowed most of them to walk away in disgust. (Read all of John 6)

In hindsight, He knew that these people were following Him for the wrong reasons. They wanted Him to be the new Moses with the new manna and then they would crown Him Messiah King. But He wanted them to believe in Him and spiritually find their life in Him. That was a concept for which they were not ready. It would be about a relationship with God through His Son Jesus Who was the Bread that came down from heaven. If you feed on this bread, you will live forever. But the Jews reacted to Jesus' words negatively. On hearing it, many of His disciples said, "This is a hard teaching. Who can accept it?." (John 6:60) Your faith should not be in the things Jesus gives you but in Jesus Himself. Jesus wants us to trust Him even if He gives us nothing. Then the passage says, "From this time many of his disciples turned back and no longer followed him." (John 6:66) Are you one of them? Jesus took away the bread and the fishes and told them they had to feed on Himself and believe in Him.

They wanted the immediate political blessings of the Messiah King of Israel to save them from Rome; they wanted manna from heaven like the new Moses Messiah figure would be; and they wanted the miracles to keep coming all the time. But what they were getting was a Savior Who would save them from their sins by His body and His blood. They did not understand the implications of this and many just did not want that kind of Messiah. But is that the Savior for Whom you are looking?

Principles
- *There are people following you for "bread and fish." When you do not give that to them, they will eventually leave you.*
- *If God gave you a vision, do not get discouraged when people leave but keep going and believing God to provide for the vision.*

Do You Remember Daniel?

Remember the story of Daniel in the Old Testament in Daniel. The law was contrived against Daniel such that no one could pray to any other god but the king, but Daniel defied this and continued to pray to the true God. As he was brought before the king to be tried, the king regretfully threw him into the lion's den. Daniel was a favoured government official but the king had to abide by his own law. So imagine how Daniel must have felt before the king when he was tried. He expected to be thrown to the lions and eaten alive. But what happened? God shut the mouths of the lions and spared Daniel. He had the faith and God enabled him to survive. Then Daniel's enemies were thrown to the lions and they were devoured.

How many of us are willing to go to that length? Are you willing to sacrifice your life for your beliefs? Are you willing to lose your life? What is more important than life? Are you willing to pay a price? Most people say my life. That is not your life. You will be remembered for the crisis that you overcome. Your level of leadership as well as maturity is measured by the obstacles and challenges that you will encounter and overcome. Some of these challenges will test your resolve.

I have been through some significant storms in my own life. I have had to learn to wait for God's help through the storms on many occasions. God did not stop the storms. They were there to test me for my faith. In John 6:35, Jesus declared, "I am the bread of life. He who comes to me will never go hungry, and he who believes in me will never be thirsty." Some people cannot survive the storms; others cannot survive success. Jesus said if you have been faithful in little things, then you will be blessed with big things

(Matthew 25:21). Whether it is survival of storms or success, we have to be faithful. So it doesn't matter if you are going through huge problems and trials that could stretch out for two years, five, or twenty years, this message is here to help you. God knows what He is doing.

God Knows Everything Before It Happens, Do You Believe This?

God knows things you do not know. I remember one day I was travelling from Tororo town in eastern Uganda to Kampala City. The driver was driving so fast that I just asked him to stop because I was scared we were about to be involved in an accident. I told the driver that the speed was very high and the road was very bad. The driver could not listen to what I was telling him. The car had 14 passengers. I pleaded with driver to drive with care and with moderate speed. The driver refused. I decided to ask him to stop and I paid him off the full fare and had him let me out of the car that was full of people. I was not happy about the decision to pay money for nothing and I had to wait for another vehicle. This crazy ride so upset me and I knew that I would have to pay even more to catch another ride to Kampala.

But in a half an hour I did get another means of transport and this time the driver was safe and friendly. Then as we drove towards Kampala, we saw the same car I had been riding in had a terrible accident that wrecked it and had overturned several times and killed everyone aboard, including the driver. There were 13 people in the car and all of them died. I was the only one who had left the car and I survived. Little did I know God had wanted to save me. Sometimes, God can do something and we get upset, but there is a reason for everything. I have learnt to let God be God. As children in Sunday school and early Christians in Mbale (Mbale is a city in Eastern Region of Uganda), one of the phrases and teaching I received was "Let God be God." It sounded so simple, but this has kept me until this moment in my life. Some people think they are powerful but believe, "Let God be God."

There is another thing you need to know in life. Everything you have or own, you will lose. There is nothing permanent. Everything is seasonal. Even your spouse will die one day. This is not a negative statement; just plain fact. Humans must get used to this approach to life. In the book of Psalms 20:7, David said something interesting: "Some trust in chariots and some trust in horses but we will trust in the name of our Lord our God." When I look around in my community, I have never seen a chariot or a horse. Many people have "chariots and horses" in which they trust. These could be your bank account, your father, mother, spouse, children, land, property, power, or your friends. Our trust should not be in all this but should be in the God Who created us.

Psalms 20:8 says, "They are brought to their knees and fall but we rise up and stand firm." David advises that those who trust in "chariots and horses" will be brought to their knees, but those of us who trust in God will rise up and stand firm. You will be able to stand firm only when you have trust in God. You will be able to win only when you have trust in God. I believe that I was able to overcome challenges as a child or teenager because of trust in God. I do not survive or exist because of the people around me but because God has given me an assignment to finish and nobody can stop God's plan. When you do not know what to do, you trust God.

Peter made the transition from seeking the physical bread to the spiritual "Bread of Life." He had nowhere else to go. He may not have understood what Jesus meant about eating His flesh and drinking His blood, but still, only Jesus had the words of eternal life. You see, Peter had true faith in Jesus and was actually doing the very thing Jesus wanted everyone to do: come to Him; believe in Him; feed on Him for eternal life. It was during this meeting when Peter was trained to be the next leader of the church. Peter got a revelation that Jesus had words of life. John 6:70, 71 says, Then Jesus replied, "'Have I not chosen you, the Twelve? Yet one of you is a devil!'" He meant Judas, the son of Simon, who, as one of the Twelve, was later to betray him.

Do not let people deter you from the Father's work or mission. Keep going when your faith is being tested. Jesus kept going to fulfill his work and mission. The suicide of his personal friend could not stop him from going ahead. Jesus' mission was to die on the cross. Judas was part of Jesus' team; He chose him. One of the things about Judas was that he was busy with private plans and doing things without informing Jesus. In life as you try to go for dreams or mission, there will be people like Judas. People whom you live with and eat with can be like Judas and be a tool of the devil. They will betray and turn against you. They will hate you. There are so many things that can happen.

As you pursue your dreams, trust God and few people who believe in your vision. Let the other people go their own way or direction. If they refuse to come with you, leave them alone and go on in your own direction. You will meet new people. You will get new relationships. You will even survive the problems that come your way and you become strong. In my life, I have experienced these thing am talking about. I decided personally that I will pursue what God tells me to do and I keep going because God knows things I do not know and cannot explain. I just keep going and I know I have a life ahead of me. I have big things to do for God. Sometimes we need to forgive people who are often against us, attacked or hated us.

As followers of Christ, we should not speak evil about them. If people leave, do not worry because they think they are important. Just keep going. I learned that when people leave you or organization, it is because they feel or think they are very important, but in fact, they are not important. If God gave you a vision for your life, do not surrender or give up to the situation because that situation comes to strengthen your faith and you need to keep going. Do not give up during times of adversity or crisis but have faith in God Who brought you to that point.

What Is Success In The Face Of Crisis?

- Sucess is measured by ability to maintain personal balance in times of turbulence, chaos, confusion, turmoil, instability, crises and storms.

- If you want to know the level of maturity in an individual, then you have to study and measure how they react and respond to chaos, calamity, crisis, disorder, or tragedy that happens to them.

- A mature person in faith is the one willing to be tried, attacked and thrown into the furnace, go through fire, or be thrown in the den of lions.

- That person is willing to pay the prince but has great confidence that victory is on the other side and will come even stronger than when they entered the furnace.

Stability In Times Of Crisis

The most important thing people need to do in times of crisis, tragedy, chaos or disappointment is to stay and remain steady. Through the fires of calamity, disaster, tests, chaos, confusion, crisis and misfortune that true maturity and leadership are tested. This is when it is proven and comes to the surface. It is after tragedy or crisis that you will know who the real leaders are.

- The key to handling tragedy is learning to expect it anytime or expecting the unexpected.

- Managing crisis requires that we have a new mindset that change will happen with or without your permission.

- Understand that change is the only thing that is constant and nothing will remain the same forever. Change is part of life and life itself goes through change.

Do Not Judge People

The Bible says in Mathew 7:1-2 that, "Do not judge, or you too will be judged. For in the same way you judge others, you will be judged, and with the measure you use, it will be measured to you." God can judge you in the same way you judge people. Be careful. Do not judge people. Leave judgment and vengeance in the hands of God. Also, let those who are qualified to judge in courts of law do it, not you.

Principle
- *Never judge people but let God do that because it is His business.*
- *Let those who are qualified to judge in courts of law do it, not you.*

Faithfulness In Small Things

Jesus told a story in Matthew 25:14-30 about three men who were given responsibilities to manage some resources on behalf of their master and leader. These men were trusted by the master when the master went away on a business trip. He came back from the business trip to check and find out what the three men had done with the responsibility that was entrusted to them. I call it "monitoring and evaluation", or I could call it "program or project review." The master was pleased with one of the servant.

This happens most of the time with human beings. Many times, your parents, friends or supervisors will give you resources to manage, but they are giving those resources to check how you manage in their absence. "His master replied, 'Well done, good and faithful servant! You have been faithful with a few things; I will put you in charge of many things. Come and share your master's happiness!" (Matthew. 25:21).

God will congratulate you when are a faithful servant. God is pleased by people who are faithful but not necessarily famous or popular people.

Principles
- *Be faithful in small things and God will bless you with big things.*
- *Be responsible in what God has given and you will be entrusted with more responsibility and resources and opportunities.*

People That History Remembers

The world has a population of over seven billion people today in the planet. Majority of these people are ordinary people and most of them will die when nobody will ever know they existed and lived on Earth. Millions of them are destroyed by poverty, conflicts, earthquakes, wars, terrorism and diseases. People who are remembered are those who have overcome the most difficult things in life. When you study those recorded in history and in God's Word, the Bible, you will find that most if not all of them overcame the most difficult times in their lives and some even died because of their faith and conviction in what they believed. They were ready to die for their beliefs and willing to pay the price. Jesus said anyone who loses his life will gain it for his sake.

Why do we remember these people? Let's examine each of them below:

Abraham, Faithful But God Tested Him To Sacrifice His Son

This man is regarded as a hero when it comes to faith. He was married to Sarah and God begun by asking him to leave his birthplace and go to a land that God was going to show him. This man did not even question God but instead obeyed and went as God told him. He never had a child and while in the land that God had given him. He was getting old. He wondered who was going to inherit the land and wealth. After years of waiting, the wife got a solution and told the husband to sleep with her maid so they can have an heir.

Due to pressure, Abraham accepted, and the outcome of that relationship was Ishmael. When he was presented before God, God said that this child would not be the seed child of the covenant

287

nation. That child would be Isaac. God promised Abraham a son but the son did not come right away. Isaac was eventually born and even then God asked for a son to be offered as a sacrifice. Can you explain God? Can you explain what was going on in the life of this man, family and community? This is the reason we remember him because he was able to overcome, the difficulties, tests and challenges. Today we call him the "Father of Faith" because he believed and never questioned God. It turned out that this was a test of faith and God stopped him from sacrificing Isaac. Check Genesis 22. Do you question God? My encouragement is that no matter how difficult it will be, believe God, and like Abraham, God will do and fulfil His plans according to His own way and time.

Jacob, Stole His Brother's Birth Right, A Thief

Jacob was a twin brother of Esau and his father was Isaac, the son of Abraham. When Isaac was old and about to die, he prepared in their tradition to bless Esau as the firstborn and as the heir, but the mother Rebecca, heard about the plan. Isaac wanted Esau to be the heir and the one with the birthright. Instead, through the collaboration of the mother and Jacob, they succeeded in deceiving the father by having Jacob dress up as Esau and mimicking him so that Isaac gave Jacob the blessing that was to go only to the firstborn. Then when Esau came back from hunting, he was surprised at the turn of events and what had been done. In short, Jacob stole his brother's right as firstborn son. The blessing could not be revoked. Jacob was a thief, but this action is why we cannot forget him because he was able to overcome the difficulties that confronted him and was able to deal with them.

This story is similar to what you might be going through. Someone might have cheated you, but do not let that experience destroy you. Use that experience to rise above what is expected of you and prove them wrong. Jacob overcame that crisis because of faith and he was later called Israel by God. God gave him the name "Israel" which means "He fought with God." I have learned that it is after your tragedy or crisis that God does a different work in you and even changes your name. This happened also to Saul in the New Testament when his name was changed to Paul.

Moses, Confronted The Egyptian Pharaoh

Whenever you hear the name Moses, you will recall that great experience of going to confront the mighty government of the Pharaoh of Egypt. The story is found in Exodus 3. Moses led a campaign to have the children of Israel set free from slavery. He did it perfectly and Pharaoh released the people as God wanted. Moses is also remembered for murdering a man who was beating an Israelite and he ran into the wilderness of Sinai. He was a murderer, and in those days and even these days, murderers were outcasts in the society. Moses overcame all this because he believed God when he was called to be a deliverer and leader of God's people. No matter what you have done, it cannot cancel God's plan, potential and purpose for your life. You should never get worried or destroy your life because of your past, but instead, be courageous to believe God because after that experience, God will turn that test into a testimony and a mistake into a miracle.

Joshua, Captured Jericho And Entered The Promised Land

Joshua was a friend of Moses as he led the Israelites into wilderness. When Moses was old, God told Moses to select the next leader, and Moses announced that Joshua was the next leader and introduced him before the people of Israel. God told Joshua that He would be with him as He was with His servant Moses. God told Joshua to keep and obey the commandments if was to be successful and prosper. Joshua accepted and did as God instructed him. Before the crossing of River Jordan and after, Joshua was confronted by capturing the walls of Jericho. Joshua together with his soldiers defeated the enemy and captured Jericho when God caused the walls of the city to come tumbling down.

This was a great battle. This is similar to what you might be going through, believe me, your battles are about to be over. You are about to take over "Jericho" but the success of this will depend on your faith and if you will believe God. You will need faith in God for overcoming and capturing Jericho. Jericho could be a situation in your life, a dream or vision that you have been waiting for years or decades, but believe God because God does not lie; God will make it happen and His promises never fail.

David, Shepherd And Second Of King Of Israel

David was the youngest son of his father Jesse. He was the least of the sons in the family and therefore the one who was to be tending the sheep of his father's flock as a shepherd. David never protested this work. David kept going, and one day, the Scripture says that the sheep was attacked by lion and David intervened. He killed the lion. Through this experience, David learned to use the rope to sling. I believe David never knew what was going to happen in his life and that is the same with some of you. You could be doing something and you think that is your final address and you want to quit and give up. Do not give up. God's plans are different but be obedient. One day, Samuel was sent by God to anoint David, a young teenager to be the king after Saul because Saul disobeyed God. God fired Saul even though he was still in "office" because David was anointed to be the next king.

Later, there was war between the armies of Israel and the Philistines and the elder brothers of David were part of the army.

The parents gave instructions to David to carry lunch for the brothers, and David accepted. The instructions were simple: "Take lunch to your brothers at the battle front." Sometimes, simple instructions can change your life forever. David went as a teenager; he was carrying stones with rope that he used for slinging. When he arrived at the place where the brothers were, he realized that there was war and there was a giant named Goliath. Goliath had insulted the Israelites and their God, and David heard this.

David asks who this uncircumcised fellow was who blasphemes against his God. David then told his brothers that he was going to fight Goliath. He moved in the direction of the giant, and the giant advanced, warning David that he would be given to the birds. However, David prayed to God and with the power of the Almighty, he put a stone in his sling and slung a rock that hit the forehead of Goliath who fell down. David ran towards the giant, cut of his head and all the armies of the Philistines fled. David became a hero. David was able to overcome a great crisis. David is greatly remembered as the person who killed Goliath.

David also did stupid things such as committing adultery with Bathsheba and then having her husband killed in battle. But these did not stop David's purpose even though he had problems. Believe me, friends, you might be having a problem or crisis, but it is only temporary and you are about to become a hero. It does not matter what you are going through; you have God's anointing. God is about to bring you to your purpose. David had faith in God and that faith enabled him to overcome the most difficult situations in his life. When you read the book of Psalms that contains David's own Psalms, you will find that David trusted God in everything. He was a king but he never trusted in the things that God gave him.

David, also knew the Source of success. Psalms 20: 4 says, "May he give you the desire of your heart."

In one of the statements and prayers by David, Psalms 57:2, it says, "I cried out to God Most High, who fulfils his purpose for me." Can you imagine a king crying out like that? But David is saying to his followers and constituents that he cried to God Most High. Why? David knew his limitations. David knew where the source of his power comes from. David knew that his assignment was only possible when God is with him. David could not fulfil his purpose without God and this made David cry out. I believe David said this prayer because things were difficult and tough. David cried out because on his own he could not achieve or accomplish his purpose.

Job was a man who was blameless before God but God allowed Him to experience crisis. The Scripture is full of mysteries and things too difficult to comprehend. Job is described as the richest man who ever lived. He had wealth and property. Most of humanity today is interested in material things, wealth, power, fame and property. The Scripture says Job lived a righteous life. He was blameless in the eyes of God. He obeyed God. He submitted himself to the will of God. The interesting thing about this man is that God allowed him to go through tests and trials.

God allowed Satan to afflict Job with pain and made him lose all his earthly wealth that he possessed and owned. Job lost everything and all things. In all this experience, Job never lost his faith in God. He lost everything but not the faith he had in God. Job knew himself. When he was afflicted, he fell to the ground in worship. Job 1:21-22 states that:

Naked I came from my mother's womb, and naked I will depart. The Lord gave and the Lord has taken away; may the name of the Lord be praised." In all this, Job did not sin by charging God with wrongdoing.

Job was aware of what he owned and the Source of his wealth. He was confident that God knew things he did not know. Job was left alone by his spouse when the life became tough and complicated. Job's wife told Job to curse God and die. This happens most of the time in life. Your family and friends will abandon you when you become bankrupt, poor and without any material possessions. When you are in crisis, you will know who the true friends are. You separate them in your heart and mind.

You will see those who are friends and those who are foes. God allowed Job to go through hell on Earth. God allowed Job to experience shame. God allowed Job to be ridiculed. God allowed Job to experience the pain of poverty and lack of material possessions. God allowed Job to experience what most people avoid. Why did he succeed? It is because of His faith in God and not the God of things. Job as reported in Job 42 recovered everything he lost after the test in unexpected quantities. Job got back as much the property as he had before the trial.

Principles
- *We as humans did not bring anything to the world.*
- *People who are remembered by history are those who have scars and testimonies or who were able to overcome tests.*

Lessons From Job's Life

- God gives everything and the devil can take everything (if God allows it).

- The God we serve as believers and followers does not protect us from problems.

- God allows Satan to test us and then after we have passed the test, God can trust us.

- God will not trust what has not been tested. God tested Abraham with a promise of a son and even when the son was born years after, God demanded for Isaac as a burnt sacrifice. God trusts only what has been tested. If you want God to trust you, you need to accept the test.

- The bigger the test, the bigger the trust God places in you. God is pleased when we have faith in Him Not His miracles and blessings that we receive.
- God is a God of faith and faithfulness. Have you entrusted your life to God? Does your life belong to you or to God?

History of Great People

The great men and women in history of humanity are those people who have endured the most difficult moments of their lives. They are those who have overcome the most challenging times, trials, setbacks, problems, hardships and temptations. They have a story of how they were able to come out of the den of lions. They have a story to tell how they were able to get out of the pit and go to the palace like Joseph. They have a story of how they ran naked when they were seduced in the palace. They have a story how they were able to come out of the gas chambers.

People Who Are Remembered

What is your story? What have you managed to overcome? How did you make it?

The people who are remembered in history are those people with convictions and courage and faith. The examples of these people are numerous and we have the list as follows: Peter, David, Stephen, Daniel, Paul and Abraham. The list is endless. Hebrews 11:32-40 has such a long list of men and women of great faith in God. You could study that text and you gain knowledge of what the achieved and went through. They were strong because of faith. How strong is your faith?

The secret to success is not to panic when things do not seem to be working out. Just believe that God knows everything you do not. You have to trust God and lean not on your understanding (Proverbs 3:5). Faith is running the race set before you (Hebrews 12:1). You need to know your faith. How do you know if you have faith? The secret is to test your faith. The only way to know if you have faith is by testing. Tests make us stronger and better. Sometimes God can promise you things and you may never see them in your life. You need to understand that this is the way God works. God promised Abraham that He would be the father of many nations but Abraham died before he could see the nations. God told Moses and showed him the Promised Land for the Israelites and Moses died on the way to the Promised Land and Joshua took His place.

Principles
- *God requires faith and faithfulness.*
- *God can show you a vision that you might not see come to pass.*
- *God rewards those who have faith in Him and His promises.*

What Is The Greatest Fight In This World?

I have been a Christian for years and I have always heard people and believers talk about fighting the devil. However, in my search for the greatest fight, I found an answer in 1 Timothy 6:11-13, which says,

> But you, man of God, flee from all this, and pursue righteousness, godliness, faith, love, endurance and gentleness. Fight the good fight of the faith. Take hold of the eternal life to which you were called when you made your good confession in the presence of many witnesses.

I used to think that we are fighting the devil. But according to the above Scripture, the fight is for our faith. Faith is belief. This is secret to the peace in my life. The fight is when you have been in the storms of life that you keep your faith. What is our fight? What is your real fight? The fight is for your belief. Do you still believe in God when you lose a job, a close relative or family member, your house, car, or friends? Do you lose your faith when you are divorced by your spouse? All you have in your life is faith. When you lose it, you have lost it all. The secret in life during tragedy is to keep the faith in God (Mark 11:22). The fight is for the belief. That is why the devil does things to stop you from believing God and yet God is more interested in people who keep their faith when life is in chaos, crisis and tragedy.

The Power of Faithfulness in God

In fact, in Hebrews 11: 6, it says, "Without faith, it is impossible to please God." Pleasing God is a result of having faith in God, so have faith in God in every situation or circumstances that might affect you. When you please God, He rewards you. The condition for pleasing God is having faith. The secret to success is having stable and strong faith in God and not the blessing that you have received and you are expecting. You need to believe in God, not your pastor, bishop, reverend, president or mayor. You need to take away your faith from people or things and place your faith in God who owns all things. I believe that the greatest source of disappointment and frustrations in life is having faith in people and not God. If you want God to be pleased with you, you need to put your faith in Him. Put your faith in God and take it away from people. People will let you down but God is faithful to Himself even when we are not faithful. God is holy and integrated. God is one. God is faithful and keeps His word.

When you put your faith in people, people might disappoint you. There are people in your circles that are or will disappoint you in a few years. I learned so many years ago that people will disappoint you. If you are going to reduce the impact of disappointment, then you must keep your expectations very low so that when you are disappointed, your level of disappointment is also low. Can you imagine if your expectations are too high? What would be the level of disappointment then? Have you heard a spouse say "I do not believe in you anymore?". It means they have lost faith in you.

Testing of Faith

I have met so many believers who think God only loves them and when bad things happen they blame the devil. This is okay to think that way. However, I have learned God does not trust what has not been tested. Jesus was led by God's Spirit to desert to be tempted. Why? Abraham was told leave your homeland. Abraham was requested to take Isaac for a sacrifice. Why? Daniel in the lion's den. Shadrach, Meshach and Abednego were thrown in a furnace.

The reasons for these tests was that God never trusts what has not been test. If you are going through any test, just know you will come out of it. What crisis or test have you passed? You will never be remembered unless you gone through a test. It is the test that gives you capacity to give a testimony. The reason Shadrach, Meshach and Abednego are in the Bible is because of the fire into which they were thrown into. They went through the fire and came out without being burnt. Read Daniel 3. These three Hebrew young men believed in God. They had faith in God, not in their strength or wisdom. These three believers never believed in people but God. Where is your faith? Do you have faith in people?

You need to learn to take away faith from people or things and put it in God. When you trust in God, your faith will not be affected by storms, crisis or disappointments. Your faith will not fade or fail. Your faith will grow from strength to strength. Your faith will be grounded under a sure foundation of the Lord of Lords. Jesus said in Mark 11:22, "Put your faith in God," because God is faithful all the time. Never put your faith in people because they can fail you. You will need to choose your friends and test their trust before you accept them as friends.

Principle
- *Put your faith in God, not humans, from now on and go after what you believe in faith.*

Put Your Trust In God, Not Family, Friends Or Jobs

We must put our trust and faith in God no matter what happens to us in life. We need to keep going and believing God in all situations. This story is packed with lessons for believers. It is usually after the tests that God blessed you with long life. To my analysis of Job's life, these are the principles and lessons I have identified.

1. The Lord restored the fortunes of Job when he prayed for his enemies. God will do the same to you after the time of testing. The Lord blessed Job more than he had at first, which was tremendous wealth.

2. People will talk about your situation or test. Do not worry about what they say, but just believe in God.

3. Pray for people who are against you during the time of trial or persecution. Do not attack or speak against them.

4. Right attitude brings blessing from God. Keep the right mental attitude even when you are going through a dark period because the there is life after darkness.
   Friends and relatives will scatter when life becomes rough. Your faith is as strong as the test that it survives.

5. Obedience to God brings or attracts God's presence. The presence of God attracts peace, love and joy.

6. Everything you lose through the tests is multiplied after the test when God restores you.

7. People will forgive you if you overcame the test because victory creates trust and integrity.

8. Keep believing God, stay faithful and steady throughout the tests.

9. There are good days after the storms, tests and challenges faced in life. Tests are temporary. There are days after storms. Do not surrender to situations. Never surrender

10. The fight is for your faith. My faith is God.

Note: Without faith, you will give up as you purse your dreams and vision. You need faith to overcome, setbacks, tests, challenges, failures and move forward with God's help. You cannot do it on your own.

CHAPTER TEN

THE FUNDAMENTAL PRINCIPLE OF TIME

"Time is money." ~ Benjamin Franklin

How Effective Use Of Time Changes Our Destiny

In 1992 I was in high school and it was holiday time. I recall one day we were at my uncle's home in Kampala and we were watching a black and white TV. We children liked it and watched it daily. There were people who were drinking " Ajono" in one part of the house. "Ajono" is a local among the Iteso of Uganda and Kenya. When my uncle came back to the house and found us as children were struggling for the TV remote. He was irritated by our actions and idleness. He mentioned something interesting to us who were there. He said something that has remained indelible in my mind:

"Please go and get something to do which is much better than watching TV all the time. He became very serious and wanted to beat all the kids who were still stuck in the living room to watch the TV. He ordered us to get out of this living room or go to other rooms and read your books instead." Then he added, "If you watch this TV you might not ever own one in your life time on earth. If you watch TV, you might never speak on TV. You might never go to the university because you are wasting time."

"What next?" I asked myself. I decided to go and borrow notes from my high school friend for my Physics class. I remember that night I did not sleep because I was busy writing and copying the materials. I realized that as you copy notes by writing them on another piece of paper, you are actually revising and learning. By the morning hours, I had completed copying the notes and I had my own notes. The topics that were in the book that I borrowed were never taught by our physics teacher. These notes helped me in one of the papers that was examined in senior six. Indeed, as my uncle had mentioned that day, those of us who left and found something to do, now own TVs, cars, and even houses. But those who continued to watch the TV do not own TVs or cars or houses. Marks of poverty are present in their personal lives. In other words, without taking the correct advice and being willing to learn, you will never succeed in your dreams.

The Examples Of Questions About Time

We ask questions such as, how old are you? How long will you be away? How long will the course take? How long will you take to reach your journey? How long will you take to finish the task? How long have you been in power, office or parliament? How long have you worked in that firm, company, organization? How long have you live in that location or place? How old is your first son? How old is your daughter? All these questions are related to time. I believe all humans have been given the same amount of time and the way we use it is what separates us. All of us are given 24 hours in a day. The use of time separates failures from successful persons. It puts human beings on earth into different positions and creates classes. There are several places in the Bible where time is mentioned and also Jesus Christ Himself spoke about time.

The Bible says, This is the day the Lord has made and we should rejoice and be glad *in it* as recorded in Psalm 118:24. This means we have to use the day that God gives us carefully because the next day or week or years has not been released to us by God. You never know if you will reach the next day, week, month or year. God gave us time so that we can start and end on what we have done in life. God gave us time so we can bring an end to "old success" and begin new successes. God gives us time so we can bring an end to failure and start again. Time brings closure to success and failure and you can rejoice in the new day.

In the book of Ecclesiastes written by King Solomon, Chapter 3 gives an elaborate and detailed perspective of time and what it means to have time when you are on Earth. Look at this Scripture again. Ecclesiastes 3:1 says, "To everything there is a season, a time for every purpose under heaven." When you continue to read this chapter, you realize that there is time for everything on Earth and when you waste the time that God has given you, you will never fulfil your purpose. When I read this as a young teenager when I was in high school, I discovered that my time of being at school was limited and not forever. I was not going to be a lifetime student in that school. Instead I would finish my time in that school and go to another school. This Scripture taught me that the time of being at school was limited to a certain period. When I read during the periods I used to go for holidays, I also noticed that holidays were not forever. When I went to the Makerere University for my undergraduate studies, I was excited about being there and I thought of it as a long period of time. This illusion also affected my friends and we all got excited as we enjoyed visiting friends and socializing.

Principles
- *Life is seasonal and things will change whether you want it or not.*
- *There is time for every purpose.*

What Is Time?

1. Time can be a blessing or a curse.
2. Time is life. When you spend your time, you are spending your life.
3. Life is time.
4. Life is defined as time.
5. Life is measured by time.
6. Life is determined by time.
7. Life is lived in time and out of time. The passing of time is the passing of life.
8. Life stops when time stops. When you die, you move out of time to enter in forever. Forever is eternity and it's a place where God lives (also known as heaven).
9. Time is a piece of forever or eternity. In Eternity, time is forever. Eternity is a tough place and everything is forever. Time is an interruption of eternity.
10. Time is measured in seconds, hours, days, weeks, months, years etc.,
11. Time is when action can take place.
12. Time is defined in seasons.

The Purpose For Time

Ecclesiastes 3: 1 and 10-12 gives clarity of the purpose for time. You may remember that God created time in Genesis 1: 14 and said everything is good in Genesis 1:18. Time is good too.

1. Time was created for everything and for seasons.
2. Time was created for the fulfillment of purpose under heaven.
3. Time was created to take you out of eternity.
4. Time was created to protect you from forever or eternity.
5. To measure the existence of life and meaning.
6. To account for your life and also to define your beginning and end or for everything.
7. God gave humans time, so we can live life in doses, hours, days, weeks, month and not one go.
8. Time separates the past from the future and present.
9. Time is measured in seasons.
10. Time will solve your problems or deal with your past
11. Your present situation will not last forever, because of time or seasons.
12. Time changes everything.
13. Time is the only commodity common to all humans. Every human everywhere is given the same amount of time.
14. The outcomes of your life depend on how time is spent and used. Time determines what you become. What are you buying? How will you spend your 24 hours? What about next month? What will you become?
15. Time gives you opportunity to change your relationship and plan a better future.
16. Time gives you opportunity to change your life.
17. Time gives you an opportunity to decide your future. What it will be in 5 -10 years from now? Time allows that.

18. Time gives you an opportunity to change history, avoid traditions, failures and write new history.
19. Time helps us to run our lives and finish the purpose in our hearts. God gave time to accomplish our purpose
20. Time helps us to learn from failure and start to succeed. God gave us time to provide closure to failure.
21. Time enables us forget the past. God gave time to push our failures, disappointments back and we can start again.
22. Time enables us not live by the past but focus on the future. God gave time to provide a new page in life to fulfil His purpose.
23. Time is given for something and that something must be related to God's purpose and our assignment.

The Principle Of Time

1. Time is just like your money.
2. Time is a resource.
3. Time can be stolen.
4. Time can be abused.
5. Time can be wasted.
6. Time can be lost.
7. Time can be squandered.
8. Time can be appreciated.
9. Time can be depreciated.
10. Time can be devalued.
11. Time can be revalued.
12. Time is leads to change.
13. Passage of time leads to change. Change can happen with or without you.
14. Change demands planning and management of time.
15. The use of time must be planned to avoid misuse, abuse and wastage.

What You Need to Know About Time

1. You can never stop time.
2. You can never control time.
3. You can never resist time.
4. You can never compromise time.
5. You can never recover wasted time.
6. You can never buy time.
7. You can never slow or increase time.
8. You can never speed up time.
9. You can manage time.
10. You can invest time.
11. You can use time to initiate, create, develop, build and add value to life.
12. Time can be used to fulfil your divine purpose.

Time Redemption Tactics

Ephesians 5: 14-18 says,

> Awake, you who sleep, arise from the dead, And Christ will give you light." See then that you walk circumspectly, not as fools but as wise, redeeming the time, because the days are evil. Therefore, do not be unwise, but understand what the will of the Lord is. And do not be drunk with wine, in which is dissipation; but be filled with the Spirit.

The Scripture is packed with insight on time which I consider as tactics of redeeming time. They are:
- Wake up and stop sleeping.
- Redeem the time because days are evil.
- We are all products of time.
- Deem means to own. To redeem means to own again, re-control and save again.

- Spend long hours working what you missed to do.
- Cut off some friendships or shut down some groups.
- Change relationships which are unproductive, toxic and not viable.
- Work a little harder than the rest of the people around you.
- Be more focused and disciplined and intentional.
- Throw out nice and unpleasable things. Start doing the important and strategic things; actions that lead to your destiny and dreams.
- Reposes or reclaim your lost time.
- Fulfil a pledge or promise.
- Convert into value
- Pay an outstanding debt on wasted time.
- Deliver on your commitments.
- Double or triple your focus on strategic things.
- Being very careful.
- Becoming wise, gaining wisdom.
- Making the most of every opportunity to go your future.
- Pursue God's will. Will means God's purpose.
- Take ownership and control your time.
- Convert into an opportunity to fulfil your purpose.
- Tap into your potential and exploit it.
- Reinvent and redesign your life and create a life of value, meaning and purpose.

How To Manage Time

- Time is like a commodity that must be managed.
- Time must be protected.
- Time must have a focus.
- Time must have a purpose.
- Time must have a plan.
- Time must have a vision.
- Time must have measureable results.

Strategies For Time Management

1. Prepare and develop a plan for your life.
2. Establish your priorities.
3. Pursue your passion only.
4. Protect your plans and priorities.
5. Identify what you value.
6. Make decisions based on your destiny.
7. Make decisions based on your vision.
8. Conduct inventory of your associations and friends, see which people cause you to waste time and drop them.
9. Review your investments, projects and do not try to please everybody.

The" Comfort" Zone

Another challenge with humans is that when we succeed, we become comfortable. We sometimes do not want close the chapter and move to achieve new successes. They get taken up by the achievement of yesterday, last week, last year and we forget to move forward for greater success, influence and impact. This is a complacent attitude. But when I finished my first degree, I did not stop. I went back to school and am currently still in school. I still spend sleepless nights reading. I also read books to learn new skills and competencies. What you have done in the past can actually stop you from advancing ahead to your new purpose and goal. My practical advice is that do not let the past accomplishments or success prevent you from getting new results or success.

Relationship Between Time On Earth And Time In Heaven

The Scripture says that God lives in heaven. God lives in eternity. Eternity is time without measure, size, amount or quantity. In other words, in eternity, there is no way you can gauge, calculate, compute, determine or even evaluate time. It is timeless. This means God lives in timeless eternity. God, on the other hand, put all human beings on Earth. When you live on Earth you are living where time can be gauged, calculated, computed, determined and evaluated. This is possible by using the seconds, minutes, hours, days, etc.

When you live on Earth you have many choices to make with how you use your time and where you spend it. Time is a resource and when you waste it, you will never get it back. It is like money. When you waste it, you will lose it. Time is life and life is time. God is wise to give us a human will. God gave this power of will to humans so that we can decide on what we want in life. God will never violate that will. God will never cross that line until we invite Him. That is why salvation is a choice we decide. God gives us opportunities, but it is up to us to take the opportunity. God will never interfere in the environment of humans. God does not speak much except He can reveal Himself if chooses.

As young people and those who have been younger longer, you need to use your time carefully and efficiently. When you look back on so many years you have been on Earth, ask these questions honestly. How have you used your time? How have you lived your life? Many of you are depressed, disappointed and angry about how you have wasted your time and life. Time is life and life is time. When you waste your time, you will regret your life one day. These are serious statements. Write that down in your journal and think about it.

The Fundamental Principle Of Time

One of the key principles I learned about this in my own life is that there is time for everything. Never waste any of your time where you do foolish things and keeping company with bad friends or groups. Use the time at your disposal to engage in things that can change and transform your life forever. Do things that will lead you to your destiny and ultimately your purpose. If you do not use time wisely, you will be frustrated one day and you will take out your frustrations on other people. You will miscarriage your dreams. There will be an abortion of your vision and never fulfil your God-given assignment and purpose.

As I live, I am aware of my death and the statement of King Solomon that reminds me that we shall all die one day. There is a time to be born and a time to die (Ecclesiastes 3:2). I am aware of life because of the experience that I have seen in my personal life and family. I was shocked when I lost my mother at age 14, my grandfather at age 15, and my grandmother at age 18. This was too much to take in and comprehend. As a young teenager, I learned big lessons that all life will end someday. In those years, I discovered very interesting things such as this, that death is not the most terrible or horrible thing to happen. But the death of a dream or dying without doing something you were created to do is a terrible thing.

One of the things that motivates me every day when I think about time of my own death. To put it another way, death motivates me to use my time effectively. I decided several years ago to use my time effectively. I wanted to make each day to count. I recall one day I was watching the TV and I saw a story of a young man who had died at the age of 20 by committing suicide. I wondered how this young man had used his time on Earth.

Another day when I was a young Christian in Mbale, I went to St. Andrews Cathedral for the normal Sunday service. The reverend quoted this passage, "There is a time to be born and a time to die for Christians." I went home I read it for myself. I was so scared about my own life and I began to think over my life. I noticed that I was wasting time with wrong people who were not helping me. So I decided to leave them alone and I went to concentrate on my books.

I remember how I used my time as a day scholar to focus on the books. There are some things you must stop doing if you are going to achieve your dreams. You must also avoid some people. I do not know how many of you reading these books have attended secondary day school. It was a unique experience where I was renting a house, looking after myself. All the while there was a war going on in my home district. I could not go there freely to bring supplies and get assistance from home. Because of these challenges, I never had sufficient time to concentrate on my studies. When the preacher talked about time, I went back home and made changes immediately to my life.

As a result, during my school days, I never went to a disco like many of my friends did. I never went even though I was always being invited. The reason to me was that I remembered how time was. I believe that I managed to progress in my education because I never engaged myself in some of the things that young people engage in today like attending these clubs.

The Benefits Of Time Management

1. **Effectiveness:** You get things done.
2. **Productiveness:** You produce more in the long run.
3. **Efficiency:** you make wise use of resources in the time you have to accomplish tasks.

4. **Confidence:** You gain self-respect and know that you can make it happen.
5. **Results-driven:** You set higher goals for getting attainable goals finished.
6. **Resourceful:** You learn all the best ways to accomplish g**oals.**
7. **Respectful:** You will feel better about yourself and others.

In the book of Paul to Ephesians, you find another powerful text on time. Ephesians 5:13-18 states that:

> *But everything exposed by the light becomes visible, for it is light that makes everything visible. This is why it is said: "Wake up, O sleeper, rise from the dead, and Christ will shine on you." Be very careful, then, how you live—not as unwise but as wise, making the most of every opportunity, because the days are evil. Therefore, do not be foolish, but understand what the Lord's will.*

- This is a powerful Scripture and I wish every Christian would read it and remember what it says. The secrets that you need to apply in life include the following simple statements.

- When you follow them and apply, you will see great changes in your personal life. You must wake up if you are "sleeping" in life. I speak about sleeping as not in the real sense of sleeping but from those things that have kept you from pursuing your dreams, goals and plans and vision.

- You must rise up from the bad company and groups or bad influences. Get out of there and be by yourself.

- Be careful how you live, and decide how you should live. Become wise and run away from foolishness. Stop being a fool! Become a wise person! Get some wisdom!

- Make the most of every opportunity in your personal life. I believe I have been effective in my life because I understood the important things I needed to be doing and the benefits of time management. Every day I have a plan of things to do and how my time will be used. Then I try to accomplish those tasks and goals with God's help.

Wake Up And Work If You Desire Success

Paul is telling people who are already awake to wake up. Paul says to be careful how you live your lives and how you understand your life. In other words, Paul is saying there are people busy sleeping, wasting time and doing wrong things. People need to stop and get up; wake up and do the things that are important. Paul is saying make every use of opportunity. This means ceasing the moment of your life when you are doing something productive and save your time. The literal Greek means for what is translated as making the most of every opportunity is to "redeem the time" or "buying up the time." To redeem has the idea of making a necessary purchase in the sense of buying something back. When you redeem the time, you are making up for lost time by the effective use of the time you have left in this world. You are making effective use of the time God has given you rather than wasting it.

Simple, But Important Ideas On Success

The greatest enemy of success is the fear that you have of failure and failing. Failure is not the end of life, but the beginning of an opportunity to learn and getting back on track. When you fail, do not sit by the side of the road and cry, but get up!

Think again, reorganize, review, re-plan, strategize, restart and move on to accomplish the goals that you want achieved.

- Set new and higher goals and strive to achieve the goals that you have created. The goals will motivate you to work hard and you notice how your life will change.

- Focus on one thing and only one thing. Do not attempt to do many things at the same time. Too many things are dangerous and can cause you more stress, pressure and discouragement.

- The previous or last success or victory can make you become comfortable and complacent. It can make you become proud and forget to dream more and want more and achieve more.

- Your success is in your hands; you should decide what you want to achieve or how you want to succeed. You decide it yourself and it is your responsibility. It is an "I can" attitude. Everything is in your hands. Trapped in a mango seed is a mango tree. So success is in you.

- Be determined at all times and your motivation will never be destroyed by discouragement.

- Do not give up. Be willing to pay the price because you cannot gain anything without pain and suffering.

- Seek knowledge and keep learning to improve your understanding of what you desire. Then you will succeed and get it.

- Become different; become unique; become like the great men of history. Dare to be a Daniel! As a teenager, I read the book of Daniel and I found where he distinguished himself as one who would not eat the meat or drink the wine of the king's table. He was given the ability to understand visions and dreams of all kinds (Daniel 1:11-17).

- Learn how to manage people, problems, challenges, situations and circumstances.

How do you manage time? Keys to effective management of time can only be managed through the following strategies:

1. **Effective Planning And Goal Setting:** This is based on an overall understanding of the mission of the place where you work or your own mission (e. g ., getting a degree).

2. **Prioritization:** If you do the harder tasks first, then when you are worn out; you will have the easy tasks to do. If you do the things that are the most in demand, then people will not be stressing you out to have what they want right then. On the other hand, if you are already burnt out on a certain job, it is better to be doing something rather than nothing. In that case you can just do what you are able to do rather than what you are unable to do.

3. **Organization:** Set up a game plan so that there is a strategy from start to finish of how tasks are going to get done.

4. **Action Implementation:** This is the action plan of your tasks. You sit down and strategize what needs to be done at a particular time.

5. **Periodic Review Of Priorities And Actions Leading To Your Vision:** This is evaluation. You need to assess whether you are doing things the right way. Maybe you need to make some changes and cut costs; be more efficient.

6. **Wisdom, Knowledge And Understanding:** Are you aware of the value of your life and time? Time is an important element of your existence. If you waste your time doing unproductive things, you will not recover it. Use the time to do things that lead you to your vision and dreams. For instance, if your vision is to be a good doctor who treats people, use your time to read books on medicine, customer care, or self-development books. Do not read books which related production of guns, cement, or other unrelated field.

Changing The Past Is Impossible But A New Story Is Possible

The past failures that have happened cannot be changed or erased. The power of your life is not in the past but in the future. You could be having regret in your life, but you need to move on to a new life and start to invest your life in the future and imagining the future. The past state of your life needs to be buried and forgotten. The focus must be pursuing the future rather than the past. If you focus on the past and your failures, you will be confused and perplexed. The past must be dealt with the new thinking of a renewed mindset.

Life is Either a Game or Not

To me life is a serious business. It is a game that cannot be understood and described. When you look at the examples of great men and women, you will notice that their lives were full of ups and downs, successes and failures. The only difference between these men and women is their attitude towards life and belief in God. One more time, let us review the lives of all these great people.

Moses

Moses killed an Egyptian. What have you done that scares you? You need to look at the example of Moses and work hard to do the will of God. You could be the next deliver of the people in your community. You need to begin to take actions and change the lives of the "slaves" that are oppressed by poverty of the mind and discouragement.

Abraham

This man was very special in God's eyes. He is referred to as the father of faith because of his belief in God. Do you know that despite his belief in God, he committed sin? He slept with the maid servant in order to conceive a son but God used that test to bless the world. God said his son through Sarah was the right seed. What have you done in the past that might be a constant threat to you achieving your greatness? The power is in your hands. My challenge is deciding to forget what you have done, even if it was adultery. Repent of your sins and decide to move forward.

Joshua

He was the second in command to Moses as the leaders of the Israelites to the Promised Land. Joshua faced the test of conquering Jericho. He was promised by God that the Lord would be with him as He was with Moses. The biggest test for him was to capture Jericho. What is your test? Do you see mountains in your life? Are you willing to move forward? You need to believe God that he will never leave nor forsake you.

David

He was the second king of Israel who was credited and honoured for killing Goliath. However, David in his weakness planned the killing of his top commander in his army in order to commit adultery with the commander's wife. This was a serious issue in God's eyes. He repented before God. David wrote his repentance prayer in Psalms 51. What then is your problem? You may not be successful because your past is a constant threat to your dreams and you are afraid to step into the future because people will talk about it. You need to learn lessons from people who were able to overcome the most terrifying situations in their lives and make history. People who have affected history have passed a series of challenges but made it to the top. You have an opportunity to make

it to the top.

Job

This man was perfect in the eyes of God and the richest man of his time. He lost everything. He lost his wealth and became the poorest man. I have learned that everything we boast of in life we shall lose. The secret is being prepared for the unexpected. I recall as a teenager, during my confirmation as a Protestant and a follower of Jesus Christ, the Bishop mentioned that in this life "we need to prepare for the worst but expect the best in life." He said life is sustained by faith not wealth and possessions. This was a crisis time when cattle rustling peaked in my country, Uganda, in late 1980s. God blessed Job with so much wealth because he made it through the test. I believe that it is usually after the test that God reveals His true nature and blesses you. Are you willing to be tested?

Jesus

The Word of God is a mystery. The Word of God says, "This is my beloved Son with whom I am well pleased." But do you know what happened to Him? Jesus was betrayed by his best friend, Judas Iscariot. The friend eventually committed suicide. Do you have people in your life who have betrayed you?

What Is The Key To Life?

I believe with all my heart and conviction that the key to life is order. Without order, you will fail. You see chaos, confusion and crisis. Order is created by law. Life without law is confusion. Law is the foundation of life. There are spiritual laws, natural laws and manmade laws. If you do no respect and obey natural laws, you will die.

Look at the fish, deciding to look for freedom from water, what will happen to the fish? So is it about you. You refuse my advice; it is up to you. Obey law and you will live. Absolute freedom will kill you. Believe me, when you obey, you are protected.

Do You Know What You Need Do Next?

You need to begin by carrying out Strength, Weaknesses, Opportunity and Threat Analysis of yourself, organization or company and work to reduce threats and maximize opportunities. Work up a plan for your life by describing your vision, purpose, goals and determine the resources you need and time it will take to achieve.

Here is a simple process that you can use to come up with important things that will lead you to desired destiny. You want to change your life here are the things you MUST do in order to arrive at your destination, desired life and fulfilment.

1. Capture And Document Your Vision

In this section write down your vision, the desires, and aspirations that inspire you or what you believe God wants you to accomplish. Make it in very few words, less than 10 words.

2. Write Down Your Purpose

Write down the reason you exist and what you need to do to fulfil that reason. Here requires you to pray and think. You need to ask God who created you to reveal this reason so you can perform and fulfil.

3. Develop Your Goals To Reach Your Purpose

Write three to five goals that you want to achieve in one, two, three or five years. Do not write many goals. Write what you think you can manage. You can write: educational goals, social goals, and financial goals. Personal development goals and Health goals. After writing the goals, write short-term objectives three of them for each and activities you will do to achieve those objectives. You also need to write about your strengths, weakness, skills and knowledge you will require to achieve it.

4. Develop Your Strategy

Think about how you will achieve the goals. How you will use the resources and things that you will need to do. Write down the choices and options available. For instance, if you what to go to your airport to catch a flight that leaves the airport in eight hours and your home is two hours to the airport, you need a strategy. For instance, your strategy will be to start your journey early to avoid traffic jam.

5. Effectively Utilize The Available Resources And Mobilize What You Do Not Have

Think about the resources, time, money, gifts, and people that you need to fulfil your vision. You will need to identify the people who will help you and work out your plans. If your vision is to build a church to serve your community, you will need to that the timeframe for starting, how much money you need and who will do the work. You cannot do things alone, you need people. Identify the people who have the same motives as you and avoid those who oppose attack or criticize you. These people are bad and will cause you to fail in your plans.

6. Identify The Right People Who Can Work With You

You also need to identify people who will help you achieve the desired goals. Choose your friends and be careful as you choose the family members to be part of the project.

7. Develop And Prepare A Work Plan

A work plan is a summary of activities that you are going to undertake each day, week, month, year etc. to achieve your vision. You can ask people to help you develop the activity plan.

8. Develop An Implementation Plan

This plan shows you which activities you need to carry immediately and which one later. Seek help also on developing the plan.

9. Design Monitoring And Evaluation Plan

This plan helps you to ensure that you are efficient, effective, relevant and impactful. It helps you to monitor if you achieving your expected results and goals. If you do not know how to design the plan, seek help and you will get someone who might help.

Note: Use your time effectively to achieve your dreams. It might take a long time to achieve the vision, but it will happen.

EPILOGUE

"You were designed for accomplishment, engineered for success, and endowed with the seeds of greatness."
~ Zig Ziglar

Welcome to the end of this book. You have come a long way in the journey and have now finished it. What have you personally gained and read?

I believe you have explored a series of basic principles that are simple, practical and workable for you to achieve your dreams and vision. The application of these principles will make you have a successful life. You have seen that all the principles are related. For example, the first principle of purpose is critical. You must discover your personal purpose. You must know if you have a passion for it. You must develop a plan, commit the principles of prayer. Further, you must remain persistent and persevere if you pursuing your dreams. Your potential must be explored, your faith must be engaged and time effectively used. The first fundamental principle of Chapter One is intentionally long so you have a better understanding.

Also, examples have been given of different people who have believed, applied and used the principles. These examples have been given to demonstrate that through the use of same principles you can obtain the same results as they did, you will also get to your dreams, destiny, and vision. However, reading is not enough. You must deliberately and persistently, go back and practice and apply all the principles. You must keep the using the principles until you are able to get the desired results.

- *"Success is no accident. It is hard work, perseverance, learning, studying, sacrifice and most of all, love of what you are doing or learning to do." ~ **Pele***

My goal of writing this book comes from my sincere to help you and millions of people who have suffered because they lacked knowledge of principles designed for success in life. It will give me great happiness and joy to know that my work in this book inspired and helped you. Personally, I have absolute confidence and belief in this fundamental principles as laid down in this book. They have been tested and proven that they work. They work and have worked.

However, we may not meet at a personal level, but in this book, we have met and interacted. I have shared my personal story and experiences. I am praying that you discover your purpose, pursue it and make a difference in your generation. Using, these fundamental principles, God will help you to effectively achieve your dreams and vision.

PERSONAL CHOICE
AND DECISION MOMENT

Establishing a personal relationship with God is the most important choice and decision you will make and never regret for your entire life. If you believe in God, you need to establish a relationship with him. God is a creator of all things in heaven and on earth. God made you and the universe. God did not start a religion that you follow but he created humans to have an intimate relationship with him in the Garden of Eden. God is like a manufacturer of a product like apple computer, iPad, or Toyota car. If a product has a problem, the buyer has to contact the manufacturer to fix or solve the problem of poor performance of the product. The manufacturer will fix the product because it gives the buyer a warranty and guaranty. You are like a product to God, just like Toyota car is a product to Toyota Corporation.

However, you might have been having problems in your life like the product which is not performing as expected by the manufacturer, and you are frustrated and worried. You are depressed, mad at people and the world. You are blind and confused in the mind. You have tried things and nothing is working. You have cursed why you are unsuccessful and failing in life and you feel empty and unsatisfied in life. You need to get back to the manufacturer so you can start to perform effectively and fulfil your purpose. If you believe and want to do that, I encourage you to surrender your life back to the creator and manufacturer of your life to correct the mistakes that you have made and you start again to perform effectively and fulfil your dreams and desires. Pray this prayer and God will start to fix your life again:

Reconnection and Salvation Prayer

Dear Heavenly Father and God of all Creation, you have created and manufactured my life for a purpose and without any mistake. I am aware that you created me to perform and fulfil my purpose. I am aware that as men and women, we have fallen and disobeyed your laws and principles and now we have lost our sense of direction and purpose in life. I am also aware that Your Son, Jesus Christ is the way, the truth and life, and without Him we can do nothing. I believe with Him I will discover my purpose and fulfil it. I therefore, ask you in the Name of Jesus to cleanse my life and send your Holy Spirit to dwell in my life and heart to reveal my purpose and fulfil it and live effectively. I surrender to Jesus Christ as my personal Savior and My Lord and I commit 100% to do your will and fulfil my purpose. In the name of Jesus Christ, I have prayed, Amen.

If you have sincerely prayed that prayer, please write to me using the following address below and share your commitment with me. We support institutions, families, churches, companies or organizations. We offer help in various areas: discovering purpose, leadership, vision, character development, leadership development, mentoring and succession planning, change management, creativity and innovation, learning organization, venture development and potential maximization.

Note: All the principles outlined in this book, must be used concurrently not in isolation.

Dr. Samuel Odeke, DSL
C/O GILBD and CTSL Uganda
P.O.Box 34820 Kampala, Uganda or
P.O.Box 2648 Mbale, Uganda
Telephone: +256783563417/782276765
E-mail: samuel.odeke@yahoo.com
Website: www.samuelodeke.com

ABOUT THE AUTHOR

Life's Story of Humble Beginining

Dr. Samuel Odeke, was born in a polygamous and a poor family and neighborhood. His parents had lots of cattle, but were stolen during the cattle raids in a single event. They lost everything that was considered a source of wealth and pride among their Iteso culture. They were 12 children with three mothers. Dr. Odeke is the first son in the family. His parents served as civil servants. However, his father lost his post due to change in government and returned back to their native home village in Bukedea. His mother continued to work moving from hospital to another, before her untimely death. Dr. Odeke attended local schools, before joining high school and later Makerere University. While in high school, Dr. Odeke lost his mother at the age of 14, followed by maternal grandfather at age 15 and followed by grandmother at age 18. His father lived a quiet life as a peasant. His high school education was supported by his father and maternal uncles and aunts.

Dr. Odeke's story is one of humble beginnings. He is married with children. The impact of losing dear ones and war did not leave him without heavy impact. It would later on form the foundation of his life. As a teenager, Dr. Odeke also witnessed the devastating impact of war, conflict and massive cattle raids in his district of Bukedea (formerly part of Kumi district) in the late 1980s, where hundreds of lives and properties were lost. On many occasions, he narrowly survived death from both government soldiers and rebels. Dr. Odeke, began to search for answers about life. He wanted to become successful in order to escape the devastating effects of poverty. He could not find answers to all his questions, but the Bible was a source of answers and inspiration. He discovered many principles including the fact that success is a result of obedience to laws or principles. He discovered that success is not accumulation of wealth, but doing what he was created to do.

Through following these principles, Dr. Odeke believes he is successful and believes that anybody can become successful. Dr. Odeke has been able to achieve some of his dreams and vision and still continues to pursue higher goals. My teenage dream was being a medical doctor which I never managed to achieve because of lack of school fees. However, Dr.Odeke earned a Doctorate of Strategic Leadership with specialization in Strategic Leadership from Regent University in 2017. He received an M.A in Organizational Leadership and Management from Uganda Christian University. He also holds a Post Graduate Diploma in Public Administration and Management and Masters of Management with Specialization in Public Administration and Management from Uganda Management Institute. Earlier, he received a Bachelor of Science Degree and Post Graduate Diploma in Education from Makerere University.

Dr. Odeke serves in various capacities such as an international civil servant, humanitarian worker, speaker, teacher, educator, leadership and management mentor and consultants for both private and public organizations. He travels to different countries annually, attends and facilitates international conferences, seminars, and workshops.

Dr. Odeke has worked with large humanitarian and development organizations among others such as World Vision, United Nations World Food Programme (WFP), United Nations Children's Fund (UNICEF) and United Nations Office for Coordination of Humanitarian Affairs (UNOCHA). He has travelled in different countries such as Kenya, Somalia, South Africa, Nigeria, Belgium, Spain, Netherlands, and the United States. Dr. Odeke believes that leadership can be developed through empowering, coaching and mentoring. He is a member of International Leaders Association(ILA), The Christian Book Sellers Association(CBA) and Africa Strategic Leadership Forum(ASLF).

Dr. Odeke, has applied the success principles laid down in this book to achieve his dreams and vision. Even though his mother's early death shocked and affected him, he has been able to achieve some of his dreams and plans. Dr. Odeke, believes that any human being who decides to study and apply these principles will be able to achieve success. Success is not about competing with other people, but doing what you are born to do and competing with yourself.

www.ingramcontent.com/pod-product-compliance
Lightning Source LLC
Chambersburg PA
CBHW051940090426
42741CB00008B/1213